THE PARADOX OF HELPING:

Introduction to the Philosophy of Scientific Practice

THE PARADOX OF HELPING:

Introduction to the Philosophy of Scientific Practice

MARTIN BLOOM

School of Social Work

Washington University
St. Louis, Missouri

John Wiley & Sons, Inc., New York · London · Sydney · Toronto

Copyright © 1975, by Martin Bloom

All rights reserved.   Published simultanenously in Canada.

No part of this book may be reproduced by any means, nor
transmitted, nor translated into a machine language without the written permission of the publisher.

Library of Congress Cataloging in Publication Data:

Bloom, Martin, 1934-
    The paradox of helping.

    Bibliography: p.
    1. Social service.   2. Counseling.   3. Social case work.   I. Title.
HV41.B45   361   74-13524
ISBN 0-471-08235-X

Printed in the United States of America

10-9 8 7 6 5 4 3

To Lynn, Bard, and Laird
and to my parents
Rose and Edward (1900—1972) Bloom

Preface

A person with a problem never runs to a theorist for help. But neither does he rush to a helping professional. Chances are that he will try to work things out for himself and hope to muddle through somehow. If the going gets worse, he might involve his family or friends, or possibly acquaintances who will listen, like bartenders. Only as a last resort and with considerable discomfort does a person with a problem become a "client" being "interviewed" by a "practitioner." Why does a person with a problem go to a practitioner? He goes hoping that this stranger with her theories, her research information, her practice skills, and a host of other abstract tools will enable him to do a better job with his problems than he by himself or with his close associates has done. On the face of it, this is a paradox: that a stranger with good intentions and viable abstractions can make a difference in problem solving. **This book discusses the nature and use of these abstract tools for helping—and the paradoxes that abound in their application.**

There are five parts in this book. The first presents some tools and a rationale for using abstractions. We begin where the client is, that is, in the world of concrete happenings. There are many ways to make sense of these events, and the client has doubtless attempted a number of them without success. Unless the practitioner can do something different from what the client has already done, there is little chance that she will be more successful than he. That difference involves the use of abstractions, representing distillations of the scientific experiences of many persons. To choose the most appropriate abstractions requires that the practitioner know the problems as clearly as possible and how they hang together. It is in large part through interviews, systematic communications, that practitioners get a clear picture of those circumstances that make up a client's problem.

The first four chapters, composing Part I, represent a way of gaining a common perspective on client problems. By taking the events that are meaningful to clients and by finding patterns among them, we can begin to share the reality that the client is experiencing. Communication is the key tool at this stage; it also provides a bridge to the reality of theorists, researchers, and other practitioners who have dealt with similar problems in other contexts.

Part II is concerned with abstractions. The four chapters of this part present the working tools of a philosophy of science—concepts, propositions, theories, and empirical statements—that helping professionals will need as they formulate their clients' problems clearly and search the literature for empirically supported modes of action. These abstract tools are used by all of the helping professions and represent a common language among them.

Part III discusses the critical task of a philosophy of scientific practice, the orchestration of professional action, information, and evaluation. The abstractions from Part II are here translated into usable forms from their original states which may not have involved practice. It is the point of view of this book that professional action, information, and evaluation are equal partners in the balanced pursuit of scientific practice and that they unfold in a systematic way which permits maximal use of the helping professional's knowledge, skills, and values. The goal of the seven chapters of this part is to introduce a relatively new task to the helping professions, developing procedures for the systematic translation and incorporation of the best available scientific information into practice.

Part IV presents further tools for helping. These five chapters introduce broader perspectives on how scientific practice might be conducted. Topics include creativity in practice, objective evaluation of client progress and outcome, the role of computers and assessment instruments in practice, and a "survival kit" for workers in the face of the information crisis. The chapters on evaluation and information science introduce some new approaches for the helping professions.

The final part of the book summarizes the entire discussion, putting the separate components into perspective with each other: from the client's world of events to the abstract world of theorists and researchers to the world of scientific practice, which incorporates and yet translates each of the other two into a working system.

This book is written for students of the helping professions whose services to people, individually or collectively, require continuing use of information (theoretical, empirical, and practical) from the behavioral sciences in the context of altruistic values. As a social psychologist who has worked closely with social workers for the last decade, I have chosen my examples mainly from this form of applied behavioral science, but the ideas developed in this book apply with equal force to workers in psychotherapy, criminal justice, pastoral counseling, education, and public health nursing. As I have observed professional helpers in action, I have tried to identify how they did what they did, that is, how they connected their theories to their practice. Paradoxically, very few practitioners could specify the rules of their actions. When I became a teacher of social work, I felt obliged to identify these rules as clearly as possible and to test them for effectiveness. This book represents my efforts toward the first task. As Einstein once wrote: "Truth is what stands the test of experience." So be it.

Experts in any of the areas discussed in this book may be disappointed with the superficial coverage given to their specialization. Very few technical terms are used. This is part of the intentional design of the book, since it is written for the student practitioner. Such a student must move through several specialized territories to a new multidisciplinary area of his own called the "philosophy of scientific practice," a term born of the enthusiasm that these disciplines bring to their convergence a potential for more effective practice. I did not intentionally do injustice to any specialized area, and I am sure that if an expert finds my approach lacking he will so inform me.

It is impossible to identify, let alone acknowledge, the many influences that have shaped this book. I have had the good fortune to know some inspiring teachers. They include philosophers Paul Henle, Abraham Kaplan, and Hans Meyerhoff, social workers Margaret Blenkner, Marcella Farrar, and Marjorie Brown, and social psychologists Theodore Newcomb, G. E. Swanson, and J. R. P. French, Jr. I can still hear their voices, although I am responsible for interpreting what I have heard.

I am especially indebted to Richard G. Lawrence, Dean at the School of Social Service at Indiana University—Purdue University at Indianapolis, for his long-term encouragement of this project. Many other colleagues and friends made important specific contributions: James Norton, Edmund Byrne, Charles Guzzetta, Jerry Ulman, Walter Hudson, and Lawrence Sherwood. I must also acknowledge several generations of students who have heard these ideas in their formative stages. I thank several who further shared their ideas and efforts with me: Steven Block, Richard Early, Mary Ghosh, Lee Grogg, Phyllis Grogg, Vernell Holley, Joan Tobin, and Kathy Willis. For yeoman secretarial efforts, I thank Eileen Daniels and Karen Neely. Special appreciation goes to Thomas Gay, my editor. Acknowledgment is also given to the seminal ideas of T. Sarbin (T. Sarbin, R. Taft, & D. Bailey, CLINICAL INFERENCE AND COGNITIVE THEORY), D. Pelz ("Environments for creative performance with universities"), and R. Stuart (TRICK OR TREAT: WHEN AND HOW PSYCHOTHERAPY FAILS), and the many others whom this book is based. These three named persons also reviewed portions of the book concerning their work.

This book was essentially written at home, amid a complex family system. My sons Bard and Laird provided a wondrous reality against which these abstract ideas were developed. My magnificient wife Lynn, busy with her three worlds of writing, teaching, and family, was never too busy to continue our

beautiful dialogue that began some fifteen years ago, much to my benefit—
and now to this book's.

Washington University   **Martin Bloom**
St. Louis, Missouri
July, 1974

Contents

THE PARADOX OF HELPING:

Introduction to the Philosophy of Scientific Practice

Part I

SCAFFOLDING

CHAPTER 1

The Critical Paradox for the Helping Professions: How Abstractions Touch People

Once upon a time, many years ago, in a kingdom by the sea, two young men were beset with problems. One young man, whom I will call Ben Doran, was incarcerated at a Scottish borstal, a training center for young criminal offenders. He had been in conflict with his society, having been caught taking something that belonged to someone else. At the borstal, he was in conflict with the staff, but only enough to annoy them without getting into major battles which might have delayed his release. In the rich parlance of the borstal, Ben was a "fly," someone who knew the limits and pushed just up to them. In addition, Ben was in turmoil with himself, alternately elated and depressed, trying to jibe his image of himself as a young, handsome, somewhat shy teenager full of the vitality of life with the image of the youth looking back at him from a mirror, pale, wearing ill-fitting prison garb, in the dull prison surroundings of stone walls and locked doors.

I was the other young man with problems. At the time, I was a student assigned (in accordance with my request) to the borstal for a month's experience associated with my training for a one-year diploma program in social study at the University of Edinburgh. The following anecdote, which is somewhat painful to me now, reveals my growing awareness that to give professional help means, among other things, that one must have professional competence in forming and using **abstractions** with people. This strikes me as a paradox of sorts—using artificial entities to influence concrete entities. Yet I believe this to be the critical paradox in the development of a professional helping person.

Consider: Here was Ben, an absolutely fascinating individual unlike any I had ever known before, with a unique set of attitudes and behavior patterns. In spite of the frustrating deeds he performed, I found him genuinely likable.

Yet I was in a learning situation. I was being urged to think about Ben in terms of complex abstractions, his "social background," his "personality," the types of "group interactions" he engaged in—ideas from many theorists from around the world, empirical research involving thousands of subjects over a period of many years. Moreover, I was being directed to combine these abstract generalizations into a precision tool detailed enough to guide my practice at this time and in this place. I was further expected, to a growing degree, to be critically knowledgable about these various forms of information—the assumptions used by the theorist, the research design used by the researcher. And, finally, I was going to be held responsible for decisions and influences that might affect Ben's entire life, based on my understanding and use of these abstract tools.

It is in guided field experience that the pressures of this paradox of using abstractions with people are eventually worked out, although not without effort. Yet, to accept the paradox is to begin to transcend it. To gain a comfortable familiarity with the world of abstractions and to retrieve them effectively as they are needed for whatever problem appears turn out to be two of the more gratifying of professional experiences—leading to the ability to offer effective help.

Abstractions, after all, are a concentration of the experiences of some persons, constructed as second-hand wisdom to help those who follow. There is nothing perfect or final about abstractions, and the user is always cautioned that he must test them in use every time. Assuming that useful abstractions can be formed at all, then what abstractions should be chosen and how should they be combined? What rules can be given to direct one in using abstractions (like concepts and theories) with living human beings whose lives may literally depend on these choices? These kinds of questions form the problems that this book considers. The answers, being abstractions as well, are also to be tested in use.

Social work education has typically involved practical experiences, such as my placement at the borstal. Consider what this means, for me, but more important, for every student at every time and place. I suddenly and literally entered a strange new world, with many cultural facets with which I was unfamiliar: the social structural arrangements of who could do what to whom and when; even the language, which I thought I knew, was now being used in different ways. To some degree, these new elements are true of every placement experience, like the middle-class white (or black) dealing with a lower-class black (or white), like being in the public schools on the inside rather than as a student, like working in some of the garbage heaps of our fantastic civilization. How is one to make sense of it all? What is one to look at and to look for? Indeed, how is one to know when something is found?

There are certain guideposts on which to hang an organization of new and confusing realities. Physical props immediately come to mind, such as the buildings into which we enter to do our field work. The borstal was located at the site of an old Scottish public school built of solid gray stone, bearing a motto over the door to the administration building, "Do or Die." One entered the grounds through an immense iron gate which was always open, along a curved road past the football pitches, to the series of gray stone boxes which housed the borstal. Going through these stone boxes, from one part of the borstal to another, required the unlocking and relocking of countless doors— one of my more vivid memories. There were borstal farmlands beyond this, and ringing the borstal were the history-filled hills of Scotland. But which of the many physical aspects of the buildings and grounds should be observed? And how were these to be integrated with other perceptions?

The social and psychological characteristics soon forced themselves on the observer. While the borstal was broken down into roughly equal-sized physical units, there were important social differences among them. As is often the case, local labels indicated the social nature of these units—one housing section was called the "gangsters," another the "gentlemen," and a third, the "loonies." In the minds of the inmates and also the staff (for allocation purposes), boys were placed according to physical and mental strengths or frailties. However, these social characteristics were not always accurate guides. At one of the boxing matches I observed, the loonies—mentally and physically frail boys— did the horrendous deed of coming within one point of beating the gangsters. It is clearly not enough to let the physical and social props completely determine our perceptions of reality if we are to use our knowledge to direct our helping behaviors. The sheer variability of people is at times overwhelming. There were some individuals in the borstal who were warm, loving, and lovable, and there were others who were just the opposite—with neither the staff nor the inmates having a monopoly on either category. Another of my insights into myself during this experience was that different people viewed me quite differently. To some I was likable; to others I was a bore. The fact of the matter is that we must contribute something to the processes of viewing and of abstracting. When we see someone as a fool, we should ask ourselves how much of this foolishness we are contributing.

I contributed a great deal—much of which I had to unlearn. Like so many other persons entering field placement, I came to the borstal full of ideas and preconceptions and no shortage of stereotypes. And I tried, as every beginner does, to impose what I knew on what I did not know. It didn't work very often, not so much because of what I knew, but rather because I couldn't translate information from lectures and texts into plans and actions. This is a distinction between intellectual knowledge and that more active knowledge formed by applying intellect and its abstractions to actual life situations. This is one major expectation of professional training: that the abstractions by which you live and work will become intellectually clearer and increasingly under your behavioral control.

The contribution that the professional must make in the process of abstracting involves both an orientation and a controlled set of questions asked of reality. Let me illustrate this with reference to my novice work with Ben. I met Ben near the beginning of my stay at the borstal, and spoke with him on numerous and long occasions, a true luxury as placements go. Ben's problems were multiple and interrelated. It was hard to unravel the threads of his story because they were in fact different aspects of the same phenomenon: conflicts with society related to conflicts with adults related to conflicts within himself.

Ben was slippery, disarmingly frank, and convincingly deceitful, all at one time. I was a bit slippery myself, an unfortunate mixture of naiveté and ignorance, which was apparently sufficiently convincing that Ben trusted me with a considerable number of personal confidences and pretended confidences. My problem was trying to sort out which were which, to try to understand his problem from his perspective, and to help, if I could.

Helping someone is a complex business. It begins with the task of finding out what the problems are for which help is needed. I soon realized that Ben did not always define his illegal behaviors as "problems" while he did view some of his "training for freedom"—this is the overall directive of borstal experience officially defined—as problematic. Ben liked to steal, so he said. It got him out of his conflict-ridden home and into exciting adventures. It paid off handsomely and he received a certain type of homage from his friends, although he had to admit that stealing had its occupational hazards. During our long conversations, I tried to reflect some reality about stealing—I have conveniently forgotten just how I did this; it probably involved a good deal of moralistic persuasion. However, it was I who was forced to concede that stealing was realistically exciting, that it could pay well for effort expended, and that it did provide some status within a certain subculture.

Somewhat in desperation, I retorted that being a criminal prevented Ben from being a "real" person. But what was a real person? This stopped Ben for a moment, as I blurted something about authenticity, the self as a composite of social actions and reactions, and the value of living freely among—not submerged beneath—one's fellowmen.

This appears to me now as a package of undigested conceptualizations on which I was totally unprepared to act. But it had an unexpected, beneficial impact on Ben which I could not then explain. It was my first paradox: What did I do that worked? If I could solve that paradox by learning the rules of successful professional action, then I could use them again in new situations, refine them, make them better. Over time I have come to realize that abstractions are not—or need not be—airy nothings but are the dimensions by which all men live, each within his own abstractions. I realized that abstractions are real in the sense that they have real effects on people, even if not the intended effects. Professional understanding means that the worker aligns his abstract ways of viewing the world with the client's view of the world—seeing what the client sees and feels. Then, utilizing his **additional** information and insight, the worker tries to convey to the client new abstractions or reorganized ways of acting that will resolve the problem.

One last lesson from the borstal: A worker never works in isolation. I have no knowledge of the long-term impact of my contacts with Ben. I have my doubts, for while I was engaged in this existential interchange, the borstal saw fit to assign Ben to a welding group, which meant, he told me, that he could learn something about his heart's desire—safecracking.

The rewards of helping are strange and wondrous; sometimes they come in unusual packages. Ben surprised me with a homemade parting gift as I said my last goodbye: a matchbox-size, wood-with-metal-inlay casket.

SUMMARY

This chapter contains a double anecdote: one about Ben, a teenager in trouble with the law; the other about a beginner in the helping professions. Ben had reacted to his problem by leaping on horseback, so to speak, and riding off in all directions. The beginner was tempted to do likewise but was restrained by a growing network of abstractions concerning people with problems. Such restraints are both necessary and occasionally painful. But if we are to do a better job of problem solving than Ben or his family or friends could do, we had better step back and see what the accumulated knowledge from scientists and other workers can tell us before we rush to Ben's aid. And the paradox of it all is that there is evidence that by using scientific abstractions, we can effectively influence concrete events like those that compose Ben's world. The nature of this paradox of helping is the subject of this book.

CHAPTER 2

Scaffolding for Abstractions: Events, Sets of Events, and Systems of Events

Every person, especially a writer, dreams that the words he launches will float on an ocean of common understanding. However, there are many currents and eddies in the ocean of words and even in the supposedly more placid sea of science. The following endeavor is an attempt to explore and to discover islands of meaning on which we can agree.

We make our way through the world of everyday reality oblivious of the fact that we are bombarded by thousands of stimuli every moment. How shall we begin to deal with this reality? Consider this analysis of the everyday world:

"I am standing on a threshold about to enter a room. It is a complicated business. In the first place I must shove against an atmosphere pressing with a force of fourteen pounds on every square inch of my body. I must make sure of landing on a plank travelling at twenty miles a second round the sun— a fraction of a second too early or too late, the plank would be miles away. I must do this whilst hanging from a round planet head outward into space, and a wind of aether blowing at no one knows how many miles a second through every interstice of my body."

Many readers will recognize this passage from Eddington's **The Nature of the Physical World** (1929, p. 342). As a theoretical physicist, Eddington is playfully taking seriously the abstractions physicists use in describing the real world. This quaint passage takes on prophetic meaning in reference to the astronauts (and the world audience through its television eye) docking their lunar modules with the mother ships far out in space. We, too, must be prepared to consider the utility—perhaps the future utility—of abstractions. Yet there are plenty of abstractions, new and old, which may never be useful. This includes some quite persistent abstractions, and some malicious ones as well. It is a difficult task to distinguish among the helpful, the harmful, and the humbug.

Let us go back to those thousands of bits of stimuli bombarding our senses every moment. From this blooming, buzzing confusion we learn to sort out, select, combine, and use certain portions of stimuli. Which portions are selected?

It would be nice to have a unit of constant size like the meter for which there is a **common physical referent**—that platinum iridium bar kept at the International Bureau of Weights and Measures at Sèvres, near Paris—or, better, a **common operational referent**—since 1960, the meter is defined in terms of the spectral line of light emitted from excited atoms of krypton-86. Imagine a "freud" (like a watt or a joule)—a unit of timeless chaotic unconscious libidinous force seeking expression at inopportune moments and identifiable only by psychoanalysts and sophomores. Or a "marx"—a unit of inevitable cyclical pressures exerted by those who produce values against those who control values and understood by everyone except psychoanalysts and sophomores. It would be nice. But we have few such units for the behavioral sciences, let alone for the applied behavioral sciences.[1] Should we abandon all hope and become physicists?

Pure science is like a virgin, shy, distant, and aloof. Applied science is more like "that sadder but wiser girl." At this time, it is a matter of values to choose to commit oneself to the behavioral sciences and to the social arts derived from them. We look in anger and frustration at much of human history, current

---

[1] Recently, some methods have been proposed to yield a metric for attitudes and opinions. For example, Wolpe and Lazarus (1967) offer a unit called a **sud** (subjective unit of disturbance). A client is asked to think of the worst anxiety he has ever experienced and to assign this a scale value of 100. His idea about being absolutely calm is assigned zero. Then he is asked to rate himself at this moment and also to rate specific aspects of his environment as to the amount of anxiety created by exposure to them (p. 73).

Stevens (1966) discusses a number of metric approaches for the social sciences, with special attention going to Sellin and Wolfgang's (1964) ratio-scaling methods. Seriousness of delinquent events (not persons as such) is one variable studied in such a way that it is possible to describe in ratio terms how much more serious one type of offense is than another. For example, "stealing and abandoning a car is only about one-tenth as serious as robbing a man of $5 and wounding him in the process" (p. 537).

Other parts of this book, especially Chapters 17 and 19, attempt to develop other metric approaches for applied social scientists working in the field with the problem events of their clients.

events, and prospects for the future, and ask what our part will be. Having chosen a helping profession, one must eventually ask how this work may be done most adequately. For many, the overwhelming answer is by systematic application of the scientific method—in spite of all the idiocies performed in that name. The scientific method is a way of dealing with abstractions about realities in order to obtain new realities about abstractions. Applied scientific methods are ways of translating abstractions to affect reality; we will discuss these methods in Part III of this book.

Even though we cannot have precisely defined units of study as in the physical sciences, perhaps we can have approximate or relative units of study so that we can get into the business of using behavioral science knowledge to help solve human problems. I am going to arbitrarily define some terms with which a scaffolding for dealing with abstractions used by the helping professions may be constructed. Eventually we will disregard these terms as the structure of applied social science shows through. But the scaffolding will give us a quick overview of things to come.

Let us use the word "event" to refer to any selected portion of stimuli that is meaningful to the person involved. I quickly learned to recognize Ben from the other boys in their purple prison uniforms, and I eventually learned to distinguish Ben-happy from Ben-depressed, but I was never certain I could tell the event Ben-honest from Ben-lying. And it never even dawned on me to distinguish Ben, the firstborn in a family of three, from Ben, born second or third in a family of three; the idea of birth order was never an event for me, though it may have been for someone else. Because something is meaningful does not necessarily make it right or wrong, real or fantasy, or connected to this or leading to that. Events will differ in terms of the number of stimuli involved, as well as how these stimuli are sorted out and organized by different people. But it is useful to know that an event has been selected; this is where we begin.

Next we may ask whether this event is related to any other events and on what basis. Often, events are related by **time reference,** like a sequence of events in which first this happened, than that, and finally something else. Or events may be related by **space reference.** As Ben and I got to know each other better, we sat or stood closer to one another, a physical indicator of the closeness of our relationship.

This idea of a physical indicator or marker is important, for while I could point to distinct physical events, it became more interesting to point to or label relationships between events, such as the growing closeness of the friendship, or whether the event Ben-happy occurred more or less often than Ben-depressed as a result of my contacts with him. Let us call those events that related to other events on any determinable basis **sets of events,** recognizing the importance of being able to apply a metric to them (number, rate, or whatever) in order to characterize the relation in objective terms.

When we include certain events in a set, we are at the same time excluding other events (if the set is not to be all-inclusive). But, like the reversible perceptual figures of the staircases going up or going down, one does not literally lose or destroy the event not seen; it can be included in another set of events, so to speak, when one looks again. Since people may combine events in different ways, we come to know another individual to the extent that we understand how he relates certain events. By applying appropriate metric notations—numbers of occasions, intensity of feelings, rate of absences—we come to understand that individual's world more accurately.

A major distinction between **events** and **sets of events** occurs under the special condition that the event is part of the set of events. Then it can be said that the set of events is more than the event alone. This unstartling but logical statement is perhaps the major fulcrum on which the social sciences hinge at this time, that relativistic content free categories involve a fixed order among them. Whatever events Ben talked about, if they were related to a set of events, then I had a basic understanding of how events meaningful to him were organized in his way of thinking. Yet we can say more. We can add a third level to an organization among events.

If a given set of events is related to one or more other sets of events, they may be so interrelated as to be referred to as a **system of events.** In order that they constitute a system, there must be such interrelatedness among these sets of events that an influence or change in one produces effects on the others. This particular definition of systems, in contrast to other possible definitions, is most relevant to living systems (Miller, 1965a; 1965b; 1965c; von Bertalanffy, 1968; Buckley, 1968). For example, when the custodially-oriented staff became embroiled with the treatment-oriented staff, the borstal boys exhibited more problematic behavior than ordinarily, even though they were not directly informed about the controversy. It appears that the tensions of one segment of the borstal system had reverberations on another segment. Sometimes, system influences are unintended and unplanned, and, of course, they are not always beneficial influences.

Now we have three terms—events, sets of events, and systems of events— relative as to size and complexity but with a fixed, logical order among them. They are content free, meaning that we can use the terms with all kinds of portions of reality, from those dealing with individuals to those involving groups and even larger segments. The overall task is to impose some order on the flow of stimuli that flood us at every moment. We all impose an ordering on events; but it appears that we impose somewhat different orders on the same sequence of events, depending on how we have learned to deal with events. Even helping professionals may see the events of a case situation differently and thus may choose different intervention plans based on their different versions of the organization of the real world. The critical issue for practitioners is the effectiveness of these different views of reality, and this we can submit to empirical test.

Typically the helping professional encounters a client who talks with him, sharing a small interpreted part of the flow of events in her life. The client has already, by her interpretation, provided some ordering of events. The worker's task is to understand the client's ordering but also to consider these same events afresh to ascertain whether there is another ordering of them that would provide information relevant to effective intervention.

For example, take this fragment of an imaginary interview of a mother who has been referred to a mental health worker for severe headaches and depression. Each statement will be numbered so that we can combine and recombine the events in ways that may be conducive to new alternative solutions to her problems.

1. ". . . Just the other day, Billy was sitting in a chair reading
2. "and was so engrossed that he hardly moved a muscle.
3. "Then Peter came in,
4. "and they started to play some game together,
5. "but in a few minutes they were arguing as usual,
6. "and I could feel a headache coming on.
7. "I just wished they would stop fighting all the time.
8. "I didn't know whether to go down to the recreation room and yell at them to stop fighting, or what.
9. "But I decided to stay in the kitchen and finish the food I was preparing for the scout meeting.
10. "And just as soon as the other scouts came in, Billy and Peter stopped their arguing and
11. "were great friends, like nothing had ever been between them.
12. "I don't know. This happens all the time, like there was some plot between those two and me. . . ."

From this portion of the interview, different workers might reasonably combine the events in different ways, depending on their purposes. All workers are, in effect, seeking some system of events because with a system one can generate ideas about what influences what and, hence, where interventions might appropriately be made. Let's look at these several statements.

The mother reports a sequence of events as a meaningful instance of her problem, and for this reason alone we must pay attention. But we need not be content with her interpretation of the events (as in sentence 12) or even with her ordering of the events. For example, she chooses to distinguish statements 1 and 2, while at the moment we might not see these as needing to be separated because it doesn't add anything to our understanding of the sequence of events. The same might be true of statements 3, 4, and 5. So mentally we combine these into one complex event. Thus we have the first event (boy reading quietly) being fairly static, while the second (boys playing) is dynamic. The term "event" is intended to encompass both static and dynamic happenings. We can always go back and separate out components if we wish.

On other occasions, we might wish to clarify the events involved, such as in statement 5. What events led to the arguing? What does the mother mean when she says that this is "usual"? When we probe, we do so in order to gain a more complete understanding of the sequence of events, that is, we are seeking to construct an **individualized system of events** concerning this client's problem situation.

Statements 6 and 7 are two other events, both internal to the reporter, although we might have seen some physical concomitant of the headache, like throbbing temples. But the wish is completely subjective and is an event only because it is meaningful to an observer. There may be events not reported, such as the mother's anger at her children which gets suppressed because of society's conventions about such feelings. As the worker seeks to identify a system of events, he may have to infer or imagine such an event as part of the system to complete the picture. Whether this inferred missing link is truly an event or just a figment of the imagination of the worker must be put to the test, usually by asking or looking for other events that would confirm or deny the hypothesis involving that inferred event.

Perhaps the worker asks why the boys' argument produces a headache in the mother. A logical puzzle has been raised because an argument between two persons does not necessarily produce headaches in a third. What is the connecting event? Let us say that the mother responds that she has failed as a mother to teach the boys to live peacefully together and that this upsets her greatly. This answer, arrived at after delicate probing, appears to provide an interactive system of events explaining the problem of headaches, but the worker may also connect this with other sets of events, like getting tired before going out to a party, feeling ill just as she was going to look for a job, and so forth. Perhaps the worker may identify a broader system of events, all having a common pattern. Thus, searching for a pattern among events has led to a tentative systematizing of these concrete instances; it has also been possible to seek abstract patterns distinguishable from any particular instance, yet which may shed light on particular events. The critical test of a system of ideas is whether it proves possible to predict future events. These concerns are the subject of Part II of this book.

But the purpose of this chapter is to emphasize the reality of events in the client's life and to learn to respect those events, which are often very painful to a client. We will soon deal with concepts like a low self-concept or whatever we might label this pattern of events in a client's life. But the helping professional, insofar as he provides effective help, must be grounded in two worlds, the world of events and the world of abstractions. Events without abstractions are blind; abstractions without events are hollow.

COMMON AND UNCOMMON SENSE AS ORGANIZERS OF EVENTS

All individuals organize the stimuli of everyday reality into various types and patterns of events. Here, for example, are two linguistic events by which some people guide their behaviors:

People are basically selfish.
There is some good in everyone.

These somewhat contradictory clichés point up the fact that people can differ in their common-sense interpretation of events. Moreover, these clichés are seen as self-validating: If someone acts selfishly, one can say "See, I told you so." If someone acts altruistically, another can say "It is the exception that proves the rule." Is there no way out of this dilemma of common sense in which contradictory statements are held to be equally valid?

In case you haven't tried, it is very difficult to argue with a person who claims to use common sense as his touchstone. You may hear words to this effect: "These blacks (or whites) are nasty, brutish, and short—I have just seen it with my own eyes." Common sense is powerful for good reason; it is often attached to a piece of reality, to a selected set of events. But the inherent deficiencies of limited personal experience generalized beyond its scope make fools of those who use only common sense. The helping professional needs an uncommon sense in addition, a perspective for seeing the set of events related to the problematic event, and perhaps new sets of events in addition. He must see the system of events as the client sees it, but he must also see systems of events, perhaps involving recombinations of the same events, which the client hasn't been able to see. The first part requires the helping professional to share in the common sense of the client, his frame of reference, which leads him to combine events into certain sets and systems. If you think you can help the client without this, think Tower of Babel. When you are working with a client, it may suddenly dawn on you that even though you have been talking the same language about events which appeared to have been public, you are in fact talking about entirely different sets or systems of events. It may dawn on the client, too, so act fast. How can we share frames of reference?

Here is where we part company with common sense per se; we turn to the critical paradox of the helping professions, that is, to use systems of abstractions which will provide an uncommon sense to the problems of the real world.

Let us look again at the term "event." Like every term, it is triangular (Ogden and Richards, 1923; Eddington, 1929; Ruesch and Bateson, 1968). At one point, it is an **idea** in our heads born of patterns of stimuli from the everyday world. At another point, this idea is translated into a **symbol** which acts as a vehicle to communicate the idea to another person. At a third point, such a symbol refers to **something in reality** (or constructed about reality) which is meaningful to the person involved. Put back together, an event is an idea conveyed through a symbol to another person in order to share a portion of reality meaningfully with that other person.

Everyone thinks he has a direct pipeline to a piece of reality—and perhaps everyone does. In addition, everyone believes he has a clear grasp of some symbol that represents the idea in his head—and perhaps everyone has this, too. But what everyone lacks is assurance that his symbol is the same as another's for the identical event in the real world. It is possible for one symbol to refer to different pieces of reality or for several symbols to refer to the same bit of reality.

The task of the person who seeks to develop control over the symbols he uses in communicating with others—and this includes the practitioner as well as the theorist—is to establish a procedure for continually testing the linkages among symbol, idea, and reality, as well as among the community of users of these symbols, ideas, and realities. This includes testing what Ben means when he says he is feeling depressed, but it also means testing whether theories of depression provide guides for action with reference to Ben. This book presents several procedures for conducting these tests.

SUMMARY

In the previous chapter, I suggested that abstractions influence people and that the helping professions must deal with abstractions, both those that guide clients' lives and those which theorists, researchers, and professionals use to understand and to influence human behavior. Lacking a constant unit of abstraction for human behavior, I offered a tentative way to attain a relatively objective and constant perspective. This involved the perception of some event, a phenomenologically distinctive portion of reality, and some sets of events related on any determinable basis. When one event is part of a set of events, we can speak in comparative terms such as one event being more than the other. When sets of events are related such that one component influences other components, we can speak of a system of events, a useful tool in dealing with complex social behavior. Thus events, sets of events, and systems of events help to begin an orderly, although content free, viewing of the everyday world.

Looking further at events, I have presented the semanticists' distinction among the idea (in the head), the symbol (public carrier of that idea), and the referent (the object or construction of reality to which the symbol refers). Even though we don't know if we are seeing the same set or system of events as our clients, by distinguishing among these three elements we can begin to focus on the communication problem—trying to see and to deal with that which is problematic to the client. And that is what the helping professions are all about.

CHAPTER 3

A Social Communication Perspective: From Events to Shared Events

Events are essentially private. It takes only one clover and a bee and revery for Emily Dickinson to see a prairie.[1] Yet, as a poet, she has set before us a field of words, a new vision of a prairie, a new event of beauty if we care to share it with her. Sharing takes effort. Although the words are familiar and the referents of the words common to our experience, we can share only a portion of her unique vision, that part she cares to share with us and that we care to attempt to understand of her. And because her communication is poetry, we don't feel uncomfortable when we admit that we may not understand all that she is saying or what we think she is saying.

Yet, how like poetry is Everyman's communication. We can share only to a degree, some more, some less, our common world. I assume that a helping professional seeks to share a large, accurate portion of her client's world in order to enter it and to help him. I also assume that the helping professional must share the worlds of the theorist, the researcher, and the wise practitioner, to learn to help her client more effectively. This chapter concerns the sharing of events.

Though essentially private, events have three aspects, of which two are potentially capable of being shared. The referent of an event may be publicly

---

[1] To make a prairie it takes a clover and one bee,—
And revery.
The revery alone will do
If bees are few.

—Emily Dickinson
(Bianchi and Hampson, 1935, p. 116)

Quotation from THE POEMS OF EMILY DICKINSON edited by M. D. Bianchi & A. L. Hampson is reprinted by permission of Little, Brown & Company. © 1935 by Little, Brown & Company.

visible and the symbol conveying the idea may also be understood by native speakers of a language. But the idea remains entirely private, locked in the mind.

The first requisite, then, for sharing events is that of **overlapping** referents or symbolic carriers. I can share with Emily Dickinson my awareness of a clover and a bee in the fields around Amherst; I can even share my understanding of the words "bee" and "clover." However, I have seen hundreds of bees and millions of clovers without seeing the prairie of her vision. Overlapping referents or symbols do not guarantee fullness of shared vision; they only provide the grounds for some sharing.

Moreover, for Emily Dickinson, "revery alone will do," when one is short of bees. I am out for a walk with my young sons. I glimpse a buzzing something and get a far off look in my eye which the boys notice. "What are you looking at?" they ask. And I say that I am thinking about a beautiful prairie that I have never seen, filled with clover and honey bees. "Like Grandpa's backyard?" they ask. "Something like that," I reply. "Ohhh," they murmur as they look off in the distance at their image of that vision. The poetic interchange illustrates another facet of sharing, that there is an **interaction** among events being shared, a defining and a refining.

The overlapping and interacting of the publicly accessible aspects of events are interesting in their own right—we could talk about shared sets of events and shared systems of events—but the important point here is to notice the primary way in which events are shared among human beings: communication.

We may be in the presence of the same event and we may actively discuss it, but we may never know exactly the idea the other person has of that event. We can at best reduce the degree of uncertainty in our dealings with the other person about that event. Whether the event concerns bees and prairies or phobias and welfare checks, we can know only a part of that other life; we live with uncertainties, but we must also act on any information which reduces uncertainty to some degree.

Uncertainty about another person's opinion regarding shared events appears to lead to actions to reduce that uncertainty (Newcomb, Turner, and Converse, 1965). In the broadest sense, all communication may be viewed as the transmission of information from one person or source to another so as to reduce an uncertainty between them. The following discussion touches only lightly on the vast topic of communications, but it is meant to serve a special purpose in the context of a philosophy of scientific practice. Referring back to our scaffolding terms, I want to note that the transmission of information between one person or source and another represents one determinable relation between the communicated events, and so communication involves **sets of events. Social** communication requires one further step to complete the attempt to reduce uncertainty: Not only is a message sent but a message must be received. Thus, social communication as used here involves a **system of events** in which one party's behavior influences a second party's behavior which, in turn, influences the first. The sender-receiver shares an overlapping and interactive event with the receiver-sender. As Cherry (1957) remarks:

"Communication is a social function. . . . Communication means a **sharing** of elements of behavior, or modes of life, by the existence of sets of rules. . . . Communication is not the response itself but is essentially the **relationship** set up by the transmission of stimuli and the evocation of responses" (pp. 6–7).

A SOCIAL COMMUNICATION PERSPECTIVE

In the space of a quarter of a century, the literature on communication has been greatly enriched by the writings of many persons. A considerable number of these writers have been in the physical sciences and technological fields, but their ideas are being translated into the social sciences as well. Weaver (1967) reduces a complex communication system to a few basic elements which are portrayed in Figure 3-1.

These terms are abstract and can be applied to any level of social communication. For example, at the individual level, I (the information source)

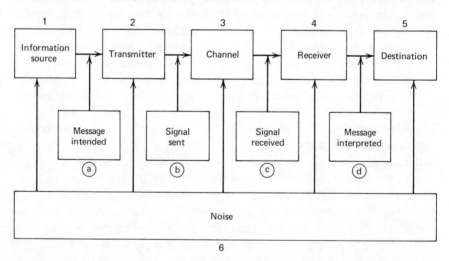

Figure 3-1—Modification of Weaver's (1967, p. 204) schematic diagram of a general communication system.

Excerpts from ON HUMAN COMMUNICATION by C. Cherry is reprinted by permission of MIT Press. © 1957 by MIT Press.

have selected the idea of one event from a larger set or system of events, and I send this intended message to my transmitter (either my vocal and gestural apparatus or my typewriter), which sends the vehicle of that idea, the public signal, across some channel (the air or the printed page) to a receiving apparatus (your ears or eyes), which picks up some signal (although not necessarily the one I sent!) and transmits it to the destination (your brain where signals are interpreted as carrying a meaning within a context, that is, as conveying some idea to your mind).

At the organizational level, the same terms may be used to describe a process involving distinct persons or roles, such as president (source) to secretary (transmitter) to office memo (channel) to mail clerk (receiver) to department head (destination), with office intrigue and gossip at all points slowing down the communication process.

The critical addition to be made to this formulation is to set it within a social context. Figure 3-2 indicates an interactive set of communicating systems, such as two persons or a person and a group. Note that the numbers and letters indicating the portions of Figure 3-2 are the same as in Figure 3-1.

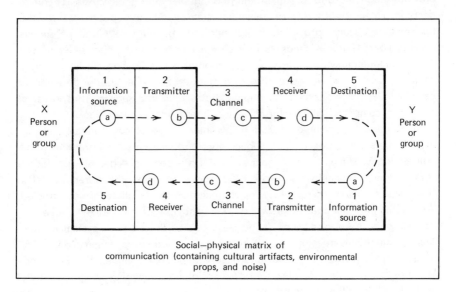

Figure 3-2—A schematic diagram of a general social communication system based on Weaver's diagram (Figure 3-1).

Diagram modified from "Information Theory—A Nontechnical Review." JOURNAL OF SPEECH & HEARING DISORDERS by permission of the Author, Warren Weaver, and the Editors. © 1952 by JOURNAL OF SPEECH & HEARING DISORDERS.

Person or group X has an information source and transmitter; X sends a signal over a channel which is received by person or group Y and delivered to its destination. Something happens to that message (indicated by the curved, dashed line in Y), and Y then becomes an information source and transmitter and sends a signal over a channel which is received by X and delivered to its destination. Thus, X is a sender-receiver and Y is a receiver-sender. The combination of two communication events (X sending a message to Y; Y sending a message in response to X) is defined here as a **circuit,** the basic unit of **social communication.** To anticipate, every one of these terms in Figure 3-2 will become a checkpoint for the practitioner in dealing with communication problems in their protean forms.

Next, let us look more closely at the curved, dashed lines connecting the receiver and the sender within one system. These represent several vital functions of the system in question, of which two are central: the decision making function and the memory storage function (cf. Miller, 1965a, 1965b, 1965c). Each decision is acted upon, even if the decision is not to act; this is the decision making function deciding how to react to a message. In addition, previous decisions and pertinent information are stored as bases for future decisions. Memory stores past communication circuits and provides the basis for sets for circuits, providing a potential for building relationships among communicants. Party X sends its half of the communication circuit—let us call this a **communiqué**—and party Y, in response, sends its half, thus making a complete circuit as we have discussed before. But when party Y sends its communiqué, party X sends still another half circuit in response. Thus, a **set of circuits** is composed of overlapping and interacting communiqués.

Information is accumulated during this interchange of communiqués, including X's expectations of Y's future behaviors and vice versa; information about values, ideas, stimulations in general—the basis for more persisting relationships among communicants. Asch (1950) spoke of "mutually shared fields" in which shared frames of reference for continued communications are constructed. As the mutual contingency grows, as the behaviors of one have to take into consideration more and more of the behaviors of the other, a **system of communication circuits** develops, an enduring social relationship (Rommeveit, 1955). These more involved systems of interactions and more complex communication patterns become the complex fabric of social life, including enduring fruitful as well as unfruitful relationships.

COMMUNICATIONS AND METACOMMUNICATIONS

Another major addition to the social communication perspective is the awareness that there are two paths along which information flows, two simultaneous events to which the receiver must respond. Various writers distinguish the verbal and the nonverbal, the content and the affect, the communiqué and the metacommuniqué, the report and the command, the spoken language and the silent language (the language of behavior), the statement and the definition of the relationship among the parties (Ruesch and Bateson, 1968; Watzlawick, Beavin, and Jackson, 1967; Satir, 1967; Hall, 1959, 1966; Day, 1972). While these concepts are not equivalent in all respects, they point to a common theme among communication writers: that the human communicator must pay attention to more than one information event, especially when the dual events may not be congruent, as when a tired child says "no" but behaves "yes."

It will be sufficient for present purposes to make the following observations pertinent to the task of the helping professional who is attempting to understand the events which the client presents to him. Content is mainly conveyed verbally, while affect is conveyed nonverbally on the whole—although this need not be so. The affect or nonverbal flow of communication can assume a variety of functions, qualifying the communiqué or report, emphasizing, denying or characterizing the communiqué according to the sender's feelings or his value preferences. It is an especially important source of information because it is used in so many different ways, and it can, with a slight change of intonation, completely modify the content message. Yet, being less visible than the message, an affective disqualification may itself be easily denied—"That wasn't what I meant at all." Thus, the affective information flow may be considered more volatile than the content information flow and perhaps a more sensitive indicator of intentions, yet may be more troublesome when it comes to a breakdown in human communication. Affective information is certainly more risky for the helping professional to interpret.

The dual communication events may be congruent or noncongruent, but they are necessarily present at every attempt to communicate, according to communication theorists. One must communicate; one can choose the timing, the form, and the content, but one cannot not communicate. One cannot not qualify one's communiqués either; one must metacommunicate the affective information that qualifies or perhaps denies one's messages. Most important, one may not be aware of the noncongruence between his communiqués and his largely nonverbal qualifications of them. For the helping professional, this takes on special meaning in how discrepancy may be indicated by an observation from the client: "You say you want to help me, but there is something in the way you say it that makes me wonder." Or the worker may comment to the client: "You say that you love your wife, but listen to this playback of a tape recording of our family interview and observe how often you put her down by the way you talk to her, rather than the specific content of what you say."

Haley (in Jackson, 1968a) points out that one can negate the effects of one's communication by denying any or all of these elements of the social communication perspective: (1) I (the source), (2) am saying something (the message), (3) to you (the destination), (4) in this situation (the social-physical matrix). For example, a spouse who was offensive to his mate after being drunk might say in words: "I was drunk [and hence not responsible for what I was saying], but I didn't say that [denial of the reported message], and if I did I certainly wouldn't have said it to you or about you [denial of the receiver and the destination of the message], and I never would have said such a thing in those circumstances [the social-physical matrix]. In some legal situations, a plea of insanity is like a negation of the source of a homicidal communiqué: "It wasn't I who murdered him; it was the demon [or the alcohol or the neurosis] which possessed my mind at that moment, and therefore I am not to be held responsible." The reality status of such "demons" in this type of defense has been questioned by some authorities (Szasz, 1961).

COMMUNICATION PROBLEMS

From the communications perspective, a problem might be defined as too much or too little information (content and/or affect) at the wrong time or place or delivered under the wrong circumstances. This includes problems in the sense of both presence of a defect or absence of a desired goal. Intervention is then defined as an attempt to redirect or to contribute information (either physical or symbolic) toward the end of producing different communication effects within the systems of the persons involved, without disturbing the communications in the larger system that contains the problem system. The helping professions are sometimes caught between these systems, trying to facilitate for one what is unacceptable to the other. Any interventive change produces new communication patterns and possibly new, unexpected problems.

The situations involving noncongruence (of content and affective information flows) constitute a large portion of the problems helping professionals encounter. Noncongruence can occur at any of the conceptual points in the social communication system (Fig. 3-2). This is the main purpose of making conceptual distinctions, that is, that they may guide practitioners to possible sources of breakdown occurring in the life situations of the clients corresponding to the parts of the conceptual system. Some of these points may have more practical import than others, but let me review the social communication system with the problem of noncongruence as illustrative of the types of practical analyses that can be made with conceptual tools.

Between the information source and the transmission of information there may occur noncongruence, even in the absence of a reply by the receiver of a sent message. "I didn't say what I intended to say very well; it came out all jumbled." This is a **social** meaning of the cybernetic term **feedback,** in which a portion of the original communiqué is returned to the sender as information about how much on target it was relative to the sender's intention (Weiner, 1950; Parsegian, 1973). Feedback serves as an adjustive mechanism in interpersonal relations. Feedback can serve to maintain a steady state in the system relative to an ideal reference point; or it can act to help the system increase its deviation from the reference point, a creative act under some circumstances, such as helping a youngster shake loose from his ties to a delinquent group.

A second place where noncongruence problems may emerge is where the receiver picks up the received message and compares it with an expectation, based on past experiences with that source. "He says he looked for work but couldn't find a suitable job. Now, in my (Protestant ethic, middle class) experience, if you really want a job, you can always find something. Therefore I conclude that he is not telling the truth." On the other hand, expectations may be helpful: "She speaks so slowly, as if she were retarded; but I must remember that this slow pace of talking is characteristic of some rural or Appalachian mountain cultures, and this would account for it, without inferring any pathology." There are various classes of expectations that are particularly troublesome in the helping professions. Since our expectations may be formed from previous experiences, including an uncritical childhood full of prejudicial learnings, we may think in stereotyped ways—we may believe in some of the many isms of our day, racism, sexism, ageism, whatever. Our expectations are built up inductively about a class, based on a limited sampling of members of that class or on false information in general, and then whenever a new member comes along, he is evaluated against this inadequate standard. Expectations are insidious because they are so pervasive and so difficult to recognize in ourselves. "That's the way we always did it." Expectations are as much a part of the client's life as ours, resulting, on occasion, in the blind retreating from the blind (cf. Mayer and Timms, 1970).

A third major location of potential noncongruence problems is the difference between the received message and the perceived metacommuniqué about that message. An eternal adolescent problem is when she says "no" but implies "maybe"; to which should he respond? I mentioned earlier the slippery but powerful force that the affective metacommunication exerts, especially when it is contradictory to the content message. Bateson, Jackson, Haley and Weakland (in Jackson, 1968a) have proposed that this form of noncongruence may be the cause of some types of schizophrenia through a double-bind situation in which a victim is continually subjected to noncongruent messages in situations of having to respond and not being able to leave the field. Not knowing how to respond to the madness of the real world, he retreats to a mad world of his own.

A fourth type of communication involving noncongruence is when an accurately received message and metacommunication simply disagree with one's point of view. "I know how you feel about X (some object or person) and I know how you feel about me, but I feel differently about X though I share the same feelings toward you." If the X is the proverbial mother-in-law and the "me" and "you" are a happily wedded couple, then one can appreciate the tensions involved. Newcomb, Turner, and Converse (1965) speak of three classes of outcomes to this "imbalanced" situation, that is, a situation in which each party receives information that the other holds a different attitude toward a common object. First, one or both parties may modify their attitude in the direction of the other. Second, there may be no change, each party either tolerating the difference with the other or ignoring the difference. Third, the system involving these parties may break up. Balance theorists offer predictions as to which alternative is likely, depending on the centrality of the object to the parties (see Newcomb, Turner, and Converse, 1965, pp. 149–151). The reaction of the other party to one's communication is another form of social feedback in which a portion of one's original communiqué—the portion that makes it through the transmission stage, the noises of the channel, the reception and interpretation on the part of the receiver and his reactive communiqué—comes back to the sender. Every reaction by another person has the effect of encouraging or discouraging change of the sender's original stance on an issue to a greater or lesser extent. The cumulative effect of reactions by significant others has a powerful influence on one's attitudes and actions. The new person on the scene—the helping professional—rarely has the power to overcome these cumulative effects; rather, intervention often involves redirecting the time, place, or circumstance under which information flows between parties in the conflicted system (cf. Watzlawick, Beavin, and Jackson, 1967).

In a broader sense, whole cultures (such as the Japanese culture or the culture of the Arabs) and subcultures (like migrant workers or the aged considered as a group) have distinctive ways in which they organize their communications. Anthropologists speak of overt culture, which can be easily described, and covert culture, which represents contexts of behavior that natives take for granted but which is invisible to foreigners (Hall, 1959). Conflicts between cultures, subcultures, generational groups, and others might profitably be interpreted as breakdowns in communications as represented by concepts in the social communication perspective: differences in expectation (of what is appropriate or desirable) and/or differences in style of transmission and reception of messages. Hall (1959) paints a vivid word picture of a Latin American talking with a North American. The former feels comfortable talking only at very close distances, while the latter needs a good arm's-length to feel comfortable. So they proceed to talk, the North American retreating backward as the Latin American struggles to get closer; the former finds the latter pushy, crowding, spraying in his face, while the latter finds the former cold, aloof, unfriendly.

Yet every person has his cultural and subcultural orientations and his individual variations on these themes. Every professional communication, such as the interview, is, in effect, a cross-cultural communication, as Kadushin (1972) points out. It is not merely racial differences that present impediments to an effective interview but also class, sex, and age differences pose barriers. The literature which Kadushin reviews shows no easy answers for the helping professional except that awareness of the problems clarifies what solutions are needed in a particular case.

SHARING OF EVENTS

The purpose of presenting this discussion of a social communication perspective is to understand the process by which events are shared between people. Recognizing the components of the communication process and the conceptual points at which breakdown in communication flow may occur enables us to understand more clearly the nature of and the extent to which sharing of events between worker and client can occur.

A client goes to an intake worker with a problem. The worker writes a summary of that interview; it may include certain demographic background information—age, sex, race, educational experiences, and other factors pertinent to the problem—as well as individualized information—the thoughts, feelings, values, and behaviors relevant to the problem. Each question asked reduces to some degree the worker's uncertainty about the client's situation. Knowing the client's age may clarify whether Medicare is a possibility or not; knowing his economic status reduces uncertainty as to whether application for public assistance is feasible. But also knowing how a person feels as a reaction to the crisis clarifies what alternatives the client might be able to use at this moment.

Moreover, the demographic kinds of information permit generalization to other factors associated through research with those categories. A considerable amount is known about the life experiences of the poor and of the aged. But this normative information must be checked against the individualizing information, lest we stereotype the particular client before us. "You know what to expect from an old woman. . . ." In fact we do know something about the class of events—the elderly—but this is insufficient in itself to predict the behavior of a particular person in that class because there are so many other variables that influence her behavior. We can not disregard normative information; but neither can we disregard individualizing information.

We share events through communication—the normative and the individualizing realities of everyday life—and we build up a picture of this client and her particular problem, an individualized system of events. Now that we have come as close as humanly possible to being with the client in her world, we must consider moving to the world of abstractions, of theories and empirical statements, of the codifications of practice wisdom, all of which will guide our professional actions. A large edifice is to be built on our communications. Yet we must never forget that we began in the stream of events that make up the lives of clients and, ultimately, we must return to this reality.

SUMMARY

Private events (and sets and systems of events) may be shared to some degree, although it is difficult to attain perfect communication, especially when the referents of the message (such as feelings) are themselves abstract or difficult to put into words. Yet, all of our social life is bound up in networks of persisting communication systems, and communicate we must.

There are several basic propositions from this social communication perspective which should influence all of our communications with clients. We haven't communicated unless the recipient responds to our message. And we must communicate over a sequence of times in order to understand the context in which the other person uses language and behaviors to describe his personal and cultural view of events. In so doing, we simultaneously join a communication system with him which is part of the way we will eventually seek to help him. We must be aware of the congruence or noncongruence in communications and metacommunications—his and ours. We must be clear about our orientation to communications as we consciously select certain types of information to seek and thereby exclude others. We must be aware of the visible and the invisible barriers that impede communication. The communication decisions we make, large and small, are ipso facto the therapeutic interventions we make.

CHAPTER 4

Issues in Philosophy of Science: Analysis of Shared Abstract Events

Here is an event:

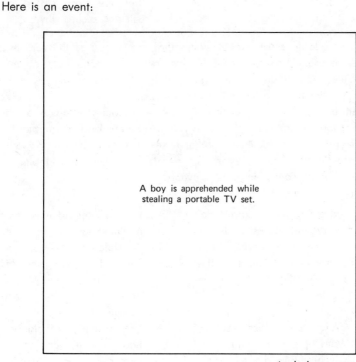

A boy is apprehended while
stealing a portable TV set.

As helping professionals,
what are we to make of this?

Standing alone, this event gives rise to any number of ideas antecedent to
the theft as well as to ideas consequent upon the boy's being apprehended.

A bit more thought would unearth some considerations about the youngster himself, perhaps about the policeman involved, and so on. The event by itself is in effect meaningless; it requires a context against which it is to be understood. And, more important, it requires a context that would provide direction for possible actions by a helping professional. Where do we begin? We begin by asking questions which uncover other events that are related to the first. We begin to identify a **set of events.**

Now what questions would you ask if you were given the core event that a boy had been apprehended while stealing a portable TV set? Perhaps these:

1. (Q.) Where was he apprehended?   (A.) He was apprehended in a department store.

2. (Q.) Was he with anyone?   (A.) He was alone when apprehended.

3. (Q.) When did this occur?   (A.) This occurred several hours after the store closed on such and such a day.

Each of these questions asks about events that are a part of the core event. Sometimes the connection is by time or place or circumstance, but we can see that all of these events are related. There are many more as well. And these are good questions, but after a long list of such questions has been asked, we may still have a feeling of incompleteness, of not being sure how all these events hang together. We may need to ask a different kind of question, one in which if one event is true then another event is likely to be true as well. In short, we begin to identify **systems of events** by asking overlapping and interactive questions concerning sets of events.

For example, we might ask:

4. (Q.) Did the boy have knowledge about and access to dealers of stolen merchandise?   (A.) Yes, he later admitted that he knew how to dispose of the stolen goods.

5. (Q.) Were there channels other than stealing for his obtaining money?   (A.) Relatively few, given his age, race, skill background, and level of employment.

6. (Q.) Were there local cultural ways of thinking and acting which might have encouraged his stealing and even attached status to it?   (A.) Yes, within his neighborhood, some groups of persons thought stealing was an easy and an appropriate way to make a living in an every-man-for-himself society.

These questions (4, 5, 6) assume that a particular system of events is operative. For example, the first connects the act of stealing with the ability to get rid of the stolen goods for profit. What makes these questions different from those event questions asked previously? And where did they come from?

It would have been possible to stumble on a system of events which connected the availability of an outlet for stolen goods with this particular boy's theft, but it was more likely to have come from the experienced observations of other persons—people who did research on patterns among a large number of individual instances of theft or people who theorized about the patterns of events surrounding theft in general. Note that both of these origins of ideas are likely to be beyond the knowledge of the client: The boy was not aware of the social forces operating on him, although he knows old Sneaky Pete, the fence.

The practitioner is, in effect, driven to the domain of abstractions in order to identify a system of concepts that can account for the individualized situation before him. One can rarely find a pattern of events easily with one individual's circumstances, although once concepts help him to know where to look, the events tend to fall into place. Thus, the most effective and economic way to deal with a person's individual problem situation is to seek aid from the **abstracted** experiences of others (theorists, researchers, practitioners) in order to find patterns which are meaningful in the specific case in question. These patterns are expressed in a new language whose analysis is part of the **philosophy of science;** we will talk about concepts, propositions, theories, and empirical generalizations as the ways in which the experiences of others are conveyed to the practitioner.

This language of philosophy of science is an involved study in its own right, but we will not get into these matters here (see Turner, 1967). Rather, let me simply point out that whereas I had spoken of events, sets of events, and systems of events, I will now discuss the idea parts of events (roughly equivalent to concepts), sets of concepts (propositions), and systems of propositions (theories, empirical statements). These will involve rules of their organization—logical or mathematical—and a number of other issues necessary to the helping professional. I will not go into great detail about the philosophy of science as such, because we need only a portion of its contribution in what is the heart of this book, the philosophy of scientific practice.

The reader familiar with the many theories of delinquency will recognize in Questions 4, 5, 6 some of the leading questions (propositions) that characterize one or another theory (Sutherland, 1934; Cloward and Ohlin, 1960; Cohen, 1955; Kvaraceus and Miller, 1959). Each theory is different; each involves different ideas and systems of ideas about the phenomenon, and a practitioner choosing among them would likely follow different paths in his practice. An obvious question arises: Which theory is best? There are two issues here: Do we mean best in terms of formal aspects of theory construction, or do we mean best in leading to positive outcomes? The first issue will be discussed in Part II of this book, the second in Part III.

OPERATIONALIZATION

For the remainder of this chapter, I would like to discuss several issues in the philosophy of science which have particular relevance for the helping professional. The first issue concerns operational definitions of concepts. Take the idea symbolized by the word "ego." I have something in mind when I think about this word; in fact, thinking of Gordon Allport's (1937) efforts at locating some 300 definitions of personality, I have a lot of things in mind when I think of the word "ego." Assuming that I can sufficiently focus my ideas about ego, when I write or speak to you about ego I hope that you will have something similar in mind. Had I used the word "egg," it would have been easier to point to an actual egg to improve communication. But even here I am reminded of Hall's (1959) story of the anthropologist who asked five children for a name when he pointed to an object as concrete as an egg. He received five different answers—the children had mistaken what he wanted named. Some named the act of pointing, the thing pointed with, the direction pointed to, the object in line with the point, a color or other attribute of the object. Thus any event is difficult to communicate about completely, and abstract parts of events, their ideas or concepts, are even more problematic.

Bridgman (1927), a physicist, formulated one approach to the meaning of abstract terms. Roughly speaking, a concept or idea is whatever the specific operations are that manifest the idea. So intelligence is whatever intelligence tests measure. One can see how such a proposal would sweep away many fuzzy ideas for which no operations were possible to give them meaning. But it becomes a matter of judgment as to what one will accept as an operation. If I choose to think that a client who can multiply two times three correctly, and then two times that answer, so long as he can get the correct answers (up to twelve times) as having certain levels of intelligence for each number of correct answers, you may agree or disagree with me (actually with Wilson, 1967; see Chapter 19), but that is one operation of intelligence. If you choose to use as a measure of intelligence a series of subtractions, seven from one hundred, seven from that answer, and so on, we would, strictly speaking, have to say we were using two different concepts of intelligence. Theories would be composed of very large numbers of ideas to match all of the operations that could be used to give them meaning, and if we must juggle very large numbers of ideas, then we gain no intellectual advantage for going to the realm of ideas as opposed to sticking with an individualized system of events.

Moreover, some ideas are not easily operationalized at all and yet are helpful in a network of ideas used to explain problem events. Let's take the concepts of the social forces acting on the boy who stole the TV set. Are we to reject an idea like social forces which was presumably inferred from the regularities among individual acts, but which had no tangible referents as such? Durkheim (1951) worked with the ultimate in individual acts, suicide, and was able to detect regularities in patterns of suicide which provided great insight about this phenomenon. Yet there is no tangible object that corresponds to the words "patterns of suicides" or to "suicide rates"; there is only the way we talk about and relate events, the collection of which provides the basis for abstracting and generalizing to the concept of suicide rates, or whatever. There is another paradox: If a concept has no clear direct operational statement, but appears to be useful in our understanding, how can we use it? One answer is to place the concept in a network of concepts, the set of which makes predictions that may be useful in guiding the practitioner.

Carnap (1953), a philosopher of science, proposed one workable solution concerning confirmability in principle, in place of absolute verifiability: If a network of ideas hangs together logically, then not all of the terms therein need to be operational. It would be sufficient that some of the terms have clear operational definitions and that the system of terms be interrelated such that measurement concerns the fruitfulness of the whole network or system of ideas rather than each specific one.

Let's examine some of the implications of Carnap's solution. Initially, we can live with any concept whatsoever, so long as it is logically tied to a network of ideas whose overall structure leads to a usable solution. This means that we must be able to operationalize the **goals** of a network of ideas and some of the **means** to attain these goals. How many of these intervening ideas we insist be operationalized is not spelled out in the solution, and it will depend on our own sense of risk. Is it worthwhile to use an expansive theory in which many concepts have no clear operational statements, or should we stay closer to behaviorally specifiable reality for our guides to action? There is no certain answer for this except the objective and systematic test of experience. The implication is that all theories must be subjected to testing and that practitioners should be appropriately sensitive to the results. In the meantime, theories carry a temporary stay of execution: Use them with care, but use them.

VALUES

The second major issue in the philosophy of science which has great relevance for the helping professions is the question of the place of values in the scientific world of fact. Every act of intervention on the part of a helping professional is directed toward the attainment of someone's valued goals (the client's goals, society's goals), and so value decisions are an intrinsic part of the act of helping. Max Weber (1949) suggested a methodological ideal long ago, that is, that the social sciences ought to be value free, that the act of performing empirical investigations should be kept unconditionally separate from the scientist's own personal evaluations of those events. The events themselves may be value laden, such as Humphreys' (1970) observation of homosexual acts which occurred in public restrooms. But analysis of the events should follow reality as closely as possible.

On the assumption that the knowledge base of the social sciences attains a reasonable degree of its value free ideal, how and when does the helping professional add values to facts in order to arrive at helping decisions?

There is no adequate solution to this problem. This book offers some observations about values in practice but mainly attempts to clarify the boundaries of the problem. For example, in Chapter 3, it was pointed out that metacommunications are an intrinsic part of all communications, and those affective qualifiers express value preferences continually. This implies that a practitioner interacting with his client is in an ongoing value interchange. Chapter 13 discusses values in the context of giving professional help. The entire book uses words like "scientific," "objective," and so forth, with the hope that these are more useful than "nonscientific," "subjective," and the like. Yet other writers present positions which are "scientific" **and** "subjective" (e.g., Combs, Avila, and Purkey, 1972). Which blend of values and facts is more useful remains to be tested in the professional arena.

So the value question persists. May its paradox challenge us all. There are, of course, many other issues in the philosophy of science, some of concern to generalists [like Kaplan's (1964) book on the logic of inquiry], others of concern to specialists [like Rychlak's (1968) book on a philosophy of science for personality theory]. But the present book has a focused concern for the helping professional, and the issues discussed above will serve as an introduction to their specialized problems.

SUMMARY

For purposes of this book, a philosophy of science is an analysis of abstract shared events which are apart from the client's world of events. The practitioner's contribution to the helping process consists in his skillful use of the abstract shared events of the theorist, researcher, and experienced therapist or interventionist. The tasks of the philosophy of science include clarification of the concept and the various kinds of relationships among concepts indicated by terms such as propositions, theories, empirical generalizations, formulations of practice wisdom.

Philosophy of science can be taken as a world apart from the everyday world, a world with its own rules of logic and mathematics and of operational definitions. Effective use of the tools of this abstract world can become the essential task of the helping professional if, unlike the logical positivists from whom I have taken much inspiration, the humanistic core of concepts-for-use-in-helping is not lost. Value considerations are a necessary assignment in any societal definition of the helping professions, and an abstract analysis of tools of these professions cannot exclude this factor.

Through the efforts of philosophers like Carnap, we have come to a better working relationship with abstract terms and their referents in the real world. But anyone who is a helping professional is at the cutting edge of the problem of integrating values in a world of facts.

Part II

PHILOSOPHY OF SCIENCE: COMPONENTS OF THE SHARED ABSTRACT EVENT SYSTEM

CHAPTER 5

Concepts: Abstracted Classes of Events

Helping professionals deal in words: "Does this **community** need a runaway house?" "Is a runaway house effective as a therapeutic **community**?" "Would the **Community** Chest support this type of nonconventional approach to counseling?"

Words, the public conveyers of meaning, take on special importance as they become the major tools for dealing with psychological and social problems. If a tool is to be properly and effectively used, then the user must know what it means and how it operates, that is, how it affects events in the world, including people, relationships among people, and the environmental stage on which these dramas are played.

Let us begin with a word that appears in each of the three lead sentences to this chapter, "community." What does this word mean? Suppose that you have lived in Tinyville all your life; this would have a powerful influence on your experiences with events referred to by the word "community." Or maybe you have traveled widely between Tinyville and Middletown, or perhaps you have journeyed extensively between 197th Street and 176th Street in Atlantic-seaboardopolis. The numbers and arrangements of people, buildings, and objects which occurred as events (or sets or systems of events) in time and space would have provided you with a beginning understanding of the term "community." But the term itself must refer to properties common to any particular Tinyville, Middletown, or Atlanticseaboardopolis. These common properties are unlikely to exist in any particular configuration of events, except as an abstraction. For example, the abstraction "territory" is common to the hills of Tinyville and the marshy plains of Middletown. In traditional philosophical language, the abstraction or general idea about a set of events is called a **class** of events.

Where do class terms come from? Some theorists suggest that individuals experience particular villages, towns, and cities, and then they mentally take note of certain characteristics, removing them from the concrete events and preserving them apart from the time and space in which they originally occurred. This general process is called **abstracting.** (Where people get these abstracted categories, whether from outward experiences or innately, is a difficult philosophical question; but the fact that abstracting occurs is not questioned.) A second step is also necessary in the development of concepts: **generalizing.** The ideas that are abstracted from experiences with concrete events are mentally combined with other such abstracted experiences, resulting in a set of abstracted ideas which are more general than the particular events from whence they came in that they can be used to characterize new experiences beyond the original ones. Growing up in Tinyville, reading about growing up in Samoa, viewing television programs about people growing up in Paris— the set of abstracted ideas from these experiences provides a class term to which another experience, New City, may be generalized.

If this abstracting and generalizing process by which concepts are developed has validity, then we may define concepts as ideas about classes of ideas derived from experience and expressed through symbols. Contrast this with the definition of events, where one has an idea of a physical referent which one expresses through symbols.

It is important to notice the role of mental processes in this development of concepts. Symbols may be formed to refer to these abstracted portions of events. These symbols then may be manipulated—combined, divided—as the vehicles for developing classes of ideas. The final product, a concept like community, is expressed by means of another symbol that summarizes the process of developing the concept. To be successful, the concept has to communicate to the audience what the speaker intends, that is, what mental processes he has used to construct the concept in just the way he did. There is nothing certain or absolute about the construction of concepts; there is no right or wrong about a concept per se. It represents the way the conceptmaker has developed the term.

If you haven't had lifelong experiences with, say, runaway persons, alcoholics, delinquents, or another of the many events we label "social problems," then you will have to depend on the descriptions of other travelers—theorists, researchers, and wise practitioners—to these regions as the basis of your own abstracting and generalizing, that is, developing your own concepts for practice. So choose your travel guides carefully.

No one can predict all of the situations in which you will find yourself in your professional practice, so in this chapter I want to convey a sense of making sense of other people's concepts. Consider the use of the concept "community" in this quotation from Maxwell Jones (1968):

"... What distinguishes a therapeutic community from other comparable treatment centres [for mental illness] is the way in which the institution's total resources, staff, patients, and their relatives, are self-consciously pooled in furthering treatment. This implies, above all, a change in the usual status of patients. In collaboration with the staff, they now become active participants in their own therapy and that of other patients and in many aspects of the unit's general activities. This is in marked contrast to their relatively more passive, recipient role in conventional treatment regimes" (pp. 85–86).

As a pioneer in the development of the concept of therapeutic communities, Jones is almost pointing to his particular arrangement at Dingleton Hospital, Melrose, Scotland, and saying: "This—all of these related systems of events—is what I mean by therapeutic community." Such a definition of the concept would then have been by means of denotation, pointing to the observable events (Greenwood, 1961). But even if we had Jones as our guide in Scotland, it is doubtful whether we could have observed the whole picture of subtle relationships among events.

Maxwell Jones has written about the therapeutic community in a variety of words, using a connotative form of definition. These other words themselves have to be attached to something meaningful, but assuming that we understand about staff, patients, or status, then we might have understood what he was implying by means of his general term. Using an ancient method of definition involving a **category** and some **differentia** within that category, he has told us that a therapeutic community belongs to the category of mental hospitals but is differentiated from conventional treatment centers by a social organization that involves patients more actively in their own and others' treatments.

As an advocate of this concept, Jones might also be seen as offering an operational definition of therapeutic community, that if you want to create such a treatment facility, you must primarily reorganize the patient/staff roles so as to involve patients more actively in their own and others' treatment by using such devices as community meetings, patient government, or staff review meetings (all of which are further defined). Like a cookbook, operational definitions must provide exact directions in order to produce or reproduce the event being described. But unlike a cookbook, it is difficult to specify all the steps to reproduce a complex concept like therapeutic community. The more precise the operational instructions, the closer the reproduction will be to the original.

Of the several ways of defining concepts, of informing others about the abstracted class of experiences one has in mind, each has its strengths and weaknesses. Some theorists, such as Greenwood (1961), see the critical need to develop operational definitions for the helping professions in order to clarify the vague terms that abound in this area. We will discuss this idea again when we consider the problem of translating from theory to practice in later chapters.

IDENTIFYING CONCEPTS IN PROFESSIONAL LITERATURE

We most often stalk the wild concept in its native habitat, the literature of the helping professions and other wildernesses. In presenting an extended example below, I want to suggest both some of the problems in sharing a theorist's ideas when we do not have him present to clarify his meaning and some of the virtues of the written statement by which we can look for internal consistencies of meaning and external tests to verify our ideas.

Truax and Carkhuff (1967) frame the central question to be asked in counseling and psychotherapy as: "What are the essential characteristics or behaviors of the therapist or counselor that lead to constructive behavioral change in the client?" Their extensive research leads them to make the following statement:

"Despite the bewildering array of divergent theories and the difficulty in translating concepts from the language of one theory to that of another, several common threads weave their way through almost every major theory of psychotherapy and counseling, including the psychoanalytic, the client-centered, the behavioristic, and many of the more eclectic and derivative theories. In one way or another, all have emphasized the importance of the therapist's ability to be integrated, mature, genuine, authentic or congruent in his relationship to the patient. They have all stressed also the importance of the therapist's ability to provide a nonthreatening, nonpossessive warmth, unconditional positive regard, or love. Finally, virtually all theories of psychotherapy emphasize that for the therapist to be helpful he must be accurately empathic, be 'with' the client, be understanding, or grasp the patient's meaning.

These three sets of characteristics can, for lack of better words, be termed **accurate empathy, nonpossessive warmth,** and **genuineness**" (p. 25).

The first thing to notice is that there are a lot of words. The first word is "despite." Is this a concept? In one sense, any word is a symbol for some idea, but in the sense for use in practice, we can ignore such words which function as grammatical or logical connectives. The first noun in Truax and Carkhuff's sentence is "array." Is this a useful concept for the practitioner? In one sense, it does present information about available theoretical tools—that there is an array of them—and this may be important in some contexts, but as we soon learn, the focus of this sentence is not about arrays. It is about common "threads" among arrays. Is this our long-sought concept? Common threads or themes are indeed labels for classes of events we are seeking, but the focus will be on different types of threads. Other parts of the sentence, verbs, adjectives, and so forth, are all vehicles for specifying these differences, de-limiting the sets of events that are to be discussed. Thus, words and sentences in scientific writing may not contain concepts significant to the practitioner, even though they provide a matrix for understanding.

The second sentence emphasizes the point that grammatical structure is not a necessary indicator of concepts. The events or ideas being focused on are parts of phrases—"of the therapist's ability," "to be integrated," "[to be] mature." The third and fourth sentences of that paragraph continue to develop the central idea, and, in the first sentence in the next paragraph, these ideas are tentatively summarized by short phrases or words. Note that "for lack of better words" the authors arbitrarily assign symbols to stand for a larger group of symbols—the word "genuineness" stands for "the importance of the therapist's ability to be integrated, mature, genuine, authentic or congruent in his relationship to the patient."

Many words are redundant—"nonthreatening, nonpossessive warmth . . . love"—because our language is about 50 percent redundant. This repetition improves the chances of being understood, although it can also work against us and can confuse the issue by having differences between the first and second versions of what is supposed to be the same idea. "Nonthreatening" may not mean exactly the same to you as "nonpossessive warmth" does to me. On the other hand, the concept which the authors are struggling to abstract and generalize may go beyond the meaning of the set of words taken one at a time. There is no one word or phrase which captures this new extended meaning—except the newly created concept. And because it is arbitrary, it may not always be clear to all users. The best we can hope for is relative consistency in the family resemblances among usages.

Because of this, dictionaries are written as guides to current usage of words. In the first Truax and Carkhuff paragraph, many complex words are used which might need defining, but if the authors had to define every concept they used, they would be writing a book of infinite length for readers who have finite patience, and they would never get anywhere. While there are a number of inexpensive technical dictionaries on psychology (such as Chaplin, 1968) and on sociology (such as Theodorson and Theodorson, 1969), there is no recent dictionary on social work (cf. Young, 1939).

Some concepts may be called "thing-concepts" as they refer to things or properties of things. For example, we might refer to a community as a piece of land or to the buildings and people who live on that land. On the other hand, other concepts called "relation-concepts" refer to the connections between two or more events. In this sense, community might refer to a sense of common bonds between people (cf. Meenaghan, 1972). Thing-concepts are easier to point to and simpler to work with, but some philosophers of science point to the development of science as connected to the use of relation-concepts (Cassirer, 1953, in Cartwright, 1959). In my terms, I would describe this as the movement from considerations of events alone to considerations of sets of events. But forming concepts has its dangers; we may pigeonhole too much and lose some degree of awareness concerning reality. The using of concepts is a constant balancing between organization of ideas and awareness of reality.

One type of organization among concepts has been called the ladder of abstraction (Hayakawa, 1972), the scope of events to which a concept can refer. The scaffolding terms—events and sets and systems of events—implies such an organization, where the higher levels encompass the lower levels, but these terms are content free. The terms behavior, empathy, and accurate empathy also constitute a series of contentful terms referring to varying ranges of abstraction: Not all empathy is accurate and not all behavior is empathy. However, if Truax and Carkhuff tried to employ behavior, the broadest term, or even the second broadest term in that series, in place of accurate empathy, the narrowest term, you can imagine the price they would pay. What would therapists need to have to be successful with clients?—Behavior, yes, but that includes too much and does not distinguish successful from unsuccessful therapists.—Empathy, yes, but only the accurate kind. Unsuccessful therapists may possess inaccurate empathy. So, we must choose the level of abstraction of our concepts according to the use to which they will be put. This is a difficult task; only a few rules of thumb exist that may be offered to make the task simpler: Concepts should be broad enough to include all of the potentially relevant events one can imagine (but no broader). Modifiers, such as **accurate** empathy, may improve the goodness of conceptual fit. As you formulate concepts, keep in mind what other events these words are supposed to deal with or influence in order to keep a comparable level of abstraction.

But here is a problem: What if we don't know what the potentially relevant events are? For example, the question of runaways captured public attention with the grotesque events surrounding the murders of about two dozen runaway boys. People had been vaguely aware that there were many cases of runaways, but they were unprepared for the estimates of one-half million to one million runaway children per year; consequently there has been no public definition of this existing social problem and little has been done in the way of services for this group. In 1972, legislative hearings were conducted by a Senate subcommittee to investigate juvenile delinquency—indicating where the concept "runaway" was placed. And, in fact, then-existing legislation dealt primarily with runaways as legal problems, youth who are truants, who steal, or who misuse drugs. It did not define the concept as involving psychological and social conditions where children are the victims, not the criminals, where running away is an act of self-defense rather than a pathological or antisocial act. The portion of the Social Security Act relevant to runaways (Title IV A) provides that money be spent only for children on welfare. While data are scanty, it appears that a large number of runaways are from the middle class. And so a legal definition of this concept in 1972 would have excluded a large category of persons in need (United States Senate, 1972).

The point is that we often do not know the demographic characteristics of a class of events in order to construct an adequate concept that reflects the problem fully. In such cases we must go slowly, collect new information to identify these parameters, and be ready to change the definition—and the service programs that follow from it.

Assuming that we have good data on the demographic characteristics and parameters of the events labeled by the concept, to what degree do we understand how a particular theorist is using the term? We cannot say precisely, but if there is an internal consistency in our understanding of the theorist's usage within the network of his theory, we may have greater confidence in the understanding of a particular term. And, as we will expand in later chapters, if we gain pragmatic control over events by using a concept as a guide, we will have another source of confidence in our understanding of the concept.

CONSTRUCTS AND VARIABLES

Constructs are concepts produced by inferences rather than by observations of concrete events. This distinction is relative. All concepts are artificially created entities, and don't have to be tied to common sense. In fact, some of the more successful concepts have been contrary to some common-sense ideas, like whether the sun moves around the earth or vice versa. Constructs are useful in interrelating numbers of concepts, raising the organization of a set of concepts to a higher level of abstraction.

Because of their distance from concrete reality, constructs are more susceptible to the temptation called reification (Greenwood, 1961), in which a creative hunch intended to synthesize diverse events suddenly appears clothed in the language of concrete reality. When a concept changes from a hypothesis to a function to doing such and such an act, then we have reified an abstraction. We no longer manipulate the symbol; instead, it begins to push us around. Every construct and indeed every concept must be carefully watched so that its logical status as an abstraction to be tested against reality is maintained.

Variables are the empirical characteristics of concepts that can take different degrees (number, magnitudes) according to the particular situation. For example, the concept "age" refers to the length of time a person has lived. But the same word is also a variable that can take a range of values depending on the number of years lived. Each event experienced can be placed in just one value of that variable; the 99-year-old can be placed only in the age group of persons living 99 years. Mullin (1971) describes the variable as a "potential empirical proxy" for a concept. Concepts are not measured directly, but are associated with the empirical indicators explicitly defined as representing those concepts. Sometimes there is no readily available empirical indicator for a concept, and so one must be constructed. Truax and Carkhuff (1967) construct a nine-point scale of empirical observations which represents the level of accurate empathy hypothesized to be operating in the real world. The many issues surrounding test construction take us far beyond the limits of this book, but some practical concerns are discussed in Chapter 19.

SUMMARY

Concepts are the prime way in which scientists and helping professionals share information and ideas. Referring to potentially observable events or derivatives of these events and carried by public symbols, concepts are a special type of idea—concerning abstracted and generalized classes of experience. Concepts are man-made, subjective, and arbitrary. They escape being utter nonsense only insofar as other persons may share the subjective experience sufficiently to be able to agree that this arbitrary way of viewing an event makes sense.

Constructs are used here as high order concepts, produced from inferences rather than from observations of concrete events by which concepts are created. Variables are empirical representatives of concepts taking on any of a range of measured values.

CHAPTER 6

Propositions: Sets of Concepts

When two or more concepts are joined together, they are wed; they have become a proposition. Their fate now hangs together, at least temporarily. Like other newlyweds, propositions may gain a large number of family relations on both sides, including associations among terms linked by natural affinities or shotgun marriages. One should be careful of conceptual match-making or one may end up with unscientific polygamy.

We spoke earlier of **sets** of events as being events related to one another on any determinable basis. This determinability usually refers to connection by time, space, or circumstance, all of which are potentially measurable. This chapter will continue to explore the determinable basis of relations among concepts. It is another paradox of human behavior that persons are intricately involved in the determination of relationships. If there is a glass tumbler and it has exactly half of its contents occupied by a liquid, it is the human contribution of an optimist to see this set of events (glass and liquid) as half full, a pessimist to see the same set of events as half empty, and a paranoid person to see these events as a plot of enemy agents to poison him. Thus, it is not only **events** which are meaningful selections from the vast flow of stimuli of which reality is composed, but **sets of events** which are also meaningful selections and combinations of reality. Both reality and human interpretation contribute to the meaning of an event.

Concepts and propositions are special types of events and sets of events, those having to do with abstracted classes of ideas and their symbolic carriers. Because of their abstract nature, concepts and propositions receive the larger portion of meaning from human interpretation rather than from reality. But what part do people play in the formation of propositions, and how are these formations tested against nature? We can greatly simplify the ways philosophers of science have analyzed the relations among concepts by reference to the following classification:

Class I.   Some relations among concepts are **assumed.**
Class II.   Some relations among concepts are **tested.**
Class III.   Some relations among concepts are **known.**

Let us look first at the propositions formed by concepts related by assumption. In traditional philosophy of science, writers speak of axioms (propositions whose truth is self-evident but in fact capable of neither proof nor disproof), assumptions and postulates (both of which are used as provisionally true for purposes of developing a further line of reasoning or as a premise in an argument). But for present purposes, we can combine all of these as types of propositions which relate concepts by assuming that they belong together so that we can get on to the next phase of our work. Such propositions are regarded as reasonable interpretations of reality or at least are not contradicted by known facts.

Propositions may also be formed by concepts related by arrangements which put the relationship to an empirical test. Terms from traditional philosophy of science include hypotheses and predictions (both of which state relationships among events in such a way as to permit observations in nature to act as a corroboration of the symbolic pattern). These terms differ in their specificity and in their formal elegance as derived from a theory, but for present purposes it will be sufficient to combine them as propositions to be tested empirically.

The third category of propositions are those whose concepts are known to be related. The basis of this knowledge, as described in traditional philosophy of science, is either from empirical laws (in which a large number of empirical generalizations have been demonstrated) or from theoretical principles (in which a logical network of propositions has been shown to exist). In both cases, the knowledge is in fact tentative and limited to the trained observers involved; it is always possible that new information may bring about changes in either laws or principles.

The paradox of these three classes of propositions is that any given statement may be interpreted as falling into any one class—one man's assumption is another man's proposition to be tested while it is a third man's certain knowledge. This does not mean that the classes are worthless; rather, it requires that we know how a person is using a proposition and see that he uses the proposition consistently in whatever class he chooses.

Reynolds (1971) makes a distinction between **existence** statements (indicating that something exists or is the case) and **relational** statements (indicating either an association or a causal relationship between events). Referring to our scaffolding terms, some propositions simply refer to events as existences: "The client is female, high school educated, self-deprecatory . . ." This type of proposition forms the great bulk of our recordings about clients. Propositions about sets of events refer to associations while propositions about systems of events refer to causal networks.

Existence statements are basically descriptive. They are vital to professional work, but they do not in themselves provide a sense of understanding of the total situation. Relational statements begin to provide this sense of understanding. "Because the client doesn't have as much education as her friends, she feels inferior. . . ." Whether the connection between level of education and degree of inferiority is a causal one or merely a juxtaposition of events which in reality have no connection to one another—this is yet to be determined. Association is not necessarily causation. It is a critical issue for the helping professional to identify causal patterns in order to intervene effectively. But it is very difficult to discover the exact causal pattern, for causality is an inference we must attach to sets of events based on certain rules such as Mill's Methods (see Copi, 1953, for an introductory discussion).

Unfortunately, existential, associational, and causal propositions may have the same form. "He is in the oedipal phase." This sentence may assert a fact of existence, suggest an association among events, or provide the listener with an idea of causal forces acting on the subject. Like any proposition, this sentence may be true or false. Presumably there should be some way in which we can test for the existence of the oedipal phase, discover whether the subject is in fact in it or not, and ascertain whether this phase influences his behavior. If we cannot discover the truth or falsity of a proposition either directly or through its network of propositions, then it is, as some philosophers used to say, a meaningless metaphysical proposition.

Consider these sentences:
1. "Sir Walter Raleigh lived."
2. "Sir Walter Raleigh smoked cigarettes."
3. "Sir Walter's life was shortened because he smoked cigarettes."
4. "Sir Walter's life was shortened because he was beheaded."

The first sentence is clearly an existence statement, and even though it has only one term, it is still a proposition because the grammatical form suggests an ellipsis for the other implied term (such as "Sir Walter Raleigh lived 66 years.)". The second sentence is an associational one, like so many of the statements social workers write in their reports. Two events occurred in such a way that a viewer saw them as a set of events (such as Sir Walter and lighted cigarettes). Let's skip to the fourth sentence; it is clearly a causal relation, beheading causing death. The critical sentence is the third one: Is it associational or causal? We can't say in the individual case; we need either a systematic network of events concerning Sir Walter's life or a large number of persons allocated to various categories being studied. In the research sense, we typically do not have longitudinal data of the first type, while we can read the research literature about surveys or experimental designs providing the second type of data. (As practitioners, we tend to have the reverse situation, with a certain amount of longitudinal information but little by way of controlled group data.)

While we don't have Sir Walter Raleigh available, we do find research statements like the following. Grannis (1970) analyzes the survival of male smokers and nonsmokers with that of females since 1900 and notes the increasing disparity in the sex ratio (the growing numbers of widows produced by the premature mortality of males) between smokers and nonsmokers. In 1960 nonsmoking males survived in the same ratio to females as did all males to females in 1900, when consumption of cigarettes was low. He cites Hammond's (1966) massive epidemiologic study of one million persons which shows that the average longevity of male smokers is about seven years less than male nonsmokers; the data also show nearly a ten-year difference between male smokers and females. Grannis' analysis suggests that these differences in longevity associated with smoking would fully account for the demographic changes over the past half century. None of the other factors commonly mentioned in this connection—wars, epidemics, changes in sanitation, nutrition— could have accounted for the kind and magnitude of demographic changes that have occurred.

The cigarette lobby and large numbers of very confirmed smokers would like to believe that these statements are merely associational, not causal. With powerful data such as those accumulated in this report as elsewhere, it begins to make **scientific** sense to consider the information as causal; it makes **practical** sense to consider intervening in the many links between decisions to plant tobacco and the medical decision that further efforts to save a life would be in vain. However, between the scientific and the practical are value decisions—"What's a life for without a lungful of self-imposed irritants" —and the political/economic decisions—to subsidize the tobacco industry and simultaneously to require the printed admonition on advertisements that smoking may be hazardous to your health. Scientific information alone is not sufficient to make changes in human behavior.

Consider causal relations at higher levels of generality. "All men are mortal" means in part that "manness" leads to mortality, to be a man is to die. However, at this lofty, abstract level, the two terms become merged or tautologous. But let us not tackle the philosophical questions in this type of proposition as we have ample questions of our own to tackle.

Let us take a more familiar sentence: "A male born in the United States in 1968 can be expected to live 66.6 years, other things being equal." These life table projections are derived from actuarial data from previous cohorts of persons. The qualification about other things being equal refers to such events as unexpected wars. Note that smokers and nonsmokers alike accept this form of actuarial statement. They also accept the demographic fact that there are millions fewer older men than older women than would be expected on an actuarial basis. It is with the set of propositions that link specific events (mass smoking behavior on the part of males early in this century) to these actuarial facts that there is dispute. The power generated by an assertive causal statement is immense, like splitting an atom. In the behavioral sciences, the practical limit of causality is at the highly probable level, which gives leeway for choosing to act or not to act on the basis of this knowledge. In the helping professions, the element of values, added to facts, further complicates human behavior and professional response. (We will return to this issue in Chapter 13 in the discussion on values.)

Let us examine the linkages among concepts more closely. Verbs connect nouns that typically are the symbolic carriers of concepts. "My client misuses drugs." The concept client is connected with the concept drug misuse. (Even if your client is a particular teenager, Alex Smart, he still belongs to the class of all Alex Smarts of which there is only one; so, by this word game, individuals can be used as if they were a class of events.) I will shortly suggest four patterns of linkages among concepts, but, first, I want to discuss word connectives among concepts, such as "and," "or," and "not," which function like logical connectives but without the same degree of clarity in everyday speech as in formal logic. For example, "or" may mean "both . . . and" or "one and only one," depending on whether your client needs a coat to keep out rain **or** sleet, or wants to spend her food stamps on bread **or** milk.

Quantifiers of propositions, such as "all," "none," or "some," also are used too loosely in conversation, not because helping professionals are malicious when they say that "all my clients are anxious," but more likely because they are imprecise. They may mean nearly all, or most, or many, or some, or the last few that now stick in memory are anxious.

Adjectives and adverbs also modify nouns and verbs. Consider such sentences as these: "A **small** group of **highly** active **nursery school** children was **constantly** moving about the room." Or "Is the **sensuous** male **existentially** hollow?" Each of these emphasized words modifies its object term. Some are clearly quantifications (such as **small** group), while others are qualifiers (such as **sensuous** male). The former may have numbers directly specified (**six** children), while the latter has to go through a two-step process before it can be quantified. First a quantifiable scale must be presumed (such as supersensuous, sensuous, and otherwise preoccupied), and then numbers may be attached to the scale.

Thus, propositions such as those found in the professional literature and conversations are constructed in a variety of ways which aim both to please one's aesthetic sensitivities and to provide information logically and clearly.

Sometimes one gets in the way of the other, and it is not clear just what is the nature of events with which one is dealing.

FOUR PATTERNS OF PROPOSITIONS

By putting together all of the words which signify concepts and the qualifiers of concepts, we can form various patterns of propositions somewhat parallel to the patterns by which numerals are assigned to objects (Stevens, 1951). For example, five persons on a basketball team may be distinguished from one another by the numerals on their shirts. This would be a **nominal** (scale) usage to show that one object is different from another. It would make no sense to add or subtract these numerals; they are simply names for different objects. However, if there was a policy to give the highest numeral (90) to the player who was the highest scorer on the team, and the next highest numeral (76) to the next highest scorer, and so on, then there would be some order among players represented by the numerals; the highest numeral would indicate a person whose scores were more than the next highest numeral. This is an **ordinal** (scale) usage, comparing more and less on some attribute. No amount of difference is implied, simply order.

If we can say not only that one player scored more than another but also that he scored a certain number of units more, then we are dealing with an **interval** (scale) usage. And if there is an absolute zero point in the situation, as there is in scoring by numbers in basketball, then we have a **ratio** (scale) usage, the ratio of times some unit is more than another unit. A player who scores 100 points is twice as high a scorer as another who scores only 50 points.

Several important points are to be made using a model of these measurement scales. First, scales differ in terms of strength; more arithmetic functions can be performed as one ascends from the nominal through the ordinal and interval scales to the ratio. Second, one's data must likewise be precise enough to permit use of these stronger scales. Third, each higher scale incorporates the functions of the scales below it, while adding a new function of its own. For instance, an interval usage not only distinguishes nominal differences and specifies the order among them but it also supplies the number of units involved in that order—though it cannot specify the ratio among those units until some absolute zero point is known.

With this as background, let me suggest that there are four corresponding patterns among propositions. I will use one example from the literature and vary the form in which these same concepts may be connected in order to illustrate the point about the strength of propositions deriving in part from their form. This illustrative proposition is borrowed from a seminal book by Goldstein, Heller, and Sechrest (1966).

I. A Nominal Proposition
Transfer of learning from the therapy situation to extratherapy situations will occur when the therapy stimuli are representative of the extratherapy stimuli (p. 226).

First, let's break down this complex statement into its underlying form. I think this can be summarized simply as if **X**, then **Y**—if you have therapy stimuli which are representative of extratherapy stimuli (**X**), then transfer of learning from the therapy situation to the extratherapy situation will occur (**Y**). This is testable; like all propositions it permits us, in principle, to judge the truth or falseness of the statement. In a sense, this proposition asserts an all-or-nothing condition: If you have **X**, then you will get **Y**; if you don't have **X**, then you won't get **Y**.

The authors probably did not intend an all-or-nothing proposition; it would be more likely that they had in mind a continuum which could be expressed as follows:

II. An Ordinal Proposition
The more the therapy situation is like the extratherapy situations, the greater will be the transfer of learning from the former to the latter.

This implies an ordered relationship among the concepts, that is, more of one leading to more of the other. The form of the sentence embodies a new organization and also gives rise to new meaning and new power. The form of the sentence suggests that there can exist degrees of relationship among the concepts and leads to a testable expectation about this relationship. As we will learn in later sections of this book, this form of proposition gives rise to action by the helping professional: The stronger the form of the proposition, the clearer guidance there is for professional action and also professional evaluation of the outcome.

So far, the form of the proposition does not tell us how much difference it will make to have the therapy situation like the extratherapy situations. For this kind of information, we must construct another form of proposition.

III. An Interval Proposition
If so many units of the therapy situation are like the extratherapy situations, then such and such a number of units of the transfer of learning can be expected to occur.

The reader will no doubt notice that this formulation is considerably more abstract and unfamiliar than previous propositions, reflecting the fact that we, in the behavioral sciences, don't see many of these types of propositions. But we can imagine statements such as this: If so many hours of therapy are spent in role playing typical life situations, then such and such a level of improved outcome can be expected when the client faces these same situations in actual life. To test this level of proposition requires considerable precision in defining problem events, baseline rates, and the like; these are difficult to obtain but by no means beyond the grasp of helping professionals (cf. Chapter 17). Such a type of statement provides the basis for asking whether the amount of effort a worker would have to engage in (the **X** of therapy) is worth the degree of effect (the **Y** of transfer of learning). In other words, this form of proposition provides the basis of a cost/benefit analysis, formally or informally conceived. This is a powerful tool for choosing among alternative plans of action. But note that as an interval type of proposition, relative magnitudes are involved.

If we had an absolute zero point, we could construct a ratio type of proposition.

IV. A Ratio Proposition

Every time one unit of representativeness between the therapy and the extratherapy situation is produced in the therapeutic context, then a ratio of an amount of transfer of learning will take place.

We might return to a concrete (but hypothetical) example to suggest what ratio statements might look like: Every time one's personal habits lead one to smoke a package of 20 cigarettes, actuarial figures suggest that this personal habit reduces one's expected life span by 33 minutes. Such a proposition would require a considerable amount of information, but it would also represent a very powerful tool for the helping professions.

SUMMARY

The combination of concepts into propositions adds something new: A proposition is more than the sum of its parts. Some propositions are assumed to be true, so that we may get on to other business by building on given foundations. Other propositions are arranged so that they may be put to the test. Still other propositions are known to be true and dependable although no proposition is absolute. Because any given proposition may be assumed, tested, or known differently by different persons, it is important to know how a person is using a proposition, and whether it is being used consistently.

Our language helps as well as hinders us in understanding how a proposition is being used, primarily because of its rich redundancy and its imprecision for technical use. This is why we have technical languages.

Of central importance for practitioners is to recognize that the form of a proposition indicates the strength of that proposition to guide our understanding about sets of events. In ascending order, nominal, ordinal, interval, and ratio types of statements give us increasing precision in describing the relation among events and will, eventually, give increasing direction in practice and evaluation.

CHAPTER 7

Theory, Empirical Generalization, and the Formulation of Practice Wisdom

"Theory" is often characterized by interesting metaphors, oxymorons, and confusions in language and in mind. For example, theories are often defined as a network of interrelated propositions which provide a sense of understanding of some portion of reality. However, such networks are required to "hold water"—which obviously requires them to be densely woven fabrics. Theories are also said to be the stuff of imagination, ethereal and inspired by the gods—which makes their threads very fine and delicate. These threads are also strong and hardy, as man lifts himself up by his own bootstraps: "The history of science demonstrates beyond a doubt that the really revolutionary and significant advances come not from empiricism but from new theories" (Conant, 1947). But beware: One man's Mead is another man's Parsons. And there is nothing as practical as a good theory (Lewin). This is why some people can't be bothered with theories; all they want are the facts. These same people usually request that we shouldn't confuse them with new facts, because their minds are already made up. Foolish consistency being the hobgoblin of little minds (Emerson) and the last refuge of the unimaginative (Camus), I approach this section on theory with more than usual fear and trembling.

FUNCTIONS OF THEORIES

Theories have many functions, which account for many of the confusions that surround them. My interpretation of these functions follows some ideas from Rychlak's (1968) penetrating discussion: First, theories are used **to delimit** the scope of events being considered, according to one's purposes in theorizing. A theory cannot deal with all reality, and the basis for setting limits is a function of the limited mind of man. In selecting events to be considered as interrelated, we make assumptions that we have identified a subsystem of a larger system (of course, with the implication that there are subsystems within our focus of concern); these assumptions suggest that it makes sense to treat these events as a relatively autonomous sector for the moment. Other theories involving related topics can be developed, and perhaps in time, groups of related theories can be joined together or a more general theory can be developed to encompass them. In the meantime, it is useful to focus our theoretical efforts on a group of events from real life. Delimiting leads us **to classify**— to group events according to their distinguishing characteristics. When we distinguish among fur, feather, and fin, we have taken the first critical step in cataloging our experiences with events. The basis on which these typologies are formed is likely to be a combination of what the events have in common and what we see (or imagine) the events to have in common—nature and man's perception of nature in interaction. A theory should state or clearly imply its limits, the scope of events with which it can reasonably be assumed to operate. If it does not, it may get top-heavy, try to be all things to all people, and resist any effort at disconfirmation which might weaken it as a theory.

A second function of theory is **to describe** that group of events. Description involves stating the manifest relationship of an event to other events. For instance, Captain Ahab looks into the water and sees an event, one of the category of things that lives in the sea, a whale. He also sees attributes of that whale, such as its size and its color. A native speaker of English, he would describe his experience as seeing a "large white whale" (not, interestingly enough, "a white large whale," but that is another story entirely). Descriptions tend to be patterns of symbols in which adjectival or adverbial events are attached to subjects or predicates of the statement; these symbols usually refer to surface characteristics of the event, in a part- (or attribute-) to-whole relationship. The descriptive function of theory has another vital use: It **summarizes** information in an economical fashion. After careful observation has yielded specific sets of events that are related to each other, then the summary statement of these observations, as embodied in a theoretical statement, stands as a major accomplishment.

A third function of theory is **to explain,** or to specify the sequence of events that describes fully the conditions under which the given events vary, including coming to be or ending. Explanations may use publicly shared symbols as descriptions do, but they need not. They may use hypothetical constructs that are created as likely or possible events which account for how the given phenomenon varies (MacCorquodale and Meehl, 1948). At this point, the theory can be free from reality. "It was an evil demon that took possession of his mind and made him do those terrible things." The willingness to use hypothetical constructs in explanation, as contrasted to a situation in which all terms have received explicit operational definitions, depends on one's willingness to use a logical network of concepts including imaginative ones for which no known referent exists in the real world. As Carnap suggested (Chapter 4), if the entire network of imaginary and operationalized concepts produces fruitful results, then one can live with the hypothetical constructs, until such time as knowledge or technology permits one to develop a better understanding of those hypothetical constructs.

With **Moby Dick,** we can use several levels of explanation, depending on what we are trying to explain. If our task is to explain how a mammal can live in the water its entire life, then we would describe its eating, sleeping, reproductive and other vital functions, the set of which explains the whale's watery life. If our task were to explain the whiteness of the whale, we would have to get assistance from specialists, such as the geneticist, to describe abstract processes of mutation and related matters. These are harder to describe, but no less useful than naturalistic observations in explaining events. If we wanted to explain **Moby Dick** as a symbol of evil (or justice, or whatever), then we would, as literary critics, find passages in which the whale was involved in our favorite metaphor, recognizing that other critics may use the same passages as evidence for different metaphors. Explanations at this level become word games, depending as much on the medium of expression as on the message itself (cf. McLuhan, 1964).

A fourth function of theory is **to integrate,** to refer to the number and completeness of the logical network of propositions. Some theories are highly structured systems of propositions, while others are much less so. Integration may go beyond description and explanation by filling in the missing pieces, usually by adding hypothetical constructs. In performing this function, integration provides an important **psychological** concomitant which is relevant to helping professionals, namely, a feeling of understanding that permits action even in the absence of details of the situation. "Because **Moby Dick's** color makes him so conspicuous among objects in the sea and so rare and awesome an event, it becomes easy to understand why readers would develop interpretations of the whale's special supernatural essence." In short, we have added subtle pieces to the story to make it into a pleasing, coherent whole. Such additions are a pleasure in works of fiction; in real life, that's another story. . . .

A well-structured system of propositions permits integration of a group of events more effectively through an organization of symbols rather than an organization of things; that is, we gain power in the affairs of men by pushing symbols around in order to help make decisions rather than by pushing people around to serve the same end. I think the analogy of mechanical leverage is useful here. Theories give theoretical leverage. We are able to pull together large portions of physical reality by means of relatively small amounts of manipulation of symbols. Theoretical leverage is a powerful tool.

A fifth function of theory is **to generate** new ideas, that is, to generate new concepts and new relations among concepts in the pursuit of new information. Theory, in this sense, is a way of looking at the world in order to look at the world in new ways. Theory provides hunches and, more formally, hypotheses. All of these **expand** the knowledge basis described by the theory. But, in another sense, for practitioners, the generative function of theory suggests **application** to new situations. This is a **use of knowledge function** to which I will return in Part III of this book.

Prediction is included under this theory function to direct the search for new information and for new ways of relating events in a system. **Postdiction**—relating past events—is a legitimate way of providing new information if the events of the past are further connected to current events. A critical aspect of prediction is its potential for **control**, that is, the ability to intervene in the course of events purposively so as to influence a new consequent event which is closer to a desired outcome than the natural event would have been.

These five functions of theories are interrelated and quite difficult to separate in some cases, but they reflect the different emphases which theories have been given. I suggest that, in the order presented, these functions of theories place increasingly greater demands on the logical tightness of the structure of propositions, which is, after all, the essence of theory. But the theories of greatest interest for the helping professions are not only those with intricate integrations of ideas but also those which provide the power to predict and, ultimately, to influence behavior. To obtain this power, there must be play back and forth between formation of networks of ideas and observations of the referents of those ideas in actual life to see whether they behave as the theory specifies they should.

Ultimately, theories are tools, never ends in themselves. Theories are never complete, but only existing in provisional states of verification or disconfirmation (cf. Turner, 1967). We next turn to empirical statements and the relationship between the theoretical and the empirical in the context of the helping professions.

EMPIRICAL STATEMENTS

There are several forms of statements concerning observations of events in the real world. One person may make a personal or **behavioral observation,** seeing that certain events behave in a certain way. We all do this most of the time. If our person were scientifically oriented, she might use more care in her scrutiny, obtaining objective and standardized observations through the use of instruments and procedures so that what she then reported could have been recounted by any trained observer under those same circumstances or could be repeated under similar circumstances. Let's grace this more scientific venture as involving an **empirical observation.**

Should several people become interested in the project or our one person make a series of empirical observations—then the statement of uniformities among events might bear the label **empirical generalization.** This is the label for the large body of statements about specific events that fills our literature. Each empirical generalization deals specifically with an isolated phenomenon, although the scale of the phenomenon may range from large to small, from the social-class status of persons with various forms of mental illness to the number of ambidextrous persons employed as secretaries. These are isolated in the sense that one statement cannot be extended to the other without new research to make the connection, say research concerning ambidextrous secretaries who have been driven mad.

When many workers come up with empirical generalizations that all point in the same direction, then one can speak of a **law,** which is an empirical generalization accepted as true by a group of qualified observers. Laws refer to very broad statements about uniformities in nature; to repeal such a law would take a great deal of new evidence, although it has been done. (Remember Copernicus!)

In real life, it rarely occurs that every empirical finding fully supports one generalization; rather one finds degrees of empirical support between empirical generalizations and laws. For example, McGrath and Altman (1966) cataloged a large number of empirical generalizations concerning variables in small group research and organized the findings in terms of thirty-one classes. The proportion of significant relationships found for any set of variables is given a descriptive label—60 percent or more is "highly related"; 40 to 60 percent, moderately related; 30 to 40 percent, somewhat related; 15 to 30 percent slightly related; and less than 15 percent, not related. To take one instance from their catalog:

> 120. Personality characteristics of members as related to leadership performance. Moderately related (in 12 out of 24 studies):
>
> > Leaderless group discussion performance was positively and highly related to ratings on personality traits such as extroversion, assertiveness, and social maturity (10/14). However, other traits

such as seriousness and general activity were but slightly related to leaderless group discussion performance (2/10) (p. 170).

Using this catalog, can we say that ten out of fourteen studies which indicate a highly related connection between two events represent a law regarding these specific traits and performances in leaderless group discussions (think of sensitivity groups as one practical application of such a group)? Probably not. First, the group of factors named—extroversion, assertiveness, and social maturity—involve an unclear underlying event to which the uniformity would refer. Would the term "socially comfortable" cover the behavioral nature of these traits or perhaps "socially aggressive"? Second, fourteen studies is not enough to make me feel comfortable as the basis of an empirical law, although there is no scientific covenant stating what number of uniformities of research constitute a law per se. However, these empirical generalizations from McGrath and Altman's catalog would be ample for me if I were going to set up a leaderless discussion group which I wanted to operate in a predictable way. And this is the purpose of group intervention methods. But given the isolated nature of empirical generalizations I would have to locate from McGrath and Altman's catalog or elsewhere each factor I wanted to control and seek to find the best combination of arrangements that would lead to the desired goal. Similar catalogs of relationships among variables are not easily found, but I will suggest in a later section of this chapter that this is one way in which practice wisdom may be accumulated. If each worker pays special attention to what professional actions under what circumstances lead to what results and if this information has a way of being formulated and distilled, then the helping professions might provide some internal sources of growth.

It is important to note the differences between even a large catalog of empirical relationships and a theory covering the same (or a similar set of) relationships. The catalog is a convenient clustering of isolated empirical generalizations; the arrangement itself may be based on a theory or on empirical observations by the authors. There may be a high or a low degree of empirical support for each particular relationship, but any cross-relationship would require additional research. In distinction to the empirical law, the conceptual **principle** represents a theory that is widely accepted as true by a group of qualified observers. The principle is a logically interrelated system of concepts dealing with uniformities of nature, usually with causes and effects, and related matters. Being a logical system, it is open to inclusion with new concepts so long as logical connectives can be found. The additions to a widely believed theory do not automatically gain the same level of acceptance as the core theory, although, again, there is no convenant to specify when the level of belief worthy of a principle is attained.

These differences between laws and principles are due primarily to their status as creatures of philosophy of science. Laws are defined by mathematical relationships among concepts involving extensive links to the events in nature— This is one instance of event X, that is another instance, there is a third; they occur in conjunction with other events Y, permitting us to calculate a correlation coefficient. . . . Principles are defined by logical relationships among concepts— If **A** implies **B** (if ambidextrous secretaries are given twice as much work as nonambidextrous secretaries), and if **B** implies **C** (if overworked secretaries get strains leading to mental illness), then **A** implies **C** (then ambidextrous secretaries are more likely to get strains leading to mental illness than non-ambidextrous secretaries). When logical concepts and networks are connected to the world of events—and there is no reason why they must be connected; some mathematical systems have no counterpart in the real world—they utilize operational definitions which are empirical statements defined as providing the meaning of those concepts.

Let us summarize some distinguishing characteristics about empirical generalizations and theories. I think it is a chicken-and-egg question to ask which comes first or which is more important. Both observation and conceptualization go on simultaneously, though with periods when one or the other is consciously predominating. In contrast to theory, empirical generalizations tend to make discrete and relatively concrete statements about events; they also make no provision for procedures to disprove their statements, while theories are in principle supposed to do so. Predictions are **logically** made from some theories, whereas one may infer speculatively from empirical uniformities. The difference rests mainly on the degree of certainty in going from what is known to what is not known. Logical networks go well together with other logical networks but less well to distant events; empirical generalizations, closely reflecting real life, are probably good guides for other real events of a similar nature but less so for the greater dissimilarity between known and unknown events. In short, there are strengths and weaknesses in both. Generalizations are relatively mechanical—they are designed to reflect empirical events closely and there is no leeway in so doing. Theories are a relatively creative process and while internal consistency is vital, the theory need not reflect events closely.

Analysis of a Specific Content Theory: Adolescent Suicide

Among the basic tasks that helping professionals are continually faced with is to read the professional literature in order to identify and to use relevant information. Theories serve a number of functions, as described earlier, and it well behooves the reader to pay careful attention to the system of propositions which focuses on a delimited content area, describing and perhaps explaining the phenomenon, integrating relevant pieces of information, and perhaps generating new ideas on the topic, particularly those applied to practice. However, like communication in general, the message the sender sends is not necessarily the message the receiver receives, especially when the communication is as complex as a theory.

In reading the professional literature, especially the theories but also the research, I would suggest that the system be identified: What interrelated group of propositions is given? On the assumption that the author did his job in making them internally consistent, can the reader re-create this consistency? I would further suggest that although not all authors write this way, a theory can be restated as a series of propositions. Indeed, if the reader understands a complex message from a given professional article, he should be able to re-construct the article as a series of propositions. Such reorganization and re-duction of a complex message enable one to retain the big picture longer and more clearly, so it is worth the effort.

In the following excerpt from a paper by Jacobs and Teicher (1967), I have attempted to include most of the elements to reconstruct their theory of attempted suicides in adolescents. Read the excerpt carefully, and then we can try to reconstruct what was said or what we think was said:

"This paper deals with an analysis of a key concept in the psychiatric literature on suicide: broken homes. By comparing the life histories of fifty adolescents, we sought to better understand the process whereby 'broken homes' and the implicit 'loss of a love object' worked to progressively isolate the adolescent from meaningful social relationships. It is this latter condition that we feel ultimately led the adolescent to attempt suicide (p. 139).

"Method: Each adolescent in the experimental group was interviewed within 24–48 hours of the actual suicide attempt by the sociologist or his research assistant and the psychiatrist. The structured interview schedule used covered the following areas: the suicide attempt, family relations, peer relations, attitudes toward and performance in school, and career aspirations. The attempter's parent was also interviewed, using a structured interview schedule which covered the same areas but with an additional section on the adolescent's 'developmental' history . . . (p. 142).

"In seeking a common denominator in the life histories of adolescent suicide attempters that distinguishes them from the control adolescents [the authors attempted] to delineate . . . formal aspects of a process through which the adolescent had to progress in order to, first, entertain, and then, attempt suicide. . . . We felt it was necessary to consider two basic aspects in describing such a process: (1) the formal aspects of the sequential ordering of the 'external' events in the everyday life of the adolescent, and (2) how the adolescent experienced these events and reacted to them (p. 144).

[The authors identify three stages that distinguish their sample of suicide-attempting adolescents from their controls:

(1) A long-standing history of problems (from childhood to the onset of adolescence)

(2) A period of "escalation of problems" (since the onset of adolescence and in excess of those "normally" associated with adolescence)

(3) The final phase, characterized by the chain reaction dissolution of any remaining meaningful social relationships in the weeks and days preceding the suicide attempt] (p. 145)

"If a series of these events occurs in the particular sequence outlined [above], they seem to result in the adolescent's experiencing extreme unhappiness and withdrawal. Why should this be? It is postulated that these events (or comparable ones) experienced by the adolescent in the right sequence will lead to his progressive unhappiness because they have led to his progressive isolation from meaningful social relationships. This isolation, in turn, is seen by the adolescent as 'the problem' and simultaneously serves to isolate him from gaining access to that segment of the population necessary to resolve the problem, i.e., help him reestablish a meaningful social relationship" (p. 144).

In reconstructing this theory, we might profitably begin by looking for constituent elements: concepts and propositions. The authors present a large number of concepts, some identified boldly, others by inference. I will list concepts as they appear in the five paragraphs; have I missed any? Have I included some that aren't relevant?

1. broken home
    adolescent suicide attempter
    loss of a love object
    isolation
    meaningful social relationships

2. family relations
    peer relations
    attitudes toward school

       performance in school
       career aspirations
       developmental history

3. process of suicide
       entertaining thoughts of suicide
       attempting suicide
       external events in everyday life
       internal reactions to external events

4. history of problems
       escalation of problems
       normal problems of adolescence
       chain reaction dissolution of meaningful social relationships

5. sequence of events
       unhappiness
       withdrawal

These twenty-three concepts are only a part of those presented in the longer article but they will serve our purpose here. Even so, twenty-three concepts can be related a million different ways in the formation of propositions, so let's return to the excerpt to see which specific propositions (relationships between or among concepts) the authors present.

In the ways of the world, it is quite clear that the concept of attempting suicide should come at the end of one proposition, insofar as events presumably caused it. What events lead up to a suicide attempt? The authors suggest several in the first paragraph:

1. broken homes ——————→ attempting suicide
    loss of a love object ——————→ attempting suicide
    (isolation + meaningful social relationships) [combined as one concept, isolation from meaningful social relationships] ————————→ attempting suicide

(Before I go on, notice that the three propositions above are legitimate propositions, but within the context of the article they are not intended to be sufficient statements of adolescent suicide. The authors have presented them literally, one at a time, but they fully intend to combine them in a particular way as part of their theory. Let us not take their propositions out of the total context.)

Continuing with the remaining paragraphs from the excerpt:

2. family relations ——————→ attempting suicide
    peer relations ——————→ attempting suicide

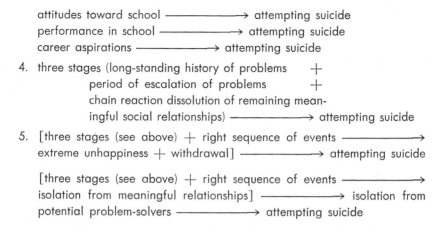

attitudes toward school ⟶ attempting suicide
performance in school ⟶ attempting suicide
career aspirations ⟶ attempting suicide

4. three stages (long-standing history of problems +
    period of escalation of problems +
    chain reaction dissolution of remaining mean-
    ingful social relationships) ⟶ attempting suicide

5. [three stages (see above) + right sequence of events ⟶
    extreme unhappiness + withdrawal] ⟶ attempting suicide

    [three stages (see above) + right sequence of events ⟶
    isolation from meaningful relationships] ⟶ isolation from
    potential problem-solvers ⟶ attempting suicide

We have reduced the twenty-three concepts to eleven propositions, a reduction in information which is very helpful but not yet sufficient to grasp in one sweep of the mind. Note that information might have been presented about the empirical findings, relating, say performance in school with suicide, or broken homes with adolescent suicide. As empirical facts, these are what they are, but they are not necessarily related. The relationship comes at the theoretical level. Suppose the authors had hypothesized:

> Broken homes lead to poor performance in school which in
> turn leads to attempting suicide.

Such an hypothesis relates two bodies of information by means of implicit arguments which, by all rights, should be stated explicitly: Broken homes lead to stresses, which produce an environment nonconducive to homework, which leads to poor preparation for school, which leads to poor performance in school, which leads to lowered feelings of self-adequacy, which leads to . . . . To be explicit would mean to specify all these additional concepts and to link them in a logical order. The body of research data might only mention the correlations between broken homes and suicide and school grades and suicide, so this would be a case in which a long, thin theoretical network is made to carry a heavy load of explanation. Perhaps too heavy.

Let us return to Jacobs and Teicher's statement of theory. If you look at my abstraction of propositions from the several paragraphs in the excerpt, you will notice a progressive accumulation of logical argument. Paragraphs 1 and 2 provide specific propositions, some of which are not utilized directly in the major statement of theory. By paragraph 4, we are offered a more complex statement, summarizing (indirectly) the earlier concepts. For instance, the long-standing history of problems may refer to family relations or peer relations. Or it may refer to something else.

In paragraph 5, the theory is pulled together. Twice. As you can see, the three-stage concept experienced in the right sequence of events leads first, to extreme unhappiness and withdrawal, but, second, to isolation from meaningful relationships. Which is right? Perhaps both are. What is the relationship between extreme unhappiness and withdrawal and isolation from meaningful relationships? Are they the same **idea**? Are they the same **concept**? Do they have the same referents in the real world?

Let's assume for the moment that these two concepts refer to the same idea. Isolation from meaningful relationships is seen by the authors to lead to isolation from potential problem-solvers, and this in turn leads to attempting suicide. Altogether, we have reconstructed a theory, a sysem of five interrelating complex propositions.

1. A history of distant past, recent, and current problems
2. in the right sequence of events
3. leading to isolation from meaningful relationships and
4. leading to isolation from potential problem-solvers
5. tends to lead to a suicide attempt.

This is a manageable reduction from the linguistic complexity of the full excerpt. This is the task of the reader of any professional article. However, whether it is a useful reduction of complexity is another story, whether it is an adequate theory, whether it is logically consistent as stated, whether there is corresponding empirical support, whether it leads us to have productive ideas with real clients—these and other questions must then be raised.

I recently spoke of the ways of the world in identifying which concept would come at the end of a proposition, namely, that attempting suicide would follow a number of other events. But the ways of science, especially from a systems point of view, do not limit us to the places where concepts are stated. What if we considered attempting suicide in another location within a network of concepts. It is conceivable—it may never be true, but one can at least imagine a situation—that an adolescent may purposively choose to threaten suicide because he predicts certain events to follow, such as stress in family relationships or the divorce of his parents resulting in his staying with the loved parent and being removed from the hated parent.

My point is simply that concepts have no natural position in a systems perspective—in the theoretical domain, everything is conceivable with a little effort. This is the power and glory of the theoretical domain, a creative reconstruction of the events of the world. It is also a potential weakness because there are a large number of ways in which such creative reconstructions can be absolutely unfruitful. A given proposition can be true or false; strictly speaking, a theory can merely be shown to have confirming or disconfirming evidence identified. Such evidence would change the likelihood of one's using the theory again, but would not, in itself, disprove the theory.

A moment ago I assumed that "extreme unhappiness and withdrawal" meant the same as "isolation from meaningful relationships." Now, let's assume that they are different. This assumption leads to another possible statement of the theory, one which involves an inner loop, that is, a set of instructions to repeat certain events until a given point is reached (in systems terms, an inner loop is like feedback):

1. A history of distant past, recent, and current problems
2. in the right sequence
3. leading to a repeating cycle of events [the inner loop] involving a tendency toward unhappiness and withdrawal leading to new levels of unhappiness and withdrawal
4. leading to a given point, isolation from meaningful relationships, and consequently, to isolation from potential problem-solvers,
5. such that all possibilities of problem solving, except self-destruction, appear to be closed off to the adolescent.

This statement may appear to capture more of the dynamic process being suggested—it may also include more concepts and it certainly raises more problems than before, such as, why suicide? Why not sex or crime as a method for release of tension?

Such internal-loop statements are useful in many ways. They require us to think in concrete terms about dynamic relationships; they provide an explanation for the presence of events without the final result occurring—there are lots of unhappy adolescents who don't kill themselves. And, interestingly, such internal loops are capable of being simulated by computers since the complexity of the accumulating effect is sometimes beyond simple calculation—how many problems and how many combinations of problems will lead a person to his breaking point? The implication of these forms of propositions for practice is immense, such as where are we able to identify accumulating pressures that may lead to a violent release of energy? Prevention is always easier than cure, but it has been given short shrift in social work, perhaps because we have never had the tools to implement prevention.

TOWARD THE SYSTEMATIC FORMULATION OF PRACTICE WISDOM

Of all the topics discussed in this book, I believe that the issue of systematic formulation of practice wisdom is one of the unrecognized critical issues of the helping professions. Vast numbers of individual and agency innovations are effectively lost to others who might profit from this knowledge. There are a small number of outlets such as workshops and professional journals, but reports of case illustrations without the accompanying conceptual analysis—abstracting beyond a particular case to derive the intervention ideas applicable to other situations—have little value beyond their human interest descriptions. Is there no way to make use of this reservoir of experience?

A conceptual analysis of practice wisdom requires first, an idea of what practice wisdom means, and second, a plan to define that in words which others can use.

Practice wisdom is, to my knowledge, nowhere defined (as distinct from professional competence which focuses on concepts of knowledge, skills, values, and professional integration). In my view, practice wisdom denotes not only a high level of competence in practice but also the possession of an individual theory of practice that represents the worker's attempt to conceptualize what he is doing.

Given this rough definition of practice wisdom, it appears to fall midway between a theory and an empirical generalization. Considering the hybrid nature of practice wisdom, we can begin considering plans to capture practice wisdom in usable words by looking at its two parents.

As a partial theory, it should be susceptible to analysis into conceptual components—concepts, propositions, and the network of statements called theory. An example of such an analysis is given in Chapter 8 using a source rich in ideas—Carl Rogers on encounter groups. Not every wise practitioner is as lucid in writing, but, in principle, it is possible to seek clear concepts and to assemble them into integrated networks. Only a given practitioner can tell us whether we have captured the essence of his individual strategy of practice. But even if we fail to satisfy the practitioner with our interpretation of his practice, we have at least developed a system of internally consistent propositions which may be tested in practice.

As a partial empirical generalization, a statement of practice wisdom should be grounded in evaluated performance. Such evaluation, as suggested in Chapter 17, requires clear specification of goals of intervention and means used. It would be possible, using procedures like those discussed in Chapter 17, to identify the wise practices and the components in them.

Then we would have to return to theorizing to put these empirically identified components into a logical network. But, again, we would have to return to a field test of these strategies in action. Hence, practice wisdom is a working back and forth between theory and experience, but again, in principle, it is possible to capture the information.

One final thought: Nothing will be done to conceptualize practice wisdom until a new professional orientation is established. It is my belief that orientation to the possibility of, and experience in, formulating what is innovating and effective service should be a part of professional education from the earliest moment.

SUMMARY

This chapter has reviewed five major functions which theories may serve: to delimit events and thus to classify; to describe surface characteristics and to summarize; to explain an event by accounting for how it changes; to integrate the conceptualization of this event with other conceptualized events, thus approximating a sense of understanding of the system encompassing the event; and to generate new ideas perhaps leading to influence over events, an applied use of theories.

These functions blur in practice and are closely connected with empirical statements, yet there are basic differences. The empirical statements—behavioral observations, empirical observations, empirical generalizations, and laws— vary in the degree of acceptance of the uniformities discovered among events.

A detailed case illustration for identifying a system of propositions constituting a theory was given, using excerpts from a journal article. This same type of activity must be performed for each analytic reading of the professional literature.

The issue of practice wisdom was briefly discussed. Problems abound in the systematic formulation of this largely untapped source of information in the helping professions, but several suggestions were offered to begin the task.

CHAPTER 8

Five Illustrative Theories in Search of a Practitioner

This chapter contains synopses of several social science theories which may be useful to helping professionals. The theories are contained in various books and articles; I offer my personal interpretations here. One is found in only one book, another in hundreds. Some of these theories are new, one is more than a century old. Each was selected to represent a dominant tradition in social psychology: the psychodynamic, the behavioral, or the existential. Each has generated empirical inquiry—this is the sine qua non of their presentation here—although research varies from a few to many thousand studies. The theories refer to individual, group, and societal levels of abstraction. The original statements of these theories offer the helping professional stimulation, challenge, and great reward.

The purpose of including these synopses here is not only as sources for illustrations in later chapters but also to exemplify the various ways philosophy of science may be brought to bear on developing and understanding theories. One statement of practice wisdom is conceptualized into a network of propositions. Another theory has some of its concepts and assumptions analyzed and criticized for inconsistencies. Still another theory is used to formulate some speculative hypotheses about historical and future events. They serve many purposes—all suggesting that theories can be among your most practical friends.

Caution: These theories are illustrations, not ends in themselves. They will be referred to in Part III of this book as we analyze the processes of selecting among theories and of moving from a given theory to practice.

IN THE PSYCHODYNAMIC TRADITION: TASK-CENTERED CASEWORK
(An illustration of an analysis and critique of a theory)

Task-centered casework, a recent vigorous offshoot from the mainstream of traditional psychodynamically oriented social work, is a theory-in-the-process-of-development (Reid and Epstein, 1972). The following brief summary of the one book in which this theory appears is intended to capture the spirit of the theory, because explicit practice strategies are yet to be derived from it. This theory is designed for use with the majority of clients currently served by social casework. Seven categories of problems are identified, which in turn guide task selection and treatment strategy. These are problems of (1) interpersonal conflict, (2) dissatisfaction in social relations, (3) relations with formal organizations, (4) role performance, (5) social transition (movement from one social position or situation to another), (6) reactive emotional distress (e.g., anxiety, depression, any feelings that may accompany other problems), and (7) inadequate resources.

Given a client who fits into one or more of these categories, this client must be willing and able to define and to act on the problem with the help of the worker. The scope of the problem must be a relatively limited and specific target. Reid and Epstein distinguish between the first-level expression of a problem and the second level, with the implication that a second level reaches a more basic concern, although this is not intended to get at personality structure and deep unconscious feelings as such. (The criteria are not yet clear by which the most critical target problem may be identified; a judgment by the worker is still required to set priorities among named problems.)

However, once explicit agreement on the target problem has been reached, certain tasks are identified which the client can perform to alleviate his problem. "The task represents both an immediate goal the client is to pursue and the means of achieving the larger goal of problem alleviation" (p. 21). The task is largely defined by the client and modified in the direction of manageability by the worker, so as to insure high probabilities of successful accomplishment.

Next, the worker and client agree on an approximate amount and duration of service. Task-centered casework is specifically a short-term service, attempting to capitalize on the rapidly changing conditions surrounding most problem situations and on the existing motivations to do something about the problem at hand (rather than long-term personality changes), thus heightening expectancy that these changes will occur in the allotted period, without straining the limits of the professional help that can in fact be offered to a client.

Based on these definitions of the target problem and agreements on tasks, the work begins. Overall, the worker must engage in two necessary but conflicting general modes of communication. The worker must be **systematic** in the sense of communicating so as to further the completion of the stage of treatment being worked on—problem identification, target selection, task formulation, durational limits, the work itself, and termination. The worker must also be **responsive** in communicating encouragement to the client, in helping him to feel accepted and understood, and in enabling him to utilize the worker's input.

The basic practice assumption of task-centered casework states that "the effectiveness and efficiency of methods normally used in casework practice can be increased considerably if they are concentrated on helping clients achieve specific and limited goals of their own choice within brief, bounded periods of service" (pp. 146, 147). Reid and Epstein summarize their practice by means of five types of specific communications used by workers. The first two lay the groundwork for the latter three, which are change-oriented techniques: (1) exploring (obtaining information and focusing its flow on relevant content), (2) structuring (explaining the purpose and workings of the treatment situation), (3) enhancing the client's awareness of his own behavior and that of others or about his situation, (4) encouraging (expressing approval by the worker of some action the client has initiated), and (5) directing (conveying the worker's advice about possible sources of action). The treatment consists of keeping the client systematically working toward his chosen task while being responsive to him as a person-solving-a-problem, using whatever techniques are appropriate toward these ends. (The theory is not yet at a state of development in which a specific technique leads to specific outcomes.)

Termination is considered in the initial phase of client-worker contact and is periodically reviewed as the goal date approaches. The termination process involves discussion of achievements and further tasks the client may carry out independently. The hope is that the client will have achieved a sizable degree of relief from the problems focused on in treatment so that "he no longer wants further help at that point. We expect that he may want help again with other variations of the same problems or with some other kinds of problems and would encourage him to return if he does" (p. 199, emphasis in the original removed). (The relationship between training for independence and expectancy of return for treatment is not conceptually clear in the theory.)

A discussion of some early research work involving tests of the effectiveness of task-centered casework is also given, as well as a review of the literature on the efficiency of short-term treatment relative to longer forms of treatment. Both lend initial support for the utility of this mode of treatment, although considerable work remains to be done (see also Reid and Shyne, 1969).

IN THE BEHAVIORIST TRADITION: BEHAVIOR MODIFICATION
(An illustration of translating a theory into a procedure for practice)

Behavior modification, behavior therapy, reciprocal inhibition, precision teaching, contingency management, behavior shaping, socio-behavioral theory, and many less mentionable epithets are labels for a family of approaches to interpersonal change derived from learning theories. While the major developments concerning learning theories and research began at about the time Mary Richmond was formulating her book on **Social Diagnosis** (1917), the flowering of clinical applications began little more than a decade ago, and applications in the natural environment (homes, schools, camps) began even more recently. However, an immense amount of research supporting the utility of behavioral techniques has already accumulated, presenting an empirical richness of a kind that the helping professions have never known (cf. Kanfer and Phillips, 1970; Franks, 1969; Bergin and Strupp, 1972).

Some of the behavior modification techniques derive from Pavlov's respondent conditioning theory which focuses on events **antecedent** to the event in question. In his famous series of investigations with salivating dogs (capping a long career that had already led to his winning a Nobel prize in physiology), he carefully paired a neutral stimulus with a stimulus that produced a desired event, resulting in the empirical phenomenon that the previously neutral stimulus would eventually also produce the desired event. Then, in an enormous program of studies, Pavlov and his colleagues tried to develop a basis for learning for almost all aspects of human behavior, including symbolic behavior. In the process, Pavlov, along with Skinner, has contributed a large number of terms to the basic psychological vocabulary we take for granted today. In their applied form, it may be said very generally that respondent conditioning methods, such as those developed by Wolpe and his colleagues, are applicable to involuntary psychological behaviors like anxiety, anger, sexual feelings (Ban, 1964; Wolpe and Lazarus, 1967).

Another group of techniques stems from Skinner's operant conditioning approach which focuses on events **consequent** to the event in question and on the manner by which the event and its consequences are connected. In highly controlled laboratory experiments, Skinner and his colleagues were able to produce immense amounts of evidence indicating that once an organism emitted a response that resulted in a consequence reinforcing to it, the organism was more likely to repeat that behavior. The experimenters controlled the delivery of the reinforcing consequences not only as a consequent event but also in the manner of delivery—continuous or intermittent reinforcement, attached to performances of behavior or to periods of time. Characteristic patterns of behavior resulted from different types of schedules of reinforcement. In experiments beyond the laboratory, Skinner and others have demonstrated the generality of their empirical laws in schools, hospitals, prisons, and many other settings. Again, as a generalization, the application of operant learning is to voluntary behavior, such as talking, acting, and thinking (Skinner, 1953, 1971).

A third approach to applications from learning theories may be termed the social learning or modeling or imitation perspective. The focus in this approach is on the person (the learner) being aware of another person as model (antecedent event) and what happens to that model as a result of an activity he engages in (consequent event). Research from this perspective has demonstrated that complex learning appears to occur, learning that may take place either immediately (as in the respondent and operant approaches) or at a great distance in time. The learner exhibits behaviors like some or all of the model's behavior or even the model's style of behaving. The implications of this point of view were brought to public attention recently with discussions of the effects of television violence on the behaviors of the mass juvenile audience (Bandura, 1969).

Even though this is merely a brief overview, we must recognize what many commentators on behavior modification have missed, that is, that these perspectives purport to deal with the full range of human behavior, not just with tiny, specific, isolated behaviors. A professional movement has developed around this approach. Specialized journals, such as the **Journal of Applied Behavioral Analysis,** bring the many empirical-clinical studies to public attention, as do the large number of books published in this area. Therefore, it is possible to describe only a small fragment of this approach to intervention. I will adapt an actual case handled by a first-year social work student to illustrate behavior modification through positive reinforcement. I will summarize the social work process by referring to a sequence of procedures described by Gambrill, Thomas, and Carter (1971) which appears to be successful in helping new practitioners achieve relatively high levels of successful outcomes (Thomas and Walter, 1973).

Joan was a five-year-old kindergartener who had come to the attention of the social service unit at the school because she was extraordinarily shy and withdrawn. The child's health record revealed that she had been severely burned in a playing accident several years earlier; the accident had resulted in large burn scars on her arms and hands. Given this background, the worker went through the following process in working with the little girl.

1. **Problem areas were inventoried.** Joan talked very little to her teacher and not at all to her classmates. She participated in class activities only if

Ideas borrowed from E. D. Gambrill, E. J. Thomas, & R. D. Carter, with permission of the National Association of Social Workers, from SOCIAL WORK, 1971, 16:1, 51-62.

directly urged to do so and then often in a pro forma fashion. The worker observed that, on several occasions when other children commented bluntly on Joan's scars, she physically withdrew. These appeared to be the only problem events.

2. **The priority problem** (or set of problems) **was selected** in cooperation with persons in the situation. Joan's teacher thought the priority problem was Joan's participation in class, both verbal and physical. (Her parents did not respond to the social work student's communications at all.)

3. **A commitment to cooperate was obtained** from the teacher who was concerned about Joan and eager to further the child's social and educational development even though it might involve extra effort. The worker provided reinforcement for the teacher by praising her interest in her students (cf. Tharp and Wetzel, 1969).

4. **Target behaviors were specified** in detail. Participation specifically meant that Joan was to move verbally or physically into class activities without individual promptings from the teacher. Many particular events might be encompassed by this specification, but the referents of the concept participation were clear in the mind of the teacher and worker.

5. **Preintervention occurrences of the targeted problem behavior were determined.** In Joan's case, this meant the number of occasions in which she did or did not participate under standard (nonintervention) conditions. It was important to take controlled observations at this point, both to determine the nature and extent of the problem and to have a reference point by which to compare the effects of intervention. Other problem behaviors might also have been observed, such as the number of unpleasant comments that other children made to Joan. Sometimes observing the pattern of occurrences among separate problem events might indicate a relationship among them which was not observed before. For instance, on days following a verbal assault from other children, Joan was even more withdrawn than usual.

6. **Identification of probable controlling conditions was determined** both conceptually, by assessments of the antecedent and consequent events, and empirically, by the hints derived from looking at the relationships among preintervention occurrences of problem events. There were very few events in Joan's school time that were sufficiently appealing to her for her to participate. Observation of her behavior showed a regular though small rise in participation when she played a particular word game at which she excelled.

7. **Social and physical environmental resources were assessed** to determine what persons, reinforcements, and intervention contexts were available in the modification. The challenge of the word game and consequent praise by the teacher and esteem from the students appeared to be relevant resources.

8. **Behavioral objectives were now specified** in precise terms. The worker

and the teacher wanted to obtain a level of volunteering for class activities significantly above the preintervention level. In practical terms, this meant a rate of participating closer to the norms of the class (which could be determined by a time sample from each member of the class, if need be). In either case, possession of preintervention data is invaluable in the formation of precise goals.

9. **A plan for the modification of problem behavior was formulated.** This combined the information on the problem behavior, the behavioral goals, the available resources, and the probable controlling conditions. The worker was concerned not to single Joan out from the rest of the class, thus calling further attention to her differences, and the teacher wanted the plan to be as simple as possible for practical reasons. The plan called for the teacher to say "That's good, Joan" immediately after she had volunteered for anything and once at the end of the day. This was thought to be as natural a reinforcing condition as possible, as the teacher praised others in a similar fashion. Short word games were to be used regularly to get Joan to participate more frequently and to receive her positive reinforcement for this participation. Nothing was done, for the time being, regarding other students commenting on Joan's scars.

10. **The plan was implemented,** with the teacher continuing to record Joan's behavior exactly as before.

11. **The outcomes were monitored,** both during the process itself as well as at the termination of service. The monitoring during the intervention process enabled the practitioner to observe closely what the on-going impact of his intervention was. Should there be a sudden change in behaviors, then he would look for new conditions to account for these changes and to react appropriately to them. Monitoring at the final outcome was a way to document the overall effectiveness of the intervention. This included a subjective impression of how well the worker had done but also independent observations (from the teacher) and other corroborating evidence (observations at recess, e.g.) that informed supervisors and agency funders precisely how successful the worker was for a given amount of time and effort. (See Chapter 17.)

12. **Maintenance of the change** was reinforced as the final step. Joan did increase her participation (statistically significant improvement at the .05 level of probability) under this regimen. The worker could have gone in several directions at that point. She could have continued to strengthen the participation so that it shifted entirely to Joan's own natural reinforcements—in effect saying "That's good, Joan" to herself when the teacher wasn't around. Or she could have dealt with the other problem behaviors of lower priority. The long-range goal is for the client to be self-monitoring, utilizing the reinforcing conditions that occur in the natural environment including continued performance even during periods of time when the natural environment is low on reinforcement.

IN THE EXISTENTIAL TRADITION: A THEORY OF ENCOUNTER GROUPS
(An example of reconstructing statements of practice wisdom into a network of propositions)

The third illustrative theory is at the "group level," that is, a therapeutic or educational intervention context in which a small number of persons interact on a face-to-face basis without a predetermined structure so that the focus of activity is on the interpersonal interactions and the intrapersonal reactions thereto (cf. Rogers, 1970). There are a variety of these interventive groups, some emphasizing human relations or leadership skills (such as T-groups) while others focus more on personal growth and awareness experiences (like encounter groups or sensitivity groups). There are numerous special-purpose groups, like Synanon or Alcoholics Anonymous, or Weight Watchers, or scout groups. Indeed the primary family and peer groups are themselves omnipresent. Why single out encounter groups for discussion in this chapter?

Encounter groups are a phenomenon of our times of which the helping professions will have to take account. From time to time, the helping professions will be faced with new interventive modes and it is worth considering how to approach such phenomena in order to distinguish the fad, the fake, and the fantastic. There are many articles and books in the professional literature which are descriptions of new methods and demonstration projects; many conversations between practitioners concern new ideas and methods. These are examples of "practice wisdom," rich statements by skilled practitioners which are not put in clear conceptual form. We must begin to make sense of these experiences, using some writing on encounter groups as an example of practice wisdom.

Carl Rogers is to be our guide; consummate practitioner as well as major contributor to theoretical and research literature, Dr. Rogers has written a lucid book about encounter groups: "At this stage of our knowledge I wish merely to describe the observable events and the way in which, to me, these events seem to cluster" (p. 15). It will be our task, using the tools of philosophy of science, to rearrange these statements to sum up the practitioner's broad experience so that we may find sound and testable advice to guide our own practice.

An underlying assumption that may put Rogers' book in perspective is that groups are vital in the formation of human personality, and when there is a breakdown (or lack of fulfillment of potentialities), the group can be a major instrument for healing or further socialization. In an overview of the encounter group process, Rogers notes that the unstructured nature of a group creates the problem of how the members are going to use their time together, whether for an intensive weekend or longer. "Only gradually does it become evident that the major aim of nearly every member is to find ways of relating to other members of the group and to himself" (p. 8). There ensues a period of milling around, of initial confusion and awkward politeness. As some members begin to express some personal facts, there is often ambivalence in reacting to this: "Do you really think it is safe for you to tell us these kinds of things?"—which Rogers sees as also expressing the questioner's own fear of revealing himself.

It soon becomes evident that the members of the group wear masks, presenting a public image while defending the private self. But, over time, in the context of a group of persons all struggling with the same concern of dealing with the substance of self rather than the illusion (and the strain which holding illusions creates), a sense of "genuine communication" is created, an expression of actual feelings rather than pretended ones. Sometimes these feelings are negative, sometimes positive, but, in either case, the person thinks that such feelings are unacceptable to others in his group. "To his astonishment, he finds that he is more accepted the more real that he becomes" (Rogers, 1970, p. 8).

A sense of trust begins to develop within the group; also "a sense of warmth and liking for other members of the group . . . Participants feel a closeness and intimacy which they have not felt even with their spouses or members of their own family, because they have revealed themselves here more deeply and more fully than to those in their own family circle" (Rogers, 1970, pp. 8, 9).

In this "psychological climate of safety" (p. 6), freedom of expression and reduction of defensiveness gradually occur as immediate feelings and reactions toward other members and toward oneself are expressed and accepted by others. Mutual trust permits members to be less inhibited by their rigid defenses so that they can receive feedback from others and test out new attitudes and behaviors, new ideas and directions. In short, the freedom, support, and challenge is present to seek one's self-actualization potentials not only in the group but beyond.

The helping professional will often encounter such writings or conversations of skilled practitioners in which information will be conveyed which offers the possibility of guidance, if one can put it together in a meaningful way. Bartlett (1970) laments the fact of unformulated and therefore often unrecognized practice wisdom, passed along if at all through one-to-one supervision. One solution for mining this rich vein of knowledge is to utilize the tools of philosophy of science, that is, to take the practitioner's statement, to formulate concepts which best capture its meaning, and to put these concepts together into propositions and networks of propositions which permit valid sharing (and testing) of experiences, so that the user may, in some degree, approximate the skills which the practitioner has achieved. In this way, the user will be able to build upon previous knowledge without forever having to retread the same grounds as previous practitioners. Testing out new knowledge is critical; it may be that the practice wisdom is too narrow, that it fits only the given practitioner who evolved it. But it is more likely that a formulated statement of practice wisdom will strike suggestive chords by which the user can develop new practice methods beyond those of his own experience. By this means, the helping professions may grow.

Turning to Rogers' views on encounter groups, I think the first step is to identify some critical concepts. It is difficult to capture and paraphrase a book so rich in experiences and illustrations, but this is the task we often face. I begin simply by selecting the concepts that seem to me to be critical: the group structure; the processes of the group; relationships (to others and to oneself)—public and private, actual and potential; communication (including self-content and affect and feedback); and acceptance and trust. On the assumption that we share an understanding of the meanings of these terms, what sense shall we make of them? It is easy to paraphrase Rogers as a series of **discrete** propositions. I am suggesting, however, that there is a critical stage in the formation of a **network** of propositions which is necessary for understanding what the practice wisdom is really about. Indeed, unless a reader can reduce a vivid experiential statement to a system of events that he can encompass within his own mind, the practice wisdom of another person is like a mirage.

As one reads a statement of practice wisdom he begins to sense a coming together of the ideas. Writing propositions about one's understanding may encourage this coming together. But it has been my experience in trying to understand another person's theory that I must combine my sense of the overall idea with the specific propositions I am able to frame regarding portions of his theory. Accumulating separate propositions won't make a network emerge from an aggregate of ideas.

What is my understanding of Rogers' major idea? It is to help an individual find self-actualization through an encounter group process. Given this understanding—and it may be an incorrect reading of Rogers—then I will attempt to formulate propositions in such a network as to achieve this goal. In doing so, I am selective in using his words, but I will account for all the critical terms as best I can.

Consider the following propositions:

1. (Assumption) An **encounter group** can generate a "psychological climate of **safety**."
2. (Hypothesis) If a person feels **safe** within an encounter group, then he will exhibit **freedom** of expression.
3. (Hypothesis) If a person exhibits **freedom** of expression, then he will provide genuine **communication** to others.
4. (Hypothesis) If a person genuinely **communicates** his ideas and feelings to others, then others will return genuine **feedback** to him.
5. (Hypothesis) If a person receives genuine **feedback**, then this will lead to **self-knowledge**.
6. (Hypothesis) If a person feels **safe** within an encounter group, then he will exhibit a **reduction of defensiveness**.
7. (Hypothesis) If a person exhibits **reduced defensiveness**, then he will have greater **self-acceptance**.
8. (Hypothesis) If a person receives genuine **feedback**, then he will obtain new **information** on other possible modes of being.
9. (Hypothesis) If a person receives new **information** on other possible modes of being, then this will lead to **self-knowledge**.
10. (Hypothesis) If a person exhibits **self-knowledge** and **self-acceptance** and if that person has **information** on other possible modes of being, then he will be more likely to achieve **self-actualization**.

Using these propositions, I can attempt to put them into a network that reflects for me the way I see the theory as a whole. I cannot stress enough that my reconstruction may not be that which Rogers intends, but it is mine; I can use it as a guide to practice, testing it out as I would any other theory to be used as a guide. And while its original statement by Rogers was intended to be suggestive, I have tried a formulation to help me benefit from his wise experiences and observations. I can look at the research literature for support for each of these propositions (see Gibbs, 1971; McGrath and Altman, 1966; Berelson and Steiner, 1964), and I can test out my understanding in practice (see Chapter 17). A reformulation of practice wisdom is a beginning point,

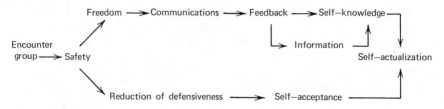

not an end. Now, consider my suggested network. I have used a word or phrase to stand for the clause in which it appears in the propositions above:

As the reader ponders the figure above, which represents one possible network among these propositions, I would also suggest that knowledge of one theory is often aided by knowing about related theories. For example, in Chapter 5, we discussed briefly some ideas from Truax and Carkhuff (1967), the concepts of warmth, empathy, and genuineness. Notice that these concepts were derived from Rogers' writing, and their discussion of these terms should broaden the network of ideas presented here.

IN THE TRADITION OF SOCIAL-CONFLICT THEORIES: MARXIAN SOCIOECONOMICS (Illustrations of a grand theory, a theory of the middle range, and a specific-action theory)

It is difficult to discuss Marxian theory in the highly charged political climate that polarizes our attitudes and allegiances today. Yet, regardless of our political views, we are all heirs of Karl Marx, including those of us who think ourselves least subject to his influence (Galbraith, 1963). In looking at the complex web of social-economic life, there are few theorists who have pulled together such a comprehensive system of ideas as Marx, the nineteenth-century scholar-radical-extraordinaire. Although times and conditions have changed, it will be instructive to review briefly some of the general propositions in this theory as a background to some current social-conflict theorists and activists.

Change—inexorable change in the way men relate or are forced to relate to one another in order to survive—this is the inner dynamic of human society. The manner by which man produces, distributes, and consumes the means by which he survives becomes the central focus for the scientist who seeks to understand society and for the man of action who seeks to influence it. Marx viewed history as a pattern of relationships between controllers of the means of production and those who are controlled, those whose labor created these valuable goods. The economic structure characterizes this fundamental relationship for any given historical period. The rest of the social structure fits around the economic, supporting it. For example, a religious organization is said to create a monumental ornament glorifying the arrangements of the existing social system, even if it has to recognize the difficult life of the controlled by promising them an opiate of heavenly reward so that they will keep the economic system running smoothly here on earth.

Marx noted that the differences between controllers and controlled tend to grow, misery tends to escalate and spiral, until a consciousness of common fate leads the controlled to rebel and "the expropriators are expropriated" (Marx, 1932, p. 204).

Behind the burning rhetoric of the Communist solution lie many remarkable insights about the nature of society and its inherent problems, the social-conflict analysis as distinct from any particular solution derived from it. A complex social system, acting out the natural consequences of its complex nature, creates stresses on its components. These components—the various groups making up a society—tend to oppose each other's interests in order to satisfy their own. Negotiations occur between those who control the goods of society and those who produce them; those who do neither are thrown on the mercies of the other two.

Marx notes that each side manipulates its sources of power in these negotiations: The controllers assert legality—for they have written the laws; morality —for they dispense salvation; and political force to back these up—for they control the police systems. The controlled assert themselves as producers of goods, without which there is no working society. Each has what the other wants to some degree, and so negotiations proceed to an equilibrium point but it is never stable, for the rebels who become the new Establishment soon have to battle the new controlled.

But Marx prophesied a coming, stable Utopia: When the workers of the world united into a system without the division of labor which enslaved the individual—such as the degradation of workers Marx saw in the industrial systems of his day—then a painful transition period would ensue, during which all remnants of the old order would be destroyed so as to establish a social system "from each according to his abilities, to each according to his needs" (Marx, 1932, p. 7). (Details of this Utopia are unfortunately few. It obviously would require planners who might become the new controlling class.)

Marxian theory contained a number of specific predictions such as the pressure on businesses to expand, to seek new methods and new markets, to concentrate in super-organizations, in order to continue to make profits in a changing world. While these have been often prophetic, other predictions such as violent class struggle and collapse of the total capitalistic system have not yet occurred. It is not my intention to discuss these points but rather to turn to contemporary analysis of social-conflict theory that may have direct implications for the helping professions.

There was no professional help-giving as such during Marx's time, although the Church and some voluntary organizations were involved with helping the new industrial poor. But Marx would have likely characterized helping professions, like social work, as being hired by the dominant controllers in order to assuage the burdens of the controlled. (Unions of the controlled were another matter, being self-help organizations.)

Contemporary writers have developed some of these ideas into a provocative theory. Piven and Cloward (1971) offer the thesis that the function of public relief-giving (public welfare) is to regulate the poor to maintain the dominant socioeconomic system. Relief-giving and the helping professions who give this relief are seen as ancillary to the dominant economic system. Piven and Cloward pose their central proposition as follows: ". . . When mass unemployment leads to outbreaks of turmoil, relief programs are ordinarily initiated or expanded to absorb and control enough of the unemployed to restore order; then, as turbulence subsides, the relief system contracts, expelling those who are needed to populate the labor market" (p. 3). Although they do not refer to Marxian theory directly, this hypothesis takes on fuller meaning within the context of a social-conflict theory such as Marx's. A corollary to the central proposition adds that some of the economically useless—the aged, the disabled —remain on welfare but are given such degrading treatment that the large body of workers will attempt not to fall into this state of affairs.

With this theory as guide, Piven and Cloward examine American history from the 1930s through the 1960s for historical evidence. For example, in the Great Depression of the 1930s, twenty million people were unemployed. Without the structuring effect of work (which Marx well noted), the social life of millions fell apart. Most were confused and ashamed by their problems, but some began to define the problem not as that of an individual failing but as collective failing. And in this latter mode, some became aggressive in seeking redress. Government action was seen in terms not of relief of widespread economic distress so much as of a balm to rising political unrest. When the unrest quickly subsided, relief was also withdrawn, forcing millions back into the labor market without hope of employment; but social stability had been recovered and the regulatory devices were not needed to a crisis degree.

During the 1940s and 1950s, when labor was needed for the war effort, the opposite occurred as persons were pushed off welfare rolls through both statutory and administrative means. In the 1960s new sources of strain occurred, creating political unrest, and, hence, requiring renewed relief efforts according to Piven and Cloward. And now we are in the 1970s. . . . Again, it is not the task of this section to analyze the arguments of these authors, but I have tried to show how a middle-range theory such as Piven and Cloward's can be derived from a general theory such as Marx's. I also want to indicate briefly how action hypotheses might be derived from this same source.

Community organizers, such as Alinsky (1971), appear to have used the propositions of conflict between groups, the power of developing consciousness of group interests toward the achievement of specific goals, and the selection of strategies of attack which fit the vulnerability of the controlling Establishment. For example, rather than going through a housing inspector to deal with the manifold and long-persisting complaints of slum residents, Alinsky organized a picket line manned by blacks around a slum landlord's nice suburban home.

It appeared to be the pressure of his neighbors rather than his humanitarian interests which got action for the slum residents. Now we come full circle. It is difficult to discuss actions based on social conflict, for one part of the helping professions is concerned with promoting social stability, while another part is concerned with amelioration of social ills—some of which may require offsetting and resetting the social order. Theories of social conflict and the part that the helping professions must play help to clarify the dilemma and, according to some (e.g., Knickmeyer, 1972), offer guidelines to surmount it. We may choose to use some theories; Marxists would say that some theories choose to use us.

IN THE SELF-CRITICAL TRADITION OF THE SCIENTIFIC METHOD: THE D K THEORY

The D K theory has not been explicated in the learned journals or in the scholarly literature, to my knowledge, but I offer it here as a vital subscript to all actions of helping professionals. D K stands for degrees of knowledge, ranging from don't know to damn konfident. One's knowledge is always limited, and yet there is a counter tendency toward seeking a completeness of understanding, a gestalt. This latter tendency is exhibited in pretending, in sliding over gray areas, in letting assumptions of expertise go uncorrected. Part of this bluff is therapeutic, similar to the trust people have in doctors (which may or may not be well-founded). But another part of the bluff is the defense of our own self-image or social justification.

The D K theory is very simply applied: To each and every professional action, the worker simply attaches a mental subscript, D K _____%, referring to the percentage or proportion of ignorance actually operating in this particular action. One must act on the best available knowledge, to be sure, but one must be equally aware of the degree of knowledge involved in one's actions.

SOCIAL WORK THEORIES AND SOCIAL WORK FIRST AID

The telephone rings and your client of several visits tells you she's had enough, she's fed up with living, and she's going to kill herself. This is not an idle threat, as you know from her past history. Then she pauses, waiting for you to speak. What do you say?

You will probably respond in whatever manner is comfortable for you. Perhaps you urge her to get out more of her angry feelings, or perhaps you point out the realities and positive aspects of her life. (Obviously, these are speculative answers for the purpose of this discussion.) Let's say that your client calms down after a while and you ask "Can you make it through the night?" She says "Yes" and you close off with a sigh of relief on the expectation that you have prevented a suicide.

After the call, you begin to think: How has all my formal education at school taught me to deal with such a situation? You mentally review the general theories of behavior and the major theories of practice and you think "too abstract." You consider the focused theories like those concerning crises, of theories about suicides, and you blink in disbelief. When the telephone call came, you forgot that you had ever heard of them and fell back on common sense. And you begin to wonder why learn theories, or research information, or the bits and pieces of practice wisdom, when they are never suitable in an active crisis of helping? I suspect that this may not be the first time this question has occurred to the reader. This incident of a suicide call actually occurred to one of my students and because it goes to the heart of professional education, it requires careful consideration.

My personal response is to distinguish between social work theories and what might be called social work first aid, that is, temporary relief in emergency situations by the simplest actions calculated to (1) do no further harm, and (2) provide immediate changes in the pressuring events so as to give relief if possible or to gain time until more comprehensive action can be taken. I would guess that anything you might say, if you show empathy, warmth, and genuineness of concern, with an indication of appropriate action, might temporarily do the trick. (You have to deliver the promises, obviously.)

But this is first aid only. The second step, after the telephone conversation has ended, is careful thinking and planning, involving the best available information. No one disputes this but still, why are helping professionals overtrained with theories and empirical information but left speechless in the face of a crisis and dependent on common sense to come to the rescue? The answer to this is that common sense is itself learned. It is likely that careful consideration of these abstract materials have their impact on common sense over time, just as they did to create your current common sense. First aid does not happen by accident. Experience provides its own serenity in times of crisis, although each time is unique. The very rehearsal of this event with this crisis call in the context of what you know will make your response to the next crisis call that much more based on knowledge and skill.

Part III

PHILOSOPHY OF SCIENTIFIC PRACTICE: THE USE OF SHARED ABSTRACT EVENT SYSTEMS

CHAPTER 9

Introduction to the Problems of a Philosophy of Scientific Practice

Any reading of a cross section of case records will show a serious gap between what is known in the profession and what is actually used by the average practitioner.

—Florence Hollis, 1972 (p. 352)

What are the requirements of scientific practice when your client of the future will have unknown problems, requiring knowledge not yet developed, perhaps to obtain goals not currently sanctioned? I would suggest that an orientation to these types of unknowns requires three major interrelated elements, the analysis of which represents the focal point of the philosophy of scientific practice. These three elements are information, evaluation, and action.

By **information for scientific practice,** I refer to the types of knowledge discussed in Chapter 7—theory, empirical statements, and practice wisdom. I will suggest later that all of this information, to be used in practice, must be translated into usable forms. I will introduce the term **strategy** to represent this translation. Steps of strategy formation involve retrieval of the best available existing information (Chapter 20), as well as the collection of new objective information (Chapter 19) and its on-going evaluation (Chapter 17). Information so obtained needs to be translated into explicit operational plans and specific steps connecting the particular case with normative data and abstract theories (Chapters 10, 11, and 12). The distinctive addition to the professional (as contrasted to the scientific) enterprise is the addition of values as a specific determinable part of the strategy for action (Chapter 13).

By **evaluation for scientific practice,** I refer to the **necessary** element of defining (Chapter 5) and measuring (Chapter 17) the existence and extent of relevant variables (problem events and other nonproblem events which might be influenced by practice) before and after intervention, so that some comparison can be made of the effectiveness and efficiency of practice. This information is necessary both for feedback on the process and on the outcome in a particular case, or types of cases, or agency performance, or the accountability of the services of the profession as a whole.

By **action for scientific practice**, I refer to forms (not the contents of a specific practice method) of intervention. The practice form equivalent to the scientific method, namely the problem-solving approach, wears many guises and can be found in all of the helping professions (Chapter 11). The issue of adding values to such a scientific-practice method poses some difficult problems for the profession (Chapter 13). Less discussed but of no less importance is the issue of creative practice, used here in the sense of innovative rule-breaking and rule-making (Chapter 16).

While all of these elements of scientific practice are currently available in greater or lesser degree, it is the integration of them which is the focus of this book. This focus conceives of the three elements as occurring in a systematic interactive way throughout practice. Figure 9-1 presents a schematic overview of the system which is to be discussed, portions at a time, in the following chapters. A final chapter (21) will attempt to pull together all of the separate themes in scientific practice, an orchestrated process requiring equal emphasis on the use of the theoretical and empirical literature, the concomitant use of evaluation procedures as feedback-monitoring devices, and the more familiar use of the intervention and problem-solving sequence.

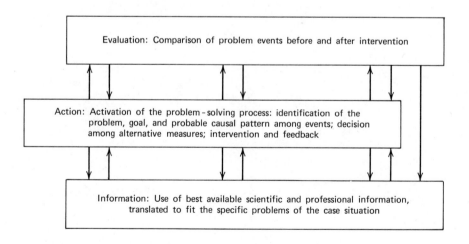

Figure 9-1—Schematic diagram of the three major elements of scientific practice, portions of which are to be discussed separately in the following chapters, with a detailed analysis shown in Figure 21-1.

Why is it necessary to emphasize the integration of these elements? Presumably, professional schools have long been teaching this, but, as the quotation from Hollis at the beginning of this chapter indicates, a systematic connection of the best available scientific information and evaluation with practice is not always to be found. . . . And, I might predict, it will never be found until the co-equal status of these three elements becomes a reality.

CHAPTER 10

Strategy: The Translation of Theory for Practice

Most of the theories we try to use in practice come in a ready-to-wear fashion, a standard size to fit the general case rather than the idiosyncratic contours of the particular case we have before us. Alterations are usually necessary to make the theory fit better. These alterations are the subject of the present chapter—how are theories used, that is, refitted, to guide practice? Far too many helping professionals are content with a comfortable hand-me-down theory which gets wrapped around every case that comes in the door, whether it fits or not. It **is** comfortable to the worker—but not to the client. The question raised in this chapter is how to improve the goodness of fit when it is needed.

Of the three components of a philosophy of scientific practice identified in Chapter 9, this present chapter deals mainly with information for scientific practice. Information involves several aspects, some of which have been previously discussed. (See Figure 10-1.) The initial aspect of information for scientific practice is the abstracting and generalizing from the flow of events the client presents. This generates the key concepts that will link the client's problematic situation with the professional literature relevant to these events. (Chapter 5 deals with this aspect of information.)

Having identified the specific concepts most pertinent to the case, we move to the second aspect of information for scientific practice. As will be discussed in Chapter 20, there are a number of avenues by which the helping professional can most effectively locate relevant theory, research, and practice wisdom bearing on a case. The third aspect, to which the present chapter is devoted, concerns the translation that must be made if the theories and research, developed in other contexts for other purposes, are to be most appropriately applied to the client's case. The fourth aspect of information for scientific

Information

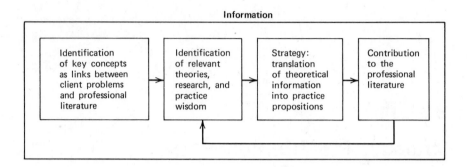

Figure 10-1—Schematic diagram of four aspects of information for scientific practice.

practice concerns the worker's contribution to his own professional literature—as innovative practice methods or problem identification, that is, as new practice wisdom. Chapter 8 and Chapter 16 discuss aspects of such contributions.

The flow of information for scientific practice occurs in conjunction with the other two major components, action and evaluation. There are numerous points at which what happens in the other two components influences information search, translation, and contribution. Chapter 21 will attempt to reconstruct this total picture.

CRITERIA FOR COMPARISON AMONG THEORIES

As we identify the key concepts of a case and begin to search the literature for information on which to base our practice, we inevitably discover that there are several ways of conceptualizing the problem, several theories claiming to be relevant. The first issue to be taken up in this chapter deals with criteria for choice among theories. A second issue concerns how a chosen theory may be translated into a tool for practice.

Beginning with the first issue, let's look at a well-known example of choice among theories. Burtt (1954) bids us consider the weighty scientific objections that could have been raised against that upstart Copernicus who first opposed the thousand-year-old Ptolemaic system of astronomy. First, there were no known celestial phenomena which were not accounted for by the Ptolemaic method—with effort. Second, any fool could see with his own eyes. The earth was a great big blob of hard material, while the sun and stars were twinkling bits of fire, and it stands to reason that the light materials would move while the heavy material would stay fixed. Third, there was a beautiful network of ideas that had categorized everything and everything had its place in that network. Moreover, the human being who constructed that category system was, of course, superior to the nonhuman things categorized, which was very comfortable. And if the truth (then known) were known, some of the assertions of the new theory were manifest nonsense. For example, in principle if you threw a ball straight up in the air, it would fall west of the starting point if the Copernican theory were correct; but everyone could see that the ball would always fall straight down. (Even Copernicus had to wait for some assistance from Galileo on this one.) On top of all this was a theological consideration which, like the political consideration of our own times, was almost too large to comprehend, let alone oppose.

Against all this, Copernicus offered an alternative theory which was conceptually and mathematically simpler. In place of Ptolemy's eighty or so epicycles, required to smooth out the observed paths of the planets, Copernicus made the heavens more orderly, using less than half of the corrective epicycles, although he had to make some giant assumptions to do this. It was a more harmonious organization of planetary events because most of these phenomena could be represented by a series of concentric circles around the sun—all except our moon which persisted in being obstinate. With facts like these, who needs enemies? It is amazing how a few pages of conceptualizations could have produced such a revolution, all because the alternative theory was relatively simpler and more harmonious than the existing one. Can you conceive of how shocked you would be if a new Copernicus would propose an even simpler theoretical explanation of our universe that scrapped that of old Copernicus? Let me list a few of the kinds of criteria which have produced other revolutions, large and small, and which, I must remind you, scientists have gone to the stake to define and to defend:

I. The following criteria, broadly speaking, concern the theoretical language level—the nature of concepts, how they are interrelated, and what functions they are to serve as theoretical terms per se.

A. Simplicity: The more simple the explanation of a given event, the more preferable (also called parsimony or Occam's Razor).

B. Logical Consistency: The more internally consistent a set of propositions is, the more preferable (also called harmony).

C. Clarity: The more unambiguous the meaning of the terms, the more preferable.

D. Derivability: The more propositions that can be derived from a theoretical formulation, thus leading to new thinking and testing, the more preferable (also called predictive potency).

E. Generality: The more events a statement of theory covers under one system of concepts and propositions, the more preferable.

II. The next set of criteria refers broadly to a theory's stance in leading to research or to the products of that research.

F. Agreement with Known Facts: The greater the agreement of a theory and its predictions with known empirical variations among events, the more preferable.

G. Objectivity: In contrast to the personal opinion of one observer, the more the propositions of a theory are publicly available for empirical testing, the more preferable.

H. Testability: The more nearly operational the concepts and propositions of a theory, the more preferable.

I. Replicability: The more easily a proposition from a theory can be repeatedly studied in research, the more preferable.

These criteria are very abstract, and partisans of a given theory will argue that, properly understood, their theory most nearly conforms with the requirements. Given the arbitrary way in which events in the everyday world are conceptualized and put into theories, it makes comparison among concepts and theories very difficult. For instance, is "self," "ego," or "personality" more "simple," "clear," or "testable"? Yet in spite of these difficulties I would encourage the reader to continue the attempt. In the long history of science, these criteria have repeatedly proven their vitality; and we can expect that they will serve the behavioral sciences as well.

If helping professionals do not choose among theories by means of such criteria, then how do they choose the theories they use? I know of no research on this point, but I would hypothesize that it largely depends on their education as practitioners. In schools, students are oriented to a particular way of thinking about problems and solutions. Sometimes these orientations become very powerful, dominating the thinking of a practitioner as to the right questions to ask and the range of admissible answers. The eclectic, by definition, is open to broader ranges of questions and answers. However, many eclectics operate within a family of possible theories such as any of the variants of psychodynamics, although they exclude the variants of learning theories (cf. Fischer, 1973). On the opposite end of the pole from the single dominant theory is the person who seeks empirical evidence for every practice action he takes and chooses to be guided by evidence alone rather than by promises of theories. Unfortunately, the nature and extent of empirical evidence do not permit easy comparison for many problems; nor are many practitioners sufficiently well trained to move freely among theories and techniques.

Kuhn (1970) points out that these general orientations, or what he terms paradigms—widely used models that for a time provide admissible problems and solutions for a community of practitioners—insulate their adherents from other perspectives. I believe that this is a critical problem during a time when theory and research are in ferment, when new ideas are becoming available if only we are open to them.

Let me provide one instance of paradigms in action in the helping professions. Reid and Epstein (1972, pp. 129–135) discuss the concept of empathy as a major ingredient for their central concept of responsiveness of communication. They acknowledge that their usage is close to that of Truax and Carkhuff (1967), and they are impressed with the latters' conceptualization and research program in support of their position. Yet the task-centered writers cannot borrow the concept as stated by Truax and Carkhuff because it is embedded in a Rogerian client-centered theory which has a fundamentally different orientation from their own psychodynamic perspective. Client-centered theory requires that the therapist reflect back what the client is expressing; the client is at the center of the growth process which is to solve a particular problem. The psychodynamic approach involves a more active role for the therapist, based on an orientation that the client needs more help than mere reflection.

Reid and Epstein go on to define empathy as involving the first half of Truax and Carkhuff's usage, the conveying of understanding of the client's view of his situation; but it does not require that the practitioner express this recognition in so many words. It is hard to say what this definition means in practice, and whether we could in fact distinguish what a practitioner from one orientation would do differently from a practitioner from the other orientation. But by rejecting the Rogerian-type concept, Reid and Epstein also do not use Truax and Carkhuff's Accurate Empathy Scale to measure their form of empathy; nor do they, so far as I know, offer an alternative measurement procedure. Thus insulated by their orientation, they—and we—are at least temporarily prohibited from benefiting from empirical research that could continue to clarify the concept, the theory, and the practice.

To continue this example of paradigms, a behaviorist looking in on this conversation from still another paradigm might object to both views because each contains too many mentalistic inferential concepts which resist accurate observation and measurement. Such a behaviorist might define empathy as giving the client positive reinforcement in the interview situation, and the behaviorist might further point out that such reinforcement encourages the behavior being presented. Now if the behavior being presented is so-called sick behavior, the argument would be that empathy operationalized as reinforcement would tend to promote the very behavior the therapist is seeking to eradicate; therefore, such empathy should be used selectively and not as an all-pervasive approach to clients.

The paradigms we hold are powerful forces in selecting the informational tools we will use in practice. We are in a time of proliferation of competing ideas, growing out of the anomalies existing in dominant orientations. Kuhn observes that crises occur leading to a new creative idea which redefines the fundamental concept; a new paradigm replaces the old, suddenly and non-cumulatively.

I think this discussion leads to a very important point for the student of the helping professions: It is necessary to remain open to, and yet critical of, all theories, being careful to weigh the evidence as it becomes available, while remaining receptive for a limited time to new theories for which empirical evidence is not yet available.

CRITERIA FOR TRANSLATION WITHIN A THEORY

Whichever theory is chosen as the beginning point in guiding practice, a second issue emerges: The translation of this theory into a form usable by the helping professional. I call the product of this translation **strategy.** Theories, whose goals include adding to knowledge through empirical investigations, must be modified as strategies in influencing the course of problem events in the lives of particular persons. Theories have relatively low value involvement; strategies are highly saturated with values. Theories spawn experimental hypotheses on classes of objects; strategies generate on-site or action hypotheses: "If I do **X**, the client will probably do **Y** . . ." (focusing the conceptual tools on the particular client). Theories tend to use more specific and molecular units; strategies are driven to include multiple systems because many spheres of life in fact influence any problem event. Theories are interested in knowledge of causal patterns; strategies are interested in intervention or prevention which may avoid altogether the question of primary causes. It is the burden of this section to offer a beginning statement for rules of strategy, making theories usable in practice.

Thomas (1964; 1967) has given the clearest statement concerning whether theoretical formulations are applicable in practice (also see Gouldner, 1957). I will reinterpret Thomas' discussion in terms of the framework of this book.

In essence, Thomas is asking how the concepts which we so carefully abstract and generalize from the events of everyday life may be returned to that reality. Since, by definition, concepts are not like a particular event, how may we know which concepts are applicable to which events? How shall we know whether it is worth the effort to make use of concepts for a given situation, and whether it is ethical to do so? Thomas provides several criteria for connecting concepts to events in real life:

1. Whether the referent of the concept—the events in the everyday world to which the concept refers—is **identifiable**. Thomas contrasts concepts having no identifiable referent, such as Jung's idea of the racial unconscious, with concepts whose referents are readily identifiable, such as group size.
2. Whether the referent is **accessible** to the practitioner, either directly or indirectly. Direct access exists when the worker can engage the events of the client's life himself; indirect access exists when the worker would have to go through an intermediary to engage those events. Another form of indirect access would be when a worker has direct access only a small proportion of the time, like one hour a week, while the rest of the week the client is on his own. Thus, access to problematic events falls on a continuum with the larger portion being indirect to most social work practice, except that conducted in some institutions.
3. Whether the referent is **manipulable** or **controllable** by the practitioner. Control is a very important concept in the social sciences, although it is handled as if it were a Frankenstein by the helping professions. Descriptively, control involves the physical or psychological pressure person **A** (the worker) can exert on a person **B** (the client) regarding movement toward **X** (some aspect of the problem situation), counterbalanced by **B**'s capacity to resist **A**'s influence attempts. The combination of these two sets of forces is needed to determine when **X** has been controlled, that is, when the one person's (**A**'s) wishes hold sway over the other persons (**B**'s) wishes. This description is not wholly satisfactory because some attempts at control may not have immediate impact; and sometimes a client will merely conform when his actions are publicly monitored, but there is no internal change. Thus, it is difficult to determine just what should be meant by the criterion of controllability.

   I would suggest an interpretation of control in the helping professions that would have the following characteristics: A referent of a concept will be said to be controllable by the worker when he can perform such actions (directly or indirectly) that the client is moved physically or psychologically a determinable distance toward some specified goal. Control is thus defined after the fact, using a measurement procedure (such as that suggested in Chapter 17 of this book) as the empirical indicator of change. By one's practice and measurement design, the likelihood of accidental sources producing the change are minimized (Campbell and Stanley, 1963).
4. Whether the referent is **potent** in influencing events in the problem situation. This criterion draws attention to the differences in potency between a con-

cept within its conceptual network and the referent of that concept in the actual world. Thomas gives the example of the conceptual importance of client attraction to the worker as affecting continuance in treatment, whereas in the practical world such attraction is reduced in potency when countervailing forces such as the costs in money and effort are considered.

5. Although not included in Thomas' original list, we may add the criterion of **durability**, that is, whether the referent is durably present beyond the worker-intervention phase into the self-maintenance phase of treatment. Will the artificial circumstances set up during any treatment find natural circumstances to take their place after the service phase is completed?

These five criteria connect concepts with referents in the context of usability. The practice context, unlike a theoretical or many research contexts, is also involved with various kinds of costs and value concerns.

6. Whether the **financial, physical,** and **psychological costs** involved in the manipulation of the client and his situation are at an acceptable level to the client, to his family and associates, to the worker as an individual and as a member of a profession, to the agency which underwrites the costs, and to society which ultimately pays the bill. As manpower and materials grow more scarce, this issue of allocation must be increasingly faced. How long should treatment be carried on without a significant change in the desired direction? Is treatment on a one-to-one basis feasible any longer? These are but some of the many difficult issues facing the helping professions.

7. Whether the professional helping is **ethically suitable.** How much reward should be administered? What kinds of inducements are bribery? When is it suitable to use punishment (electric shock, solitary confinement, forced association with other so-called disturbed people, legal obligation to attend schools that are unstimulating and unproductive) with our clients? The mechanisms for determining ethical suitability are vague, except for the most blatant violations (Shore and Golann, 1973).

There are probably other criteria, but these will do for discussion purposes. Thomas goes on to note that some theories can pass muster on all of these counts, while others can pass on only a few. He notes that these criteria may be differentially applicable: Some may be immediately applicable for direct action or for complementary or indirect action; others may be hypothetically applicable for direct or indirect action because parts of the theory have failed to meet some of the preceding criteria but not critically. This means that more research may be needed, but no disconfirming evidence is available as such. Still other theories are totally inapplicable by virtue of having failed to meet critical criteria. Unfortunately, what **is** critical is not necessarily agreed upon. For instance, Anastasi (1968) writes of projective techniques as psychometric instruments: "Yet after three decades of negative results, the status of projective techniques remains unchanged."

Even though science is not fully self-correcting or professional practice fully self-monitoring of its ethics, it is not an exercise in futility to discuss the criteria above. Raising the level of consciousness of the helping professions about these issues will help to avoid the pseudo-criteria which either prematurely exclude knowledge or hastily include anything with the label of "social science." Taken as a group, the Thomas criteria offer the soundest beginnings available for translating theoretical materials into tools for use. If a concept or a theory that has earlier caught our fancy should not pass muster on these criteria, what then? Since the ultimate goal of the helping professions is to help, not to please the fancies of the helpers, I would recommend that we follow the directives of these criteria and measure the outcomes, letting the empirical results be our guide.

These criteria may also apply differentially to theories; for example, one theory's concepts may be more identifiable than another, but the second theory's concepts may be more potent than those of the first. Thus, these criteria present to us not so much final answers as statements of the risk we undertake in following one or another theory. I will develop this idea of risk in later chapters, but it is well to note that it begins with the initial selection of concepts and theories for practice.

ILLUSTRATION OF A THEORETICAL TERM TRANSLATED INTO A STRATEGY TERM

On the premise that a little help given at the right time and place is more effective than a lot of help given at a time of less emotional accessibility, Golan (1969) presents a theoretical approach to identify a client in crisis so as to give that bit of well-timed help. The theoretical task she undertakes is to distinguish a crisis from a noncrisis problem situation. Apparently a bizarre or poignant presenting problem is not sufficient to define a crisis, nor is the lack of such dramatics sufficient to disqualify a problem from being a crisis, for a quietly desperate applicant determined not to give way to panic may constitute a crisis.

Golan offers four subconcepts ("diagnostic abstractions") concerning the main term of crisis, recognizing that no one client will necessarily present clear

Excerpts from "When is a client in crisis?" SOCIAL CASEWORK by N. Golan are reprinted by permission of the author and the Editor. © 1969 by SOCIAL CASEWORK.

pictures of each in this order. A **hazardous event** is defined as "the initial external blow or internal change that triggers a chain of reactions leading to a crisis" (p. 390), which may be anticipated or unanticipated. A **vulnerable state** is defined as "the individual's subjective reactions to the hazardous event either at the time of its occurrence or subsequently" (p. 391). These may be perceived as a threat, a loss, or a challenge, with accompanying appropriate affects (anxiety, depression, or hope). A **precipitating factor** is defined as "the final link in the chain of stress-provoking events that converts a vulnerable state into a state of disequilibrium" (p. 393). And a fourth term, state of **active crisis,** is defined as "the stage of disequilibrium, when tensions and anxiety have risen to a peak, and the individual's built-in homeostatic devices no longer operate" (p. 393). Active crisis involves dysfunction of the affective, the perceptual-cognitive, the behavioral, and the biophysiological spheres, as well as social and institutional roles.

Are the referents of the concept crisis and its subconcepts identifiable? Some are and some are not. Hazardous events may have to be identified "through an inferential reconstruction of events leading to the current situation" (p. 390), while the precipitating factor would likely appear as the identifiable present-ing problem. What about accessibility? This depends on the identifiability of the referents; the time may have passed for the cause of the crisis to be accessible, while the current forces comprising the crisis may be accessible.

Are the referents of active crisis controllable? We are directed to consider a wide number of factors which make up an active state of crisis—from the affective to the social. One must consider the particular case and ask if the affective state is identifiable, accessible, and controllable. (And so on with the behavioral and the social factors.)

But we are not directed by the concept to identify active crisis in affective states. Conceptual circularity involves the dilemma of having to identify the specific events involved in active crisis in order to know when a state of active crisis exists so as to identify the affective, behavioral, and social components of the crisis. The other criteria of potency, durability, cost factors, and ethical con-cerns all depend on the controllability criterion, and so I would conclude that the concept **active crisis** is not yet conceptually clear, according to my interpreta-tion of Thomas' criteria.

The question is not whether all the subconcepts are translatable, but how much risk do we take in using this theoretical approach which is not as yet at the point of clear conceptual statement? Some subconcepts are translatable, and others might be viewed within a network of terms, the whole of which is to be tested for its conceptual fruitfulness (cf. Carnap in Chapter 4 of this book). By identifying the concepts that are not translatable, we might begin to probe the assumptions underlying them. For example, with hazardous events, we might inquire what does the knowledge of such an inferred event do for current practice? Is there an assumption that the hazardous event represents an underlying cause which must be known before the intervention may be effective?

What strategy emerges from this analysis of Golan's theory concerning active crisis? There are three major options. One is to go along with the theorist in using the network of concepts, seeking to test the fruitfulness of the whole network even though some concepts have been shown to be difficult to translate into practice terms. At the same time, one must be aware of the strategic weak points, for example, that inference to the hazardous event may in fact be a self-fulfilling prophecy stemming from one's initial theory.

A second option is to regroup the clearly translatable subconcepts into a more limited conceptual network but one which is more usable in practice. In Golan's case, such a regrouping of terms would focus on the here-and-now but would do little to distinguish an active crisis from any other problem event which brought a client to a professional helper. Whether this is sufficient is up to the worker.

A third option is to add new concepts to build a new network. Perhaps a concept concerning intensity of problem or susceptibility to influence might be added, if practical indicators could be found to translate these concepts. The point is that the worker is a theorist in his own right, and he must face the same problems in constructing strategies for action as does the theorist who develops abstract networks of ideas. We will pursue this notion of the worker as theorist in later chapters.

SUMMARY

This chapter has focused on those criteria for choosing among theories which more closely approximate the ideals of science, e.g., simplicity of explanation, generality of application. And once having selected appropriate theories, a second set of criteria was presented for translating a theory into a strategy for practice, that is, for setting up a network of propositions that might enable the practitioner to be guided in his dealings with events in the real world.

The translation from theory to strategy is aimed at clarifying the risk a worker undergoes when using this information for his guide to action. Three major options are open to him, once he has analyzed the concepts in terms of criteria for development of usable tools. He may continue to use a whole network of ideas, testing the fruitfulness of the whole system of propositions while being aware of its strategic weak points. Or he may reduce the network to the translatable terms only, if these could give him enough guidance. And, finally, he may add new concepts as needed, in effect creating a new practice theory.

CHAPTER 11

Problem Solving:
Design for Professional Action

Imagine yourself in London nearly a century ago, staying in an apartment at 321B Baker Street. As chance would have it, you happen to be situated just a floor above the famous "unofficial consulting detective," Mr. Sherlock Holmes, and a floor below that renowned epidemiologist, Dr. John Snow (MacMahon, Pugh, and Ipsen, 1960). One evening, as a Gothic fog settles over London, you find yourself in the company of these two gentlemen just as they are discussing the approaches they take in solving problems. Holmes, a young man puffing on his brier-root pipe, listens as Dr. Snow, now an elderly physician, reminisces about the great cholera epidemic thirty years ago. . . .

Dr. Snow is speaking: "Now, of course, this was many years before Koch [Dr. Robert Koch, the German bacteriologist] discovered the cause of cholera. All we knew was that we had a large number of cases of this dread disease on our hands. One area in particular, the Golden Square section of London, St. James and Berwick Streets, was especially hard hit."

Holmes: "I know that area. There is the large workhouse, and a brewery near by on Broad Street."

Snow: "That's the place. There were some small factories in the district at that time as well, plus many tenements where huge numbers of persons lived. In order to grasp hold of the total picture, I made a spot map of the cases in this area of London."

You ask: "What events were you looking for?"

Snow: "Since cholera is characterized by severe intestinal problems, I began by looking at common sources of food and drink. I simply marked on a map significant features of the area—the workhouse, the brewery, the streets, the stores and factories, the water pumps where the residents fetched their water in those days, and the like."

You. "What pattern of events did you find?"

Snow: "A number of interesting but separate facts emerged. For example, the workhouse had some 535 inhabitants. They were more or less self-contained, with their own water pump and other facilities on the premises. There were only five cases there. But very nearby were extremely large numbers of cholera victims, except at the brewery where some seventy persons worked and no cases of cholera were reported. Mr. Higgins, the proprietor, mentioned that the workers were allowed a certain ration of malt liquor, and I daresay that it was quite possible that the workers didn't drink anything else while they were at work.

"In contrast, there was a percussion-cap factory on Broad Street where eighteen cases were reported among the 200 workers. The one significant feature near the center of the largest number of cases was the Broad Street water pump. I asked people who lived near the Marlborough Street water pump where they got their water, and they told me that the water smelled so badly that they walked the longer distance to the Broad Street pump too."

You: "What system did you see among these patterns?"

Snow: "Looking at the map of instances of cholera and significant events in the human ecology of the area, I reasoned backward, so to speak, from the occurrence of the disease to what might have caused it. Now I didn't know the specific cause, but I could identify the fact that the water pump at Broad Street was associated with the distribution of the disease in time and space. We had the pump closed, and the incidence of new cases of cholera fell sharply."

At this moment, **Holmes,** who had been listening intently, leaped up and verily shouted: "Aha! Fascinating, Snow. Your method of solving this problem involving populations of people is exactly like my own methods of solving problems involving population of events. By starting from the known (the crime), I reason backward to what must have happened just before to lead to the crime, and what must have happened just before that, and so on."

You: "What events do you look for?"

Holmes: "At first I look at everything. And I mean really looking at things with magnifying glass and tape measure. Observation is the first requirement of a successful detective. Then, by deduction from what is known to what is unknown, I begin to look for answers to specific questions. Finally, I connect these deductions with the best available information on the general subject in question. The explanatory hypothesis that emerges deals with the specific case, leading to a highly probable conclusion as to who committed the crime."

Snow: "Fascinating, Holmes. Would you have a bit more tea?"

Holmes: "Indeed I would. You don't get tea like this very often that has been carried by camel over the Gobi desert by a five-foot-tall sea-faring Swede with a limp."

Snow: "Why, Holmes, that's extraordinary. How did you know that?". . .

You: "Fascinating. I'd like some tea too, please. I was talking with Charles Babbage some time ago. Do you know his work with the Analytic Machine [ancestor of the modern computer]? He predicted that he would be able, not merely to calculate differences among numbers, but to analyze the patterns among numbers to solve problems. I would guess that he might have taken information like rates of cholera as distributed in time and space, or a whole sequence of events surrounding a crime, and analyze out the same patterns that you two gentlemen did, but in a much faster time."

Snow: "I wouldn't put much stock in that. Babbage is just an Irascible Bombastic Machinist. . . ."

THE FORM OF PRACTICE: PROBLEM SOLVING

Throughout history men and women have always solved problems more or less well, and have thought about how to solve problems better. Polya (1957) paraphrases the ancient mathematician Pappus on his method of analysis or reasoning backward: Starting from what is given, one inquires from what antecedent such an event could have been derived, and then again from the antecedent of that antecedent until one comes to the set of events which is known to be true.

With reference to the helping professions, theorists have focused their attention on how persons solve the problems of everyday life, and how practitioners might facilitate the natural problem-solving process of the client. For example, Perlman (1970, p. 131) sought to view casework as a "forward moving course of transactions between active agents"; she suggests six stages of problem solving in a blend of Deweyan pragmatics and Freudian psychodynamics. First, the problem must be identified by the client—it must be recognized, named, put into the center of his attention—but also the worker must identify the problems she is aware of, recognizing that such identified problems may not be the same as those of the client. Second, Perlman states that the client's subjective experiences of the problem must be identified, such as how he feels about the problem and how he interprets it. Also to be identified is what the client does to affect the problem. This identification of the client's subjective perceptions is distinguished from the third stage, identi-fication of the facts involved in the problem—what are its causes, its effects, within the person's life situation.

The fourth stage involves a search for possible means of solving the problem, a consideration of such means by exchange of ideas and feelings between worker and client, as a kind of rehearsal for action. A fifth stage is the arrival at a decision, based on thinking through and feeling through the alternatives that seem most likely to optimize the solution of the problem. The sixth step is action based on these preceding considerations to test out the pragmatics of the decision. The results of such actions feed back into the client-worker relationship as grist for revising or improving the plans for solution.

While this broad framework nourished many generations of social work students, new questions have arisen placing new demands on theories of problem solving for more precision and hence more control in the problem-solving process. Skinner (1966) notes that the behavior seen when a person solves a problem involves a change in other parts of his behavior. Crudely put, a person does less of the ineffective behaviors and does more of the behaviors that get reinforced by their consequences in the real world. Looking at just the observable behaviors and events involved, Skinner would define a problem as that for which at the moment there is no answer (no known set of behaviors that will take a person or group from the current state of affairs to some desired state). Problem solving would constitute those behaviors which bring about this change to the desired state; the new, effective behavior would be termed the solution. So defined, problem solving, like all operant behavior, depends on the consequences of the person's behavior, and these are subject to influence by the helping professional on a planned basis—as well as by forces antagonistic to the client on planned or unplanned bases. Problem solving involves looking more closely at events which surround a behavior (individual or collective) to identify the pattern of positive reinforcers and aversive stimuli that influence this event. Having identified these stimuli and having acted to manipulate them, the practitioner and the client together solve the problem when new contingent reinforcements are created which lead to new nonproblematic behaviors. Problem solving becomes as precise as the extent to which the reinforcing stimuli are identified. Problems are controllable to the extent that those reinforcers can be influenced to generate nonproblematic behaviors. Evidence is accumulating that this approach affords the opportunity for precision social work.

There are other approaches to learning and problem solving in addition to the behavioral. Newell, Shaw, and Simon (1958) provide a simulated analysis of problem solving by building certain innate capacities into a computer, so that the computer can generate solutions to novel and complex problems. The elements of their theory simulate human problem solving and therefore raise a number of interesting questions. I interpret their discussion as follows: The mind is like a control system that connects the receptor inputs with the effector outputs. This control system contains memories of symbolized information, a number of primitive information processes which operate on the information in the memory (e.g., like mathematical operations of addition and division, or logical operations like implication or negation), and a strategy for processing information. These strategies are called **programs,** perfectly definite sets of rules for combining bits of information and information processes. Working backward, these authors suggest that an explanation of an observed event will be provided by knowing the program which generated that observed event.

Newell, Shaw, and Simon then set a computer to work. They gave the computer memory unit symbolized information—axioms from Whitehead and Russell's **Principia Mathematica,** the classic of modern symbolic logic. They built in primitive information processes together with a program called the Logic Theorist which was composed of certain rules of logic such as the syllogism. (For example, if "**A** implies **B**" is a true expression from preceding information, and "**B** implies **C**" is another true expression, then "**A** implies **C**" is also a true expression.) These elements constitute operational statements of the postulates of their theory.

Next they presented the computer with the first fifty-two theorems from Chapter 2 of **Principia Mathematica** in the sequence in which they occurred so that when the computer proved one theorem, it stored that solution in its memory to be used in later problems. It turned out that the computer solved the logical proofs—well, 73 percent of them—and this allowed the authors to claim to have displayed the structural basis for a generative problem-solving process. I interpret these authors to be saying in effect that they have demonstrated problem solving in operation because they have constructed a working model in which a known strategy for handling information has successfully generated solutions to novel and complex problems.

As an analogue to human problem solving, this challenges us to inquire about the components of our own problem-solving behavior. What sorts of scientific and professional information do we need in our memories to be effective problem-solvers? What primitive information-processing talents does a person need to deal with social work problems? What are the strategies for the use of theoretical information in practice? Other chapters in this book will deal with these questions, especially the first and third.

Of the three components of a philosophy of scientific practice identified in Chapter 9, this present chapter deals mainly with the problem-solving process as the **form** of professional action. This form of professional action is presumed to be relevant to any theory of human behavior applied to practice, as well as to all levels of social behavior. Following the general organization of D'Zurilla and Goldfried (1971) on the consensus among writers on the problem-solving process, I will present seven stages designed to focus on the helping professional. It is important to note the addition of a value dimension to each of these seven steps, as well as the fact that each stage refers both to worker and to client (See Figure 11-1).

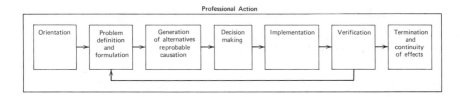

Figure 11-1—Schematic diagram of seven aspects of professional action for scientific practice.

Stage I: Orientation Toward Problem Solving

D'Zurilla and Goldfried (1971) begin their review of the theoretical and research literature on problem solving with a discussion of people's orientation toward the nature of problems in general and toward the ability to deal with them in particular. The first observation concerns realistic expectations about the occurrence of events in everyday life that upset the equilibrium of one's social-physical environment. As Ellis (1962) has pointed out, unrealistic expectations may set the ground for frustration and maladaptive behavior. A second observation concerns the confidence with which one approaches problems. Bloom and Broder (1950) note that successful problem-solvers had more confidence in their prior problem-solving abilities than did nonsuccessful problem-solvers.

Within the social work literature, the classic study by Ripple, Alexander, and Polemis (1964) discusses, among other things, the orienting concepts of discomfort and hope which the client brings to the helping situation. The proposition connecting these two variables states in effect that "even before work on a problem can begin the client must have discomfort about the present 'state of affairs' and hope that something can be done about it, and the worker must have empathy for the client's discomfort and must identify with the client's hope" (p. 206). Empirical evidence from this study supports the crucial role that the balance between discomfort and hope plays in regard to outcome of treatment.

In a broad review of the literature, Goldstein (1962) presents findings on therapist and patient expectancies in psychotherapy. In many circumstances, expectancies have been found to be a "major determiner of human behavior" (p. 111). Confirmation or disconfirmation of expectancies was shown to have predictable effects and may be interpreted to have practice implications. For example, therapist prognostic expectancies, that is, degrees of anticipated patient improvement, have been shown to influence treatment outcomes. From this Goldstein infers that a given patient be assigned to that therapist whose expectations that such a patient will improve are strongest among available therapists. With regard to patient expectations of improvement, Goldstein summarizes the psychotherapy research literature to suggest that moderate patient expectations, in contrast to very high or very low goal setting, appear to be related to the largest amount of therapeutic gain. The practice implication which Goldstein derives from these findings is for the therapist to present a realistic picture of the effectiveness of psychotherapy, that under- or overselling may have negative consequences with clients.

Thus there are many aspects of orientation toward problem solving which appear to be relevant to the task itself. Many of the research findings appear to have practice implications for optimizing successful outcome.

Stage II: Problem Definition and Formulation

When the worker and client come into contact, a process begins of problem definition and formulation which has been described in many ways in the professional literature. In essence, these descriptions all involve identifying the sequence of events which indicate where the client is now and where he wants to be, with some understanding of the events that stand in the way of connecting these two sets of events. For the worker, the problem definition involves another step, the abstraction and generalization from events to concepts which can provide an analytic perspective on the problem and which permit the worker to connect this particular situation with the empirical and theoretical literatures for guidance from the experiences of others.

Problematic occurrences may be viewed as discrete events or as sets or systems of events. Problem definition involves identifying the specific facts in the situation, the complete range of related facts, as well as the exclusion of irrelevant detail; to borrow a phrase, this is to obtain the truth, the whole truth, and nothing but the truth. What may be discrete problematic events to the client may be more usefully viewed as a problematic **system of events** by the worker, because with a system, one may locate the most accessible and controllable elements which may influence the whole network.

A considerable amount is known about the various ways of obtaining information about events. (Some of these matters are discussed in Chapter 19.) The helping professions rely heavily on interview information, slightly on standardized instruments and measuring procedures, and almost not at all on unobtrusive and nonreactive measures (such as those described by Webb, Campbell, Schwartz, and Sechrest, 1966), in spite of the weaknesses of the first method of gaining information and the strengths of the last two. Thus information obtained for formulating the problem may be limited or inaccurate, making definition of the problem, the whole problem, and nothing but the problem all the more difficult. Further study of this situation is called for.

Stage III: Generation of Alternatives Regarding Probable Causal System

D'Zurilla and Goldfried (1971) review the research literature on studies of generating alternative solutions to problems. The underlying assumption is that many alternatives will increase the likelihood that better plans will be distinguished from less effective plans and that these better solutions will be chosen for implementation. Osborn's (1963) method of brainstorming sets up the principal hypothesis of this stage which may be in summary phrased as follows: The greater the quantity of all ideas relevant to the general area under discussion, generated in a setting free of criticism of any idea but in the cooperative quest of expanding on and combining ideas, the better the quality of the final plan. The research evidence reviewed by D'Zurilla and Goldfried tends to support this hypothesis.

For the practitioner, this idea of brainstorming translates into consciously seeking alternative interpretations of the problematic events so as to generate different individualized theories about the client and his difficulties. Each individualized theory presents its suggestion as to the probable causal system and hence leads to alternative intervention plans. It would be my suggestion that a practitioner should begin by considering the several major theoretical alternatives, such as learning theories, dynamic theories, existential theories, and sociological theories, simply to draw the large outline of alternatives. Then, within these bounds, one would focus on specific theories that present practice differences by accentuating certain concepts to the relative exclusion of others.

Stage IV: Decision Making

The theory of decision making is a complex study in its own right, involving at least two major variables, utility and probability, and the complex relationships between them (Edwards and Tversky, 1967). Giving a brief introduction to these variables here, I will continue the discussion in Chapters 12 and 13. The utility of any decision is based on the desirableness of the expected consequences of the action. The probability of any decision is based on how likely the expected consequences are to occur. Utility and probability may vary independently; what is more valued is not necessarily more probable. Hence, decisions often mean practical compromises between some combinations of utility and probability.

To make matters more complex, it is also true that decision making takes place in contexts that differ on the basis of how much information is available about the events and their consequences (cf. Richmond, 1968). For example, if we aren't sure of the consequences of our actions—especially when these depend on the decisions of other persons who may oppose our interests knowingly or not—then it is harder to calculate the utility and the probability of our actions (see Chapter 13).

Stage V: Implementation

Not included in D'Zurilla and Goldfried's (1971) list of stages of problem solving is implementation, used in the sense of the direct or indirect changing of events (or sets or systems of events) in ways predicted to achieve specified goals. The conceptual network selected as the best guide to this problem situation must be translated into practice strategies and converted back into concrete events of professional action. Professional action always involves an action hypothesis: "If I do **X**, then it is likely that the client will do **Y**." Acting without some hunch about what the effect will be is acting blindly, not professionally. The hunch or hypothesis may be proven wrong, but this becomes important information in the formation of the next hypothesis.

Stage VI: Verification

Verification involves a person's actions being guided by a test of the consequences of his actions compared with the goals he is seeking. Miller, Galanter, and Pribram (1960) offer a heuristic model of verification: Test-Operate-Test-Exit (TOTE). The first test concerns comparing the present state of affairs with the desired goal state. If the two are not congruent, one needs to continue operating on the environment. The second test again compares the present state of affairs with the desired goal state, and if the two are congruent, then one may exit from this planned sequence of interventions—perhaps to go on to others not yet attained.

Verification may concern three distinguishable phases. There may be verification of the effectiveness of the on-going process as a sequence of means or intermediate goals; verification may concern the attainment of the ends or outcome goals; and one may verify the effectiveness of specific actions. For each phase, there is a formal and an informal evaluation. The formal evaluation test uses some scientific procedure in comparing the present state with the desired state; the informal evaluation employs a rough pragmatic approximation to the scientific procedure. I will return to these distinctions in Chapter 17 where statistical and practical significance are discussed.

For each phase of verification, a different type of hypothesis is used. For verification of specific actions by the helping professional, we may speak of action hypotheses for which evidence supporting or not supporting the hypothesis is immediately forthcoming; either the client responds or does not respond to our communication as we predicted. For verifying the ends or outcomes of service, we may use an outcome hypothesis which explicitly states the system of events constituting the goal of the case such that we can compare the current system of events with the goal. Usually this hypothesis requires precise statement of the frequency, magnitude, or organization of the events in order to make the statistical comparison.

Verifying the effectiveness of the on-going process as a sequence of means or intermediary goals is much less discussed in the literature. This type of verification would require what might be called a directional hypothesis concerning the course of events over relatively short periods of time (days in short-term treatment, weeks in regular therapy or community organization work). The type of reasoning that pertains to runs tests in nonparametric statistics could provide the measurement rationale for directional hypotheses: How unlikely is it that a certain observed sequence of events departs from the expected distribution of events in the desired direction?

Stage VII: Termination and Continuity of Effect

This final stage in my conceptual account of problem solving is also an addition to D'Zurilla and Goldfried's analysis, again as directed toward the helping professional in contrast with the researcher or theorist. It is intended to call attention to the practical implications of successful verification, that the practitioner may end the problem-solving contact in such a way that the learning, growth, or structural maintenance provided through service is continued beyond the worker-supported intervention period into the client's natural environment. It is not sufficient to prove that a client can master a given problem; it must also be known that he can continue to master that problem and related others when separated from the artificial dependency which any service from a helping professional necessarily provides.

In addition, new problems may be prevented through the development of generalizable problem-solving skills evolved from the specific problems of the case. We know very little about this generalizability, in part because we have paid little attention to it. But if we are to help clients break out of the cycle of continuing to need help in problem solving, then we must give this topic careful consideration. Prevention becomes an orientation to the possibility of future problem solving, and so the last stage of problem solving returns to the beginning stage.

Values: Substratum for Each Stage of Problem Solving

Valuing is omnipresent: As we orient ourselves to problem solving, our presuppositions shape our ideas about what we are dealing with; our personalities are the cumulative history of value decisions we and others have made. Defining and formulating problems involve selection and priority among events, as well as the construction of what a desired state of affairs would be. In generating alternative causal systems and deciding among them, our expected utilities play a large part, but our values are also present as we select admissible theoretical solutions and use cost and ethical criteria for translating them into practice strategies. Implementation through interaction with others is a continuing series of communicative acts whose metacommunication aspects represent expressions of affective concern. Verification involves selection among methods of evaluation and the degrees of risk we are willing to entertain in choosing to continue or to modify our intervention plans. In considering termination and the continuity of effect of service, we are demonstrating concern with the quality of life beyond the quality of immediate service.

Because of the omnipresence of valuing in the helping process, we must be explicit about the effects our values have in our practice. Chapter 13 deals with this difficult issue.

SUMMARY

Problem solving, whether by Sherlock Holmes, epidemiologists (cf. Cockerill, 1962), mathematicians, or helping professionals, seems to have a common form. Some writers, such as Skinner, emphasize the external aspects of behavior having to do with solving problems, while others, such as Newell, Shaw, and Simon, emphasize the internal aspects of the cognitive process. Others, Perlman, for instance, emphasize both. Following D'Zurilla and Goldfried's analysis of the literature, I have presented seven stages of problem solving as the form common to the several theories discussed in this chapter. In summary, I would like to offer this checklist of questions by which a worker can test whether he is considering the major issues as a professional problem solver:

I. Orientation Stage

    A. Is the client realistic about the occurrence and recognition of problems in the course of everyday life?

    B. What expectations does the client bring to the helping situation? What level of discomfort? What level of hope?

    C. Does the client have impulsive or immobilization tendencies in the face of problems?

    D. How confident is the worker in his ability to affect a favorable outcome in this case?

E. How shall the worker orient the client to the task of working together? What are the pertinent client characteristics and worker characteristics?

II. Problem Definition and Formulation

A. Specifically, what is the problem? With what frequency, magnitude, and direction do the problem events occur?

B. Who has the manifest problem? Who else is involved (contributing to, affected by, involved in defining the problem)?

C. What is the relation between this problem and other problems in the larger social system of which the client is a part?

D. What is the connection between the overt behavior and the reported or inferred feelings or thoughts about the problem?

E. What is unknown? Is the problem system complete and sufficient to account for the problems known?

F. Would it be helpful for intervention to know how the problem came to be as it is now? What parts did individuals play? What part did the environment play? What about interactions among them?

G. Have other instances of this problem been seen before, even in other guises? What can be learned from past experience, either with this client or with others?

H. What other information is needed? What key concepts emerge from the system of problem events that can provide access to information in the professional literature?

I. What are the goals, immediate, intermediate, and distant? What specific system of events is desired by the client? What is socially permissible?

J. How will the client's attainment of his goals affect others involved in the problem situation?

K. How will information about the problem be obtained so as to maximize veracity and to minimize our own intrusion into that information-gathering process?

III. Generation of Alternatives Regarding Probable Causal System

A. What theories and translated strategies are available to guide understanding and action in this situation? What combinations of theories and strategies might be even more relevant?

B. What patterns among events are apparent? What concepts label these patterns? What is known about these concepts in the literature? Are new ways of organizing events suggested?

    C. Does reasoning backward from the desired goal state help to generate new ideas—the antecedent sets of events that would be needed to attain the goal state?

    D. Does consideration of auxiliary problems or related case situations generate any new ideas in the current case?

IV. Decision Making

    A. What are the valued goals active in this situation? What is the relative value of each possible goal?

    B. What is the probability of the occurrence of each of these systems of goal events?

    C. Given the assigned values and the probabilities of occurrence of various goal states, what is the optimal combination of utilities and probabilities represented by a single course of action?

V. Implementation

    A. How are the abstractions from the theoretical language to be translated back into events which the worker directly or indirectly activates?

    B. How can each professional action be purposeful in serving an action hypothesis, so as to advance the intervention toward its goals?

    C. What are the costs of implementation? The resources to be used? The time, energy, and money, for the client, worker, agency, and society? How are ethical considerations systematically included in professional action?

    D. How can the worker choose those intervention methods which are most likely to affect positive change for the least cost?

VI. Verification

    A. How clear are the immediate, intermediate, and distant goals? How closely do they compare with the current state of events?

    B. How will the feedback from the case situation be used to modify plans so as to more effectively attain desired goals?

    C. How will formal evaluation methods be used in conjunction with informal evaluation methods? What if there are discrepancies between them?

VII. Termination and Continuity of Effect

    A. When has the new nonproblematic system of events been stabilized to a sufficient degree that the client may be presumed to operate on his own?

B. How can long-term monitoring or, preferably, self-monitoring by the client, be achieved?

C. Has the client been helped to make use of present problem-solving skills for new situations?

D. Has the worker given attention to prevention of new problems, both in the individual client and his environment? Are new service programs needed?

CHAPTER 12

The Helping Professional: Connecting Strategy and Action

This present chapter suggests two mechanisms by which events (sets and systems) described in Part I of this book can be connected with the networks of concepts and propositions described in Part II, namely, by deductive and inductive methods. The worker already has an acquaintance with many elements from each; she knows about many events in the client's life situation and she knows about many theories and empirical generalizations. Moreover, both events and conceptual information are continually changing, regrouping, as new information comes in, as new associations among ideas emerge. The process of knowing is aptly described as fluid; for at any particular moment the worker utilizes the existing organization of knowledge as the best available information on which to base her actions.

But at some point the worker must bridge the world of real events and the world of abstracted and generalized ideas. In brief, the deductive mechanism begins in the world of abstractions—scientific knowledge is viewed as a body of systematically interconnected information and supporting empirical generalizations. When a client comes along with a problem, the worker locates a theory or a portion of a theory of which the problem is an instance and then is guided in practice by the derivations from the theory. In practice usage, these derivations do not have the invariant certainty of deductive syllogisms, but rather may be shown to be probabilistic, hence providing the worker with a statement of the risk involved for choosing to be guided by this particular theory.

The inductive mechanism begins in the world of events. The worker seeks to identify sets and systems among the events the client presents. Using these events as cues, the worker infers to what conceptual patterns these events might be a part. There is only a probabilistic connection between events and the inductively connected conceptual network, which, for the practitioner, provides a statement of risk involved for choosing to be guided by that theory. (A more complete discussion of these approaches to connecting events and theory will be presented below.)

Thus, both mechanisms connecting events and theories provide indicators of risk in using conceptual guides. This simplified introduction to these complex topics is intended to provide a point of departure for the helping professional in clarifying her own style or practice model, in making it a more effective tool by being subject to critical analysis and evaluation. We will also discover that in practice we will move back and forth between these two approaches in connecting abstractions and events.

A DEDUCTIVE APPROACH

Sarbin, Taft, and Bailey (1960) have addressed themselves to our basic issue of connecting events from reality to our conceptual networks. Their book concerns clinical inference as it is influenced by a cognitive dimension of the helping professional and the ecological dimension of the environments in which the client system exists. They distinguish among **formal inference,** as in classical logic in which explicitly stated axioms and postulates are combined according to certain patterns to provide invariant outcomes; **statistical inference** based on mathematically defined operations to yield probabilistic and variable outcomes; and **clinical inference** which combines both forms—the major premises are achieved through deductions from the clinician's cognitive structure, while the context of decision making is formal, with the clinician acting as if invariant patterns were involved. It is this last-mentioned form of inference which will concern us here.

Sarbin and his colleagues offer a six-stage process of clinical inference which has some basic similarities to the stages of problem solving discussed in the previous chapter. The **first stage** concerns the **postulate system of the inferrer.** This includes the accessible and inaccessible beliefs, attitudes, and presuppositions, as well as the categorical systems and dimensions which hold them in a cognitive network. These various beliefs and attitudes emerge in various ways: inductively, from multiple experiences with the world; deductively, from others or their own beliefs, both scientific and fantastic; and so forth. From these various sources, a person develops a system of interlocking cognitive dimensions which exist in his mind until a problem is posed when, in the context of action, these postulates are called into play.

The **second stage** is the heart of Sarbin, Taft, and Bailey's model: the **utilization of the categorical syllogism as a model of clinical inference**, with considerable modification of this classical logical form to fit the context of the practitioner. First, a reminder about syllogisms. A syllogism is a form of reasoning in which two statements are combined in such a way as to determine the truth or falsity of a final statement. The two preliminary statements are known as the major and the minor premises, while the final statement is the conclusion. It is important to note that the logical form of the argument, not its content, determines the validity of its conclusions. In clinical practice, including social work, we must be concerned as well with the content, the material truth as logicians might say. There are various forms of syllogisms, but the one these authors use, the categorical syllogism, may be demonstrated to be equivalent to the other syllogistic forms. There are, in turn, various forms of categorical syllogisms, but the authors use the one in which both the premises and conclusion are universalistic (concerning all or none) and affirmative. For example:

All men are mortal.   All **X** are **Y**. (Major premise)
All Greeks are men.   All **Z** are **X**. (Minor premise)

Therefore, all Greeks are mortal. ∴. All **Z** are **Y**. (Conclusion) This is fine, if you are working with all Greeks, etc., but most of the time clinicians deal with one person or small groups. No problem, to wit:

Plato belongs to the class of one ("Platos") which consists of men.
All Platos are men. All men are mortal.
Therefore, all Platos (of which there is only one) are mortal.

Notice something else, more familiar. The syllogism is a proposition containing two concepts, one part of which is known as the subject term, the other part is known as the predicate term. In the example above, one term or concept (**X**) is shared in two of the premises. This is vital for drawing logical conclusions, just as it was essential for sharing experiences in communication (Chapter 3).

In logic, the terms have a single meaning, whereas in clinical practice, there are usually multiple meanings of the terms. This presents some difficulties for the logical model applied in practice but not insuperable ones as we learn to tie our meanings down more firmly to more objective behavioral events. Also, practice situations rarely have all or none as true modifiers; for example, "all older persons are harmed by relocation from their own homes to institutions." There may be some evidence that some older persons are harmed in some ways but not all. Using such evidence as premises in logical syllogisms leads to indeterminate conclusions:

Some older persons are harmed in relocation to institutions.
Methuselah is an older person.
Therefore . . . nothing.

Methuselah may or may not be part of that concrete group of older persons who are harmed, but we cannot logically predict this. The major modification in logical form suggested by Sarbin, Taft, and Bailey is to use probabilistic statements as premises and to act **as if** these were universal propositions:

All older persons are harmed in relocation to institutions—this is a proposition which has a probability of being true in (let us say) 50 percent of the time as indicated by research.
Methuselah is an older person.
Therefore, the best available evidence suggests that Methuselah faces a risk of being harmed by relocation to an institution about 50 percent of the time.

This is an important modification, not without its critics, but it permits us to consider probabilities of risk even for unique individuals (cf. Allport, 1937).

Postulates are brought into focus in the context of action on a problem. Postulates give rise to propositions that serve as **major premises.** The referents of these premises are in the cognitive structure of the inferrer, but as Sarbin, Taft, and Bailey point out, the key issue is to make them correspond to the relevant aspects of social and physical ecology so that tests of truth will be possible. Unless our practice concepts and propositions have some operational linkage with the social and physical reality in which our clients live, we will be spinning stuff and nonsense rather than providing therapeutic intervention.

The **third stage** is that of **observation leading to the construction of the minor premise.** The authors discuss strategies of search which are seen as samplings from all the possible behaviors that the client might manifest. We see only a tiny sampling of a person's life. As Virginia Woolf, novelist and brilliant character analyst, once wrote, "A biography is considered complete if it merely accounts for six or seven selves, whereas a person may well have as many thousand." I doubt whether the clinician knows more than one or two selves, a point we must never forget. Our sampling provides only partial information.

One can **scan** for obvious signs about the client; one can **scrutinize** the client for unfamiliar signs; and one can **probe,** that is, elicit responses from the client. These strategies of search provide input which can become cues for the worker in constructing the **minor premise**—the one which will be specifically about the client, stemming directly from his social and physical ecology rather than from the cognitive workings of the practitioner. Cues are manifold; they differ in their degree of potency, multiplicity, and relevance for the given problem. But they mediate between the cognitive structure of the worker and the ecological scene he is observing. Such mediation may be valid or ambiguous or misleading, or it may have no significance at all for the problem at hand. These are risks the worker takes in using any given cue. We met these problems before when we spoke of events as being meaningful.

The **fourth stage** of the inference process occurs when the worker decides that **some occurrence is a member of a given class by virtue of having the properties which define that class.** The worker, for example, may have several defining properties of the class of old people in mind, such as being over a certain age, showing signs of infirmity, exhibiting certain attitudes and behaviors. (These defining properties of classes need not be accurate; unfortunately, many persons are guided by inaccurate stereotypes.) The worker may notice some features of his client, Methuselah—his age, his possible hearing disability, and his ultra religious philosophy—and may decide that these indeed fit his conception of the class of older persons. The fact that Methuselah is physically facile, has a clear mind, and has fathered a number of children into very late old age presents some problems about including him in the worker's definition of the class of old people. This points up the fact that the overlap between the subject term in the major premise and the predicate term in the minor premise is a matter of degree, yielding a probability of fit. Let us say, for example, that Methuselah is like older persons to a certain degree, perhaps 90 percent, given the worker's definition.

For a perceived event to become an instance of a class term which is part of the minor premise, the worker must (1) observe the occurrence itself; (2) identify the defining characteristics of the class; and (3) specify that the occurrence is a member of that class. One can do this in a variety of ways, the authors point out, such as if the occurrence is like an exemplar of that class ("he's as old as Methuselah") or by analogy. The point is that input from a client's social and physical ecology should be sufficiently **aligned** with the concepts in the worker's cognitive structure to make the connection between ideas in the worker's head and events in reality sensible and testable. I discussed some of these ideas earlier in connection with Carnap's freeing of the strict operational definition of all theoretical terms in favor of testing a network of terms; now the idea has come home to roost in practice situations as well, but with a vital difference. Whereas operational definitions are one-way connectives between concepts and research operations that measure them, alignment is a two-way connection following communication-systems theory where the worker sends one message (his view of alignment) and the client returns a confirmation or disconfirmation.

The **fifth stage** is the **drawing of the conclusion from the premises.** Basically, Sarbin, Taft, and Bailey suggest that these conclusions just occur: "Although few of us could recite the axioms of the syllogism or the formulas for constructing valid inferences, most of us do employ syntactical rules in analyzing propositions and can recognize the more common logical fallacies" (p. 53). On the other hand, they cite countless examples of illogical thinking on the part of professionals, where the content (and the desire to conform to our sovereign theories) pushes the inferrer into illogical forms. For example, the fallacy of **affirming the consequent:**

If Oedipus identifies with his father, he will be similar to his father.
Oedipus is similar to his father.
Therefore, Oedipus identifies with his father.

This fallacy becomes clearer with new content:

If this object before me is a dog, then it is a mammal.
This object before me is a mammal.
Therefore, it is a dog.

Put formally:

P implies **Q**.
Q.
∴ **P**.

Note the identity of the forms of the argument above. Now, another classical fallacy, the **undistributed middle:**

Creative people produce original responses on the Rorschach Test.
Schizophrenics produce original responses on the Rorschach Test.
Therefore, schizophrenics are creative people.

Again, with a different content, and in a formal pattern:

All dogs are mammals.	P implies **Q**.
All cats are mammals.	R implies **Q**.
Therefore, all cats are dogs.	∴ P implies **R**.

On the other hand, some classes of fallacies are semantic in nature. Here is **equivocation:**

Some clients have complicated problems. [Some = unspecified number]
My client has complicated problems.
Therefore, my client is **some** client. [Some = unusual]

Or **parts to wholes** (and vice versa):

Every welfare worker in this agency is a fine person.
Therefore, this welfare agency is a fine agency.

Of course, there is nothing to prevent a person from having false premises and a true conclusion, together with a valid form of reasoning:

All telephone poles are in the helping professions.
All social workers are telephone poles.
Therefore, all social workers are in the helping professions.

The reality and the concepts which refer to real events have to be aligned. There are many sources in which variation in alignment and possible errors can occur. Sarbin, Taft, and Bailey review some of these sources by going over the steps in the inference process and pointing out how personal differences bring in different inputs, organize them differently, and produce premises and conclusions. Implicit is the idea that there are better and worse ways of achieving goals—not a single best way, but perhaps several ways that maximize the probabilities of reaching the goal. A syllogism may serve to summarize their discussion about the conclusion:

Major premise: All **X** are **Y** [e.g., all old people are harmed by relocation to an institution—this statement has a probability of being true in (let us say) .50 of the time as indicated by research.]
Minor premise: Client is **X** (e.g., Methuselah fits the worker's definition of old person in nine out of ten defining attributes of the class of old persons, a probability level of .90.)
Conclusion: Client is **Y** (e.g., there is a **joint probability** of .50 times .90, giving .45, that Methuselah faces a risk of being harmed by relocation to an institution.)

The **sixth stage** is that of **prediction**. Inferential activities are a vital preliminary to constructing and carrying out **action hypotheses**. Such hypotheses are behaviorally specific and also have a clear future referent—what the client will do under certain conditions—in order to determine the utility of the syllogism as a guide to practice. Like any other hypotheses, these action hypotheses can be proven logically true or false, but, in real life, such all-or-nothing outcomes are rare; we typically see partial evidence emerging from the worker's contribution to the client's world of events. The worker has entered his client's world through communication, he has sent a purposively influential communiqué (based on the information he has amassed and analyzed), so he makes a prediction as to what effect it will have on the client. The client's response offers information to confirm—and hence to pursue the matter along certain lines—or to disconfirm—and hence to pursue the matter along other lines. So long as a hypothesis is framed, communications from the client provide information to move the case forward. Professional communication without hypotheses is meaningless. Continual formation of action hypotheses is obviously an ideal to be approximated in real practice, but this is the heart of scientific practice.

USING THE DEDUCTIVE MODEL

The model suggested by Sarbin, Taft, and Bailey is intriguing. It offers one approach in connecting portions of the scientific knowledge base to the events in the client's life, even though it requires numerous assumptions to make the model operative. Yet it appears difficult to use by those who lack sophistication in logic (so as to identify invalid logical forms) or in patience and vision (in constructing strings of syllogisms with just one sentence in each of the major and minor premises and in the conclusion). Of course there are logical shortcuts such as the sorties and other forms of contracted syllogisms, but human problems are more easily expressed in complex packages, and scientific knowledge also comes in conceptual networks rather than in logical strings. Because we may do more harm than good to the common forms by which our information comes to us if we put them into logical strings of syllogisms, I am going to propose a modification of Sarbin, Taft, and Bailey's model, a suggestion offered in the spirit of an hypothesis to be tested.

In the place of a major and a minor premise, each with its probability statement attached and a conclusion with its joint probability statement, I would propose a general statement (statement of theory or set of empirical statements), the individualized statement of the client's problems, and a plan for action, respectively. In place of the probability statements attached to the major and minor premises and to the conclusions, I would propose attaching probabilities based on empirical statements concerning the fruitfulness of the conceptual networks as tested in research; the observed preintervention expression of the client's problem; and the joint expression of these two as a level of risk one faces for using such a theory with such a client. This suggestion is presented graphically below:

Sarbin, Taft, and Bailey's
Deductive Model

My Modification:

Sarbin, Taft, and Bailey's Deductive Model	My Modification:
Major premise with probability statement	General statement with empirical support as averaged percentage of validated outcome; if no research, then estimate translatability using Thomas' criteria (Chapter 10)
Minor premise with probability statement	Individual statement with pre-intervention measurement of problem events (see Chapter 17)
∴ Conclusion with joint probability statement	∴ Plan for action with level of risk indicated

In the next few pages, I will attempt to explain this modification so as to make the deductive model usable by helping professionals employing conventional tools at their disposal. First, the order of the categorical syllogism, major, then minor, premises, then conclusion, is not the order of events in helping. Usually, minor-premise information is constructed first; it is the individualized statement of the client's problems. Then, using key concepts from this statement, the literature is searched to find relevant theories and empirical information as well as practice wisdom; this is comparable to major-premise information. A conclusion and decision step is then made, a plan of action using the combined picture of the client's conceptualized problems and the conceptual networks from the literature.

Let us take an illustrative case situation. A 19-year-old college student comes to a counselor for aid with several problems: His grades are poor and he feels uncomfortable in class because contributing ideas to class discussions is difficult for him, and a forthcoming assignment requiring him to make a presentation before his class has him petrified with anxiety.

Following my modification of the Sarbin, Taft, and Bailey model, let's see how one might proceed. First, there is the statement of the client's problems. These concern grades, speaking in class discussion, and making presentations in front of a class. These might be reconstructed as propositions, but, more than that, they are susceptible to careful observation and measurement (see Chapter 17). For example, his grades are a matter of record; his contributions in class discussion might be recorded (by the client himself) on a calendar during the class periods between the intake interview and the first interventive session. Likewise, some operational indicators of anxiety in public speaking might be found, such as observation by the instructor of how many seconds it takes the client to get to the front of the room to present his speech and how many seconds his speech lasts as compared to the others in the class. Let's say we find that the client has a 1.5 grade average (out of 4.0); that he spoke only once in the two weeks between sessions (four class sessions in which students spoke on an average of twenty times per session); and that he has the longest latency time getting up to speak, and the shortest speaking time in the class.

On the face of it, we have two clusters of problems, although we can see how grades and poor communication in the classroom might be related. These statements of the problems also provide concepts as entry points for whatever professional information is available on these topics (cf. Chapter 20). Let's deal with the speaking anxieties first. In Chapter 11, it was suggested that practitioners have a good working knowledge of the major approaches to problem solving, such as learning theory, dynamic theory, existential theory, and theories of the group and larger collectivities. In addition, the concepts describing the particular client may also stimulate identification of special theories, for example, special theories about test-taking anxiety. There may be no theory which focuses on just the problems one's client presents, in which case one must improvise by reconstructing pieces of available theories. Let's say that a search of the literature turns up no special theories, and all the worker has to go on are the broad directives of general frameworks, learning and dynamic theories in particular. I will reconstruct the deductive equivalents of the major and minor premises and the conclusion for each theory, and then I will compare the two.

Deductive Use of the Dynamic Theory of Anxiety

The equivalent of the major premise is the statement of the theory or portion of the theory relevant to the client's problem. Anxiety, within the broad Freudian conceptual network, is bound to relations between ego and id ("neurotic anxieties") and between ego and superego ("moral anxieties"). The adult has achieved some working balance among id, ego, and superego, but there remains an unconscious threat that id or superego will assert itself inappropriately (either impulsively or overly self-punishing). The experience of anxiety is a danger signal, and the client has learned to make adaptations to the unconsciously feared outbursts which have taken their toll in terms of manifest symptoms (cf. Levitt, 1967).

Equivalent to the minor premise is the individualized statement about the client's problems. These were given above as the indicators of grades and communication. I must add that different theories might pick out additional minor-premise material, sensitized by the different perspectives each follows.

The conclusion equivalent presents a statement like the following: The client's anxieties in communicating are related to unconscious conflicts within aspects of his personality due to his developmental experiences; current problems are symptoms of these more deeply buried conflicts and are to be resolved by giving the client gradual insight into the nature of his personality, within a benign therapeutic setting.

Now the question is what probability statements may we attach to each of these portions of the modified deductive model? So far as I can discover, there is very little empirical evidence, one way or the other, for this dynamic interpretation of anxiety as related to speaking. Since little empirical evidence is forthcoming, we turn to some estimates of potential use by employing the Thomas criteria (Chapter 10) such as identifiability and controllability. Classical dynamic theory has long presented difficulties in translation to observable events, leading to circular explanations, such as those which identify a set of behaviors—nervousness, heavy breathing, perspiration, flushed face—as "anxious behavior," and then noting that these behaviors are attributable to an underlying unconscious phenomenon, "neurotic anxiety." Because some major concepts of this theory are not translatable into events helping professionals can use does not mean that the entire theory must be scrapped. The worker has three options, as discussed in Chapter 10: to continue to use the theory, recognizing that its untranslatable concepts represent a threat to accurate understanding of the theory; to take only the translatable portions of the theory as guides; or to add whatever is necessary to make the translatable portions of the theory more nearly usable. But, in present contexts, we must assign the theory as a whole a low probability of leading to a successful intervention as based on the rules established above. The actual percentage attached is up to the worker, to his experience and education. Based on general information about success rates of dynamic theories, I would offer a 50 percent rate, that is, no better than chance alone that a client would be helped using this theory.

What probability figure may be attached to the minor-premise equivalent? Here we are on stronger ground, having obtained observations and reports about the problem behavior specifically defined. Yet it is difficult to offer clear rules for attaching rates to events. For example, each student speaks about one time per class session; because the client spoke only once in four sessions, we might attach a rate of .25. On the other hand, the client was the slowest to rise to speak and the fastest to present a speech, so we might put him in the lowest portion of his class, the bottom centile or about .10. What would be the combined rate then for his speaking problems? A rough guess would be an average of these figures, say about .20 of nonproblem behavior or .80 problem behavior.

The equivalent to the joint probability of the syllogism's conclusion is the combining of the rate attached to the theory and the individual's problem (considered as a proportion of the class of problem events described in the major-premise equivalent): .50 times .80 yields .40. Our risk in using this theory with this case is about six times in ten of not achieving success. We may still choose to use this theory for other reasons, but the statement of risk is a reasonable estimate, given the reasoning of the modified deductive model.

Deductive Use of Learning Theory Regarding Anxiety

With learning theories, we have access to a number of empirical studies concerning work with specific anxieties, including anxiety about speaking in public. One series of studies on speaking anxieties (Paul, 1966; 1967) is immediately brought to attention because of the high quality of its research design and because of the fact that it is a comparative study utilizing a dynamic as well as a learning theory approach, plus a placebo situation in which subjects received attention through nonspecific social influences like therapist attention and warmth. Two other control groups were used: a no-treatment group which received all the measurements as did the preceding three experimental groups and a no-contact group which did not.

College students in a required public speaking course were the subjects of this study. From a group of students identified as highly anxious about public speaking, the experimenter randomly distributed them to the three treatment conditions. The therapists were all insight-oriented psychotherapists who had to be specially trained to give one form of behavior modification, a systematic desensitization which involved pairing deep relaxation with graduated stages of anxiety-arousing stimuli. The theory suggests that the stronger stimuli of deep relaxation will allow the client to experience a weaker stimulus, a formerly anxiety-producing event, without feeling any anxiety. By learning that anxiety need not be attached to such stimuli which are in fact not harmful, the client progresses to the point where the full-blown event occurs without arousing the neurotic (i.e., learned) anxiety danger signal.

Paul used a variety of behavioral, physiological, and self-report indicators of anxiety. Clients met with their therapist for five sessions in six weeks, at the end of which time a second test of their anxieties in the face of public speaking was administered. On all three measures—behavioral, physiological, and self-report—the data for "improved" or "much improved" showed 90 to 100 percent positive change in the desensitization group, 50 to 60 percent in both the insight and the attention placebo groups, and about 20 percent in the no-treatment control group. Follow-up studies six weeks later and again two years later showed that the effects of treatment were maintained. Moreover, no evidence of symptom substitution was encountered (Paul, 1967).

How much weight can be placed on one series of studies by one researcher? Or on reviews of the literature concerning this method? There can be no certain rule except that we should use these types of information at face value as the basis of our forming our own deductive plans of action. Let us try to place probability rates on this approach.

Equivalent to the major premise is the systematic desensitization method, presumably operationalizing a portion of learning theory (cf. Wolpe and Lazarus, 1958). This very well-done study offers evidence of 100 percent improvement after a brief time of treatment, with 80 percent continuing over a two-year follow-up. While other results from the literature are not as strong as Paul's results, the general trends are supportive of these findings. Thus, one might entertain the idea of attaching an 85 percent rate to this method derived from a learning theory, emphasizing the follow-up data.

Equivalent to the minor premise is the statement of the client's problem as an instance of the class of problems dealt with in the theory. As mentioned before, minor-premise-type statements should be roughly similar across theories, except as a theory will pick up on some special factors, modifying the individualized picture somewhat. The previous statement of the minor-premise equivalent will do as well for the learning approach as for the dynamic approach, namely, .80 rate of problem behavior.

Equivalent to the conclusion is the plan of action for this learning approach. .85 times .80 yields .68, that is, that our risk in using this theory and its derived methods with this case is about three times out of ten of not achieving success.

Comparing the risk levels of the two theories and methods of dealing with speech anxieties, we have .40 and .68, numbers resulting from a system of rules which is attempting to utilize as much of objective evidence as possible in arriving at appropriate choices among several methods of professional action. Attached to this modified form of the deductive model is the requirement of evaluating one's own interventive efforts, in order to modify major-premise-type information with one's own style of practice. For example, if over time one's own success rate using a dynamic theory were .75, then one would weigh this with a general success rate of .50, resulting in a risk factor close to that of the learning theory. In such a case, preference would initially go to the method with which one had greater experience—until case evaluation suggested a new method of intervention was needed.

AN INDUCTIVE APPROACH

The work of Kenneth Hammond (1967) and his associates provides another fruitful insight into clinical inference, the process of making judgments about events even when given insufficient information, which is the normal state of affairs for helping professionals. Hammond is most concerned with inductive inference, the process of reasoning from the particular event to the general case. Is it possible to formulate the rules guiding such intuitive inferences, and, especially, the special class of clinical inference?

Hammond suggests some provocative ideas and demonstrates the potential fruitfulness of this approach in research on inferences in nursing. He utilizes both the objective and the subjective probability approaches. I believe that these same procedures are relevant to social work, although with even less clarity than in nursing research which can point to relatively determinate states of the patient as the general class of events one wishes to infer to: Does this particular symptom or cue suggest that general class of events called state of shock? To what corresponding state of the client does social work apply? Unhappiness? Anxiety? Financial worries? Interpersonal problems?—hence the problem of relating a given cue to the general case. But, in principle, the procedure applies, and I discuss Hammond's work because of its potential value as social work becomes clearer and more clearly measures its general state of affairs and its behavioral cues.

Hammond distinguishes among the same inference concepts Sarbin, Taft, and Bailey (1960) discussed previously but in a different way: **Formal inference** involves deductive logic. **Statistical inference** belongs to true inductive inference and refers to results obtained from a sample generalized to a population by means of reproducible statistical procedures yielding probabilistic outcomes. **Intuitive inference** is also inductive inference made on the spot without special tools other than our own mental processes. However, Hammond does not assert, as do Sarbin and his associates, that clinical inference (as one form of intuitive inference) operates in the context of formal decision making and hence is deductive in nature, even though the outcomes are probabilistic. Rather, Hammond argues for a fully inductive model which I will attempt to translate into social work terms.

By and large, when dealing with human concerns, uncertainty is the context in which all persons operate, going from the known to the unknown, without knowing when the unknown goal has been reached except by the response of the environment and our own sensitivities that we are there. Actually, this is a pessimistic statement of clinical inference because there are many sources

Excerpts from "Clinical inference in nursing: Revising judgments." NURSING RESEARCH by K. Hammond, R. Kelly, R. Schneider, & M. Vancini are reprinted by permission from the first author and the Editor. © 1967 NURSING RESEARCH.

of response to our behaviors that act pursuant to our inferences. These responses lead us to revise our judgments, to refine our critical actions. This is the end point, a complex series of actions and reactions. Let me begin more simply, using Hammond as guide.

A Single Behavioral Cue

What can we infer from one event concerning the state of affairs of a client (that is, his problem)? (I know that we never have just one event from which we infer a problem, but we can isolate one event at a time—and this one event by itself may sensibly be related to a problem. This illustration is not an oversimplification; it is an analytic exercise. The synthetic exercise will follow shortly.) The inductive inferential logic Hammond uses is closely connected to statistical association, and it may be most clearly understood in statistical terms. I believe that Hammond is suggesting something like the following: When we observe a single cue and attempt inductively to reach a general statement about the client's problems, we must use probabilistic inference. The basis of this probabilistic inference comes from empirical generalizations or empirical findings which are often stated in correlational terms of some sort. Of a group of events, some are found to be associated with other events in certain patterns. For example, of one hundred observed events, let us say that fifty fell into cell **A** of the table below, that is, when the cue was present, the problem condition was present too; and fifty events fell in cell **D**, that is, when the cue was absent, the problem condition was absent too. These circumstances taken from empirical research and usually without connection with the client himself would indicate a perfect positive relationship between the cue and the problem condition for other persons including our client. Yet, note that this is still inferential. On the next occasion, research or practice might turn up another pattern.

	Cue Present	**Cue Absent**
Problem condition present	A	C
Problem condition absent	B	D

In a sense similar to Sarbin, Taft, and Bailey, Hammond is suggesting that the worker use the research probability statement as the best guess as to the meaning of the observation he has made with his client.

In statistics, there are certain types of errors inherent in associational methods which are likely carried over to the practitioner who would risk using research

information as the basis of his informed action. The type I (alpha) error refers to rejecting a true hypothesis, while a type II (beta) error refers to not rejecting a false hypothesis. Because information from research rarely is distributed in neat packages as described above, it is not usually possible to make any decision whatsoever from any research whatsoever. The worker has to be willing to tolerate the risks of error he must make to come up with the inferences based on this research. The table below, especially lines 3 through 6, illustrates these types of risks (Table 12-1). Unfortunately, research information is not often presented in a form that permits making these kinds of distinctions that enable a worker to know what types of risks he takes for using the results of the study. Correlational statistics are very useful but they tend to mask the patterns which appear to be important to the decisions of practitioners. One can easily imagine the same correlation being produced by different patterns of events which represent types of risk a worker would take if he were guided by their results.

Table 12-1
Illustrative Correlational Data Patterns

| | | Information which the worker has | | |
| | | Some Cue About the Client Is Present +C | Some Cue About the Client is Absent —C | |
Line	Information Which Worker Is Trying to Predict			Comments
		Different patterns of information from the research literature:		
1	Some problem state is present +X	50 observations in which both X and C are known	0	These 100 observations give perfect positive association between cue and problem state.
	Some problem state is absent —X	0	50	
2	+X	0	50	Perfect negative association
	—X	50	0	
3	+X	25	25	Zero association, no information
	—X	25	25	

TABLE 12-1—Continued

Line	Information Which Worker Is Trying to Predict	Information which the worker has		Comments
		Some Cue About the Client Is Present +C	Some Cue About the Client Is Absent —C	
4	+X	40	10	False negative:
	−X	0	50	There will be some occasions when the cue isn't present, but the problem state is.
5	+X	50	0	False positive:
	−X	10	40	There will be some occasions when the cue is present, but the problem state is not.
6	+X	40	20	More false negative than
	−X	10	30	false positive, but both risks are present.

Translating this statistical approach into one usable by helping professionals, I would suggest the following. First, an action hypothesis should be formed. This is different from the statistical null hypothesis, for in the action arena all hypotheses are directional. The worker says in effect that such and such an intervention will make a difference in the desired direction. However, because this is a directional hypothesis, the worker is not absolved from being aware of alternative hypotheses. In effect, such alternatives would suggest that if the action hypothesis is not supported, then certain alternatives must be entertained. Entertaining does not mean marrying; in the dynamic interaction of client-worker communication, the nonsupport for one action hypothesis does not mean that one divorces oneself from the whole strategy, but that one may be seeing an additional risk of using the given strategy. Because of the speed of forming and testing these action hypotheses, one can also try out any given one in a number of forms before it is ruled in or out. (This is the major advantage over the laboratory hypothesis where feedback is usually slower in coming.)

A second step in statistical hypothesis testing is the stating of the level of significance. This represents the risk we face for rejecting a true hypothesis or accepting a false one. In action hypotheses, we may start at a prior task, formulating nominal propositions about events, in order to find our general direction. For example, we ask a client, "Can you tell me whether events **A** and **B** are related?" A yes answer begins the construction of a system of events within the client's life space. A no answer leads us to consider events **A** and **C**, etc. There is nothing corresponding to the statistical .05 level or the .01 level of significance in social work action hypotheses. We may wonder how much evidence we will require before we believe we are on the right track. But we have as yet no terms to indicate any degree of precision of our certainty in believing or acting on information. Consequently, we cannot form any decision rule as to when we will or will not accept or reject information regarding our hypotheses.

The next steps in statistical hypothesis testing are to choose the statistic to be used, to perform the test, and then to reach a conclusion based on the resultant information—having defined in advance the grounds that one would use in reaching a conclusion. In social work practice, we rarely use statistical or even psychometric techniques or procedures at all. Our informal ways of testing our action hypotheses may be highly misleading and conducive to self-fulfilling prophecies. Yet, practitioners dealing with action hypotheses cannot utilize all of these tools; some compromise is called for. Perhaps it is sufficient for the present moment if a behaviorally specific event is identified as a goal and then is noticed as being present or absent in greater or less degree after intervention than before (see Chapter 17).

Multiple Behavioral Cues

Hammond presents a basic situation when one behavioral state is associated with three cues:

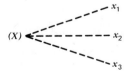

When the problem state (**X**) is present, cues 1, 2, and 3 may **sometimes** be present. (And when the problem state is absent, cues 1, 2, and 3 may **sometimes** be absent.) In this uncertain situation, if the practitioner always infers the presence of the problem state when cue 1, 2, or 3 is present, he will likely make false positive judgments (where the cue is present, but the problem state is not). If the practitioner refuses to depend on uncertain information at all, he will likely make false negative judgments (where the cue is not present, but the problem state is). The practitioner must either use or not use information, and so he had better be aware of what he is using and what type of error of judgment he may be making. In the medical profession, if false positive judgments are made, no fatal problems occur—just enormous hospital costs and the patient's time and energy are wasted. But a false negative judgment leads to serious health consequences. . . .

Multiple-Cue, Multiple-Problem Behavior States

More complex and more realistic is the situation when many cues are present and they point to many problem states. To simplify, consider two problem states, **X** and **Y**, three cues related to each (stated in lower-case letters), and three combinations in which these relationships may occur:

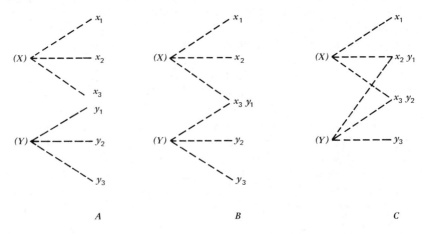

In situation **A**, there is no overlap between cues and their related problem states, but in **B** and **C**, the degree of overlap increases. In situation B, the occurrence of cue x_3y_1 means that a second stage of information must be gained before a determination of the problem state can be made with a high degree of probability. Likewise, in situation C, a third stage may be needed if either x_2y_1 or x_3y_2 occurs, because available information does not sufficiently clarify whether **X** or **Y** exists.

Because of the increasing complexity among multiple cues and multiple-problem states, some researchers have turned to the computer as a diagnostic tool (Overall and Williams, 1964, reported in Kleinmuntz, 1969). For example, in the diagnosis of thyroid functioning, Overall and Williams analyzed 879 cases of clinically diagnosed thyroid patients and identified 27 factors related to thyroid functioning—hypothyroid, euthyroid (normal), and hyperthyroid. They developed empirical generalizations as to the relative frequencies of occurrences of these 27 factors for each of the three thyroid-functioning groups. Then, when a patient is tested for these 27 factors (or some portion of them), the symptoms are combined by the computer to yield a probability statement of the patient's characteristics belonging to each of the diagnostic groupings. Overall and Williams report that the computer's success rate approaches and sometimes surpasses that of the clinician, given the same set of data on a client. In principle, this same approach is applicable to social work problems when they are behaviorally specific.

Inductive Inference: Subjective Probability Approach

On the face of it, a subjective probability approach—such as the Bayesian theorem which begins with incomplete information and includes a hunch in the form of the probability estimate, but then when information is available, revises its estimate with the best current information—this seems to be a more nearly adequate description of how helping professionals work than the objective probability approach (Neyman-Pearson hypothesis testing approach). While this approach is used extensively in business and economics and in psychology to a lesser extent, there are few examples of its application in social work. Therefore, I turn again to Hammond for inspiration (Hammond, Kelly, Schneider, and Vancini, 1967; but see also Schmitt, 1969).

In this exploratory study, Hammond and his associates compared whether nurses made decisions about states of their patients by optimally using information. By controlling the inflow of information and asking nurses to make decisions at several points, the authors were able to compare the nurses' actual decision making against the Bayesian theorem which provides the optimal revision of judgment after receiving new information.

One form of the Bayesian theorem is provided by Hammond:

$$P(H/D) = \frac{P(H)P(D/H)}{P(D)}$$

where **P**   = probability

P(H)   = prior probability, the probability of the hypothesis about the state of the patient **before** observing a given datum (**D**)

P(D)   = probability of the datum

P(H/D) = probability of the hypothesis about the state of the patient **after** observing a given datum

P(D/H) = probability of the occurrence of the datum given the hypothesis about the state of the patient

Hammond further translates this formula into nursing terms:

$$P(\text{state of patient/cue}) = \frac{P(\text{state of patient})P(\text{cue/state of patient})}{P(\text{cue})}$$

and he offers a much more familiar interpretation: The probability that a state of the patient (specifically, a cold) is present if a given cue (coughing) is present is equal to the probability that a cold is present at any time times the probability of coughing, given that a cold exists, divided by the probability that the cue coughing is present at any time (p. 39). Hammond points out that in fact portions of the formula are familiar to medical personnel, although they may seem strange, put in the fashion entailed by Bayes. In any case, it becomes possible to study how professional nurses utilized information given in sequential fashion about patients. The sequencing is indicated by the following excerpt. (A mechanical device was built in which the nurse could respond by moving a marker on one of three bars divided from .00 to 1.00.)

Sample dialogue: (state of the patient—presence or absence of post-surgical shock).

Experimenter: Before you begin seeking information which will enable you to confirm the presence or absence of post-surgical shock, what is the probability of finding post-surgical shock in any post-abdominal surgery patient? That is, how many times out of 100 would you expect to find post-surgical shock?

Subject: (moves marker to indicate .50—the halfway mark)

E: Now, what is the first cue about which you would like information?

S: Low, unstable blood pressure.

E: All right. Before I tell you whether low, unstable blood pressure is present or absent in this case, I would like you to indicate how important this cue is. On the top bar, when post-surgical shock is present, what percent of the time would you expect to find low, unstable blood pressure?

S: (moves marker on top bar to .80)

E: Now, when no post-surgical shock is present, what percent of the time would you expect to find low, unstable blood pressure present?

S: (moves marker on second bar to .25)

E: Low, unstable blood pressure **is present** in this case. Does this alter your probability of finding post-surgical shock in this case?

S: (moves marker on third bar to .65)

E: Now what cue would you like information about? (p. 42)

USING THE INDUCTIVE MODEL

There are many difficulties in translating this inductive procedure into social work language. The following illustration of an obese client highlights some of the principles and problems involved in this translation.

Philip Edacious was advised to see a medical social worker because his obese condition was having deleterious effects on his health, his social life, and his self-esteem. The worker collected a number of facts on the face sheet of his record:

1. Male, age 26
2. Weight, 300 pounds
3. Height, 5'8"
4. Living at home with parents
5. High school graduate
6. Semiskilled occupation
7. Never married
8. No known medical problems

Given these facts as the initial set of events, to what concepts (conceptualization of problems) may these events be connected? Let us take events 1, 2, and 3, a male of a certain age, with given weight and height. It is wise, even for nonmedical persons, to check out the possibility of a medical problem, as in the following hypotheses:

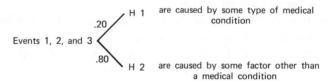

What is the likelihood that this set of three events is connected to a medically or nonmedically caused factor? Answers to this type of question require consultation with appropriate specialists. Let us say for purposes of discussion that the empirical literature suggests that 20 cases out of every 100 appear to have some medical factor as cause of obesity.

Even with such (hypothetical) information, we still have a choice whether or not to accept the more probable nonmedical cause of obesity as being operative in the case of our client. We can be wrong in rejecting the non-medical causation hypothesis when in fact this is the cause for our client (a type I error); but we can also be wrong in accepting the nonmedical causation hypothesis when in fact there is a medical cause in our client's case (a type

II error). We can choose, in effect, how much risk we want to accept in being wrong or right about attributed causation and hence the intervention plans that follow from this presumed causation. The level of significance we choose defines that probability of making the first type of error described above. For instance, we may set a level of .001 which is to demand that only once out of 1000 times could the false results appear true. In doing this we have greatly reduced the likelihood of rejecting a hypothesis that is in fact true. But because of the interrelationship between type I and type II errors, we have greatly increased the likelihood of accepting a hypothesis that is in fact false. By setting a less stringent significance level, say at the .05 level, we have reduced the type II error while increasing the likelihood of a type I error. The smaller the probability of making a type I error if the hypothesis is true, the greater the probability of making a type II error if the hypothesis is false. The implications of these interrelations in the helping context have yet to be spelled out for the working practitioner.

For example, we may know that being overweight increases the risk of premature mortality in connection with some diseases such as diabetes. But since the client has no known medical problems (fact 8 above), we might be more inclined to link events 1, 2, and 3 to the nonmedical causation hypothesis since the gravity of an error (rejecting a medical causation hypothesis when in fact this is true) is minimized. Thus, we may choose the more probable hypothesis with an added bit of security that even if we are wrong, the risk of a fatal outcome is yet not likely. While this is reasonable to our common sense, we have no procedures in the helping professions for making these kinds of judgments systematically.

Suppose that we are aware of Mayer's (1968) data that the prevalence of obesity in women belonging to the lowest social class is seven times higher than in women from the highest social class and that there appears to be something about the life style of members of one social class that differentially affects the likelihood of obesity as compared with members of another social class. We do not know the extent to which such findings may be generalized to men, but we note that facts 5 and 6 would place our client in a lower social-class status. Our inference choice is:

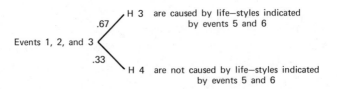

Events 1, 2, and 3

.67   H 3   are caused by life–styles indicated
              by events 5 and 6

.33   H 4   are not caused by life–styles indicated
              by events 5 and 6

Because the data from the literature are not exactly similar to our client's characteristics, we must make some tentative guesses as to the probable connections between events 5 and 6 and hypotheses 3 and 4. Let's say that the data derived from women apply to men less strongly; and let's say about 67 out of 100 times men's obesity is affected by their life-styles linked to their social-class status. Thus far, we have inductively inferred that our client is highly likely to be obese through nonmedical causes and that it is somewhat likely that these nonmedical causes are linked to his social-class style of life. This is like a branching series of choice points:

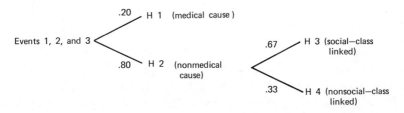

For each choice point, we attempt to find empirical evidence as the basis of an inductive choice which leads to one type of conceptual analysis rather than another. There are many such events to be linked in this fashion, but these will suffice for this illustration.

SUMMARY

All of helping practice involves a weaving back and forth between the world of the client's problem events and the world of theory, research, and recorded practice wisdom. However, this chapter has pointed out two major bridges between these worlds. The deductive approach makes more use of established systems of concepts by extracting deductions that apply to the individual case. Sarbin, Taft, and Bailey suggest a procedure by which the individual problem situation may be aligned with the general statement of theory in order to make such deductions.

The inductive approach begins with the events and proceeds either by sticking strictly with observed frequencies or by using tentatively one's subjective hunches that are later modified by observed frequencies.

These are complex statistical matters, and this chapter does no more than scratch the surface. But I predict that, with the development of advanced technology in manipulating information, these probabilistic models will become increasingly used by individual practitioners on the line, rather than with researchers behind the lines.

CHAPTER 13

Values in a Context Professional Action

Tradition has it that scientists deal with facts, that is, deal with what is, while other people (philosophers of ethics down to the man on the street) deal with values, that is, deal with what ought to be. This distinction doesn't hold up well under scrutiny (Churchman, 1961), particularly for the helping professional who, as applied scientist, is perforce engaged in dealing both with facts and with values. And yet it does serve to introduce one of the more paradoxical aspects of being a helping professional, that is, how values are applied in the context of action.

What are values? Good question. One can locate a literature on this topic that is 2,000 years old, or at least a rich summary (Kluckhohn, 1952; Buhler, 1962), or a lengthy bibliography (Albert and Kluckhohn, 1959). But it might be useful to accept philosopher G. E. Moore's (1908) statement which bypasses this philosophical thicket: "Good is good, and that is the end of the matter." Rather we will focus on what values look like as expressed in action. This is the only way we can know values, that is, by inference from events, sets, and systems of events. This is the arena in which the helping professional deals with values by dealing with persistent patterns of choices among alternatives. Note that among these choices are the client's symbolized ideals, which function in his cognitive system as they get expressed in actions.

Thus, for the helping professional, the "what is desired" and the "what is desirable" are operationally collapsed into the persisting patterns of choices the client expresses in his behaviors. This may not be congenial with our personal views on values as eternal verities or whatever, but if we are to deal openly and objectively with our own and our client's values—to say nothing of the values of our profession and of our society—then we must begin to seek operationally clear statements of values so that their place in our professional action can be known.

A client by the name of Alice comes to a would-be therapist by the name of

C. Cat with the presenting problem of being lost in a spooky wood. She asks the therapist to tell her which way she ought to go from here. And the therapist replies that that depends a good deal on where she wants to get to. Alice continues by informing him that she doesn't much care where she goes. And the therapist logically points aut that, in this case, it doesn't matter which way Alice goes to get there. If Alice had a specific goal in mind, a specific idio-syncratic value preference, then the therapist might have been able to say, in effect, that if she went to the right, she would have a 75 percent chance of finding that goal. And if she went to the left, she would have only a 25 percent chance. The percentages might come from large-scale empirical research, personal experiences, or an abstract theory C. Cat had evolved on how to get There from Here. We would call these kinds of advice forms of knowledge, and we would assign different degrees of confidence to them; or, to put it another way, each form of knowledge has a different degree of risk in following it as a guide to action.

Knowledge from any source used in the service of a client's preferences becomes value-touched. Practitioners probably never use information in a value-free context. Values become attached to knowledge about events in the very process of communicating them. I spoke earlier of the metacommunication aspect of information delivery as being largely composed of affective com-ments about the message (Chapter 3). We get very close to undefinable basic terms when we say that a certain event is preferred, that is, that a person assigns a positive or a negative affect of a certain degree to that event in a certain context. The closest we can come to observing this preference is to communicate with a person and be clear about his affect regarding possible events. Value preferences may also be expressed directly in a message, although even here the metacommunication comments on that message, possibly qualifying it.

As practitioners, we come to know about the values of clients as we predict how the client will act under certain conditions. We locate evidence for this prediction: "If the client values X, then he will tend to exhibit a pattern of behaviors described by A, B, and C." Like any other hypothesis, the evidence for or against it will likely be relative, resulting in a probability statement being attached to the value hypothesis, that it was supported (for example) 60 percent of the time when put to the test. This provides the worker with information so that when the next act involving the client comes along, the worker's best prediction of demonstrated values will be at the same rate as his previously tested expression. In other words, such a percentage expresses how important it is to the client to be consistent in this value, especially when it stands in competition with the other things which the client values. The more central the value, the higher number of times it will be expressed regard-less of what other values it conflicts with.

If it were possible to measure the pattern of behaviors that operationally defines a client's values, then we could have an indicator to apply to a deductive model such as was discussed in the previous chapter (Chapter 12) which would represent a value weighting. Given certain facts, how strongly does the client value them to act on them in the face of alternative ways of behaving? **In principle,** this should enable us to apply numbers (representing the persisting patterns of behaviors which is our operational definition of values) to the individual statement of the deductive model. The same process would be true of the general statement, but here the persisting patterns of behaviors would be represented by norms and laws. I say "in principle" for this is still a vague set of specifications on the use of values in practice. Yet I think this is the direction the future will take.

To summarize the discussion to this point: The worker has five essential tasks in using values in practice. First, he must be aware of the events that are open as options to a client. Second, he must know what the probable outcomes are for each of these options. (I will have more to say about this in the section to follow, on contexts of information.) Third, he must have ascertained the relative importance of each outcome to the client in terms of how much persistent effort the client has undergone in the past to obtain each goal. This becomes the best estimate of current values for the client in the present context. Fourth, he must overtly combine the probabilities of outcomes with the degrees of preferences to arrive at a weighted series of evaluated options. Fifth, the worker must measure the degree of attainment of the valued goals and give feedback to the client so as to modify the available options and the new values attached thereto.

CONTEXTS OF INFORMATION

I spoke earlier of a preference as being an assignment of a positive or a negative affect of a certain degree to an event in a certain context. I want to expand on the phrase "in a certain context" because such contexts play a very large part in value decisions. There are five principal decision contexts of relevance to helping professionals (cf. Richmond, 1968; Halpert, Horvath, and Young, 1970).

First, there is a **no-choice context** which really isn't a decision context at all, but is included here for completeness and in hopes that the helping professional will recognize this context when it occurs. If there are no viable alternatives of action, then the decision is already made. If a state institution is the only facility available to take care of an older person in need of acute medical care, then there is no use speculating over the desirability of **unavailable** relatives or friends willing and able to help out in the older person's home, of **nonexistent** homemaker services providing paraprofessional aid under the guidance of a health professional, or any other nicety which good professional training bids one consider in the development of a plan for a client. At this time and place, it simply doesn't exist. This decision context should be the beginning point for appropriate social action.

The second decision context involves **complete information** available about alternatives. This is ideal for decision making; just look at the probabilities of the alternative outcomes and the preferences assigned by the client to these alternatives, and then pick the best combination. (As you can see, this is the context for placing values in action which I was presenting in the previous section of this chapter.) Complete information assumes knowledge of all the major factors in the situation so that the client can place value preferences on them. It assumes that the client is open to a series of alternatives and that he will consider them without rigid biases in a reasonable and honest manner. Needless to say this decision context is very rare, although some practitioners act as if all major information were known, and fall heir to unknown degrees of ignorance and misguided planning; they would do better to recognize that a different context of information is present and to act accordingly.

The next three types of decision contexts involve uncertainty in one or another aspect of the situation, while the worker is seeking to make an optimal decision given limited information.

A third decision context involves a **conflict-of-interest** situation. It is assumed the client has an opponent who is trying to win the game, or as many of the rewards of a situation as he can—at the client's expense. The winner wins from the loser—this is called a **zero-sum** game in game theory. There is another type of game called a **non-zero-sum,** in which it is not the case that one person's win is another's loss. This type of situation permits the formation of cooperative arrangements. The cooperators are playing against nature, so to speak—what they together don't win, nature does. There is an element of the insurance perspective here, where risk is shared by people playing against nature. Optimal decisions involve reference to an analysis of the situation in which the possible courses of action of the persons involved are laid out, and the value of each possible outcome is indicated for all possible combinations of events to the extent that actions not under the client's control can be guessed. Approaches, such as minimizing the maximum possible loss (minimax), are used in economics, political science, the military, and the management sciences to some degree. Its direct application of helping professions is in its most elemental stages. Yet the safeguards offered by the minimax approach should be part of a worker's perspective.

A fourth decision context is that involving **limitations.** This would include problems in which allocations of scarce resources were involved—which is the constant state of affairs in the social welfare field. It would also include problems involving sequencing and routing, that is, finding a sequence of events so as to minimize the time and effort required to perform a service. For example, why should clients sit in welfare offices or hospitals for hours when they could be invited to come in a sequential way, thus contributing to the betterment of clients and workers, to say nothing of humanizing the system. The solutions of such cases are largely a mathematical programming of events, where the most-valued outcomes are arrived at with relative ease.

A fifth decision context is that involving degrees of **ignorance**. We may not know how likely any specific outcome of action might be, or we might not know what value preference a client assigns, or both. Yet we must act. This is a particularly difficult context of information from which to make wise choices, but the following rule of thumb may be offered: Project possible plans of action involving likely facts and preferences, fitting in available information to the extent possible. Such projections will be contingency plans, should new information show the error of one's present course of action.

ATTACHING NUMBERS TO VALUES: AN ILLUSTRATION

Let us join a group of persons trying to decide on priorities in services to a neighborhood group (Riesenfeld, Newcomer, Berlant, and Dempsey, 1972). The neighborhood is a complex social system, with many elements interrelated in cooperative and competitive ways. Resources are scarce, and choices must be made among the leaders of the neighborhood on who gets what, when, and how. There is an implicit understanding that all seek the betterment of the neighborhood, that all must work together toward that distant abstract goal, and that the leaders will abide by some rational decision rule for allocating scarce resources.

One such approach is called the Delphi method; this does not refer to the oracle with its infallible but tricky predictions, but rather to a procedure of seeking consensus on value judgments. Assuming that if everyone knew all of the options and how segments of the neighborhood felt about these options, then a consensual decision might be reached. How can this be attained? All parties (or their leadership representatives) come together in a meeting on values, i.e., to allocate resources to services in a neighborhood. Options and preferences (and the reasons behind them) are communicated—but through written messages which are summarized by the chairperson. The reason for the written message is the avoidance of various group and individual pressures and the equalization of talkative versus quiet persons. The messages are structured by the chairperson so that everyone indicates an opinion on all options.

At the end of the first round of written messages, the chairperson summarizes the results and reports to everyone the reasons behind these choices. By previous consent, if 50 percent or more of the group agree on a given item (say to allocate 30 percent of available resources to neighborhood recreation facilities), then value consensus is achieved, and this becomes part of the group's agreement. (The remaining 70 percent of the resources are next considered in the following rounds.) New information (preceding consensuses, opinions of others, changes of mind) produces new expressions of values and hence new group averages leading to additional consensuses. This process continues until all resources are allocated. Each representative has contributed to the group's decisions and presumably feels a commitment to the action.

While this example has used a group as a vehicle for value consensus, there is, in principle, no difference between such a method as used with married couples, families, or individuals alone (with their competing values). (For the basic research on the Delphi method, see Dalkey, 1972.)

SUMMARY

Let me summarize what was **not** discussed in this chapter. I did not discuss the traditional social work values of individuality, self-determination, and the like, because as I understand the research literature, there is little need to convince persons who have selected themselves for advanced training in the helping professions to learn to accept these values; they already hold them (McLeod and Meyer, 1967). I also did not discuss the definition of values or any of the magnificent philosophical problems that surround their study because I probably could not convince anyone anyway.

What I did attempt in this chapter was to force values out into the open, to put them together with professional action in a way that might, in principle, show that they can be held accountable in the same fashion that our empirical knowledge can be held accountable. By collapsing what is desired with what is desirable, I pointed to the only operational form by which a client's values may be known—the persistent pattern of choices among alternatives. Having a measured count of the behaviors that express client values gives us the best estimate of these values which we might combine with our knowledge of available options and their likelihood of occurrence.

This is a prolegomenon for further research rather than a directive for practice. We are left with the overwhelming conclusion that research on how we add values to what we do in giving professional help is still essential. No less important is putting our values squarely in the open and being held accountable for them. Our professional values are one of our strongest assets; let us not hide them from the light—or from ourselves.

CHAPTER 14

Analysis of a Philosophy of Scientific Practice: Worker-Generated Strategy

Let us now praise anonymous men and women, those who by birth or accident of circumstance become innocent victims in human history. From that legion of the anonymous, I want to tell the story of one, an old woman whose major crime was that she lived too long in a society that then allowed her no meaningful social role and few means of human existence. I present Miss Maude West, a case in disguise, but she remains as vivid to me as the day I last saw her, struggling for individuality against assaults from within her own brain and from without by those who were malevolent or indifferent, and perhaps even from those who were helping professionals.[1]

EVENTS

Miss West, age 87, came to the attention of the city health department because neighbors were worried about her. What were their impressions of Miss West? They boiled down to four: (1) Miss West was very talkative, even to strangers, (2) she cut out clippings from newspapers and hoarded them, (3) she talked to her dead sister, (4) she was malnourished.

Obviously, some impressions capture the eye of one person which might not attract another. Even if various people observed some common event

---

[1] This case illustration is derived from my experiences at the Benjamin Rose Institute of Cleveland, Ohio, some time ago (Blenkner, Bloom, and Nielsen, 1971). As a member of the research team, I was an observer at close hand of the events I report here; I also had access to the social worker's reports at the completion of the study. Permission to use this case has graciously been given by that agency, long a leader in serving the aged.

Case illustration is derived from unpublished records of the Benjamin Rose Institute, Cleveland, Ohio, and is used (and disguised) with permission of the Executive Director, M. Hemmy.

about Miss West, they might interpret it differently. And even if they interpreted something in the same fashion, there still might be a difference in evaluation. A social worker, therefore, is asked to meet Miss West to assess the situation. Some neighbors have signaled that there is a problem existing; this is where a study begins. What are the events in this situation? From these events and the patterns among them will be formed the concepts that are the keys for finding relevant information from the professional literature, for developing the theoretical structures which will offer tentative guidelines in the therapeutic situation, and for evaluating the outcome of service.

Events are meaningful portions of reality. Miss West was watering her garden when the social worker arrived. Miss West does indeed talk to strangers—the worker didn't have a chance to introduce himself. Miss West invited him to chat. The worker noted that this propensity to talk to strangers might be unsafe, but in an old residential suburb of a large city, it was not an immediate problem. Still, it was a piece of reality to be kept in mind.

After he discussed the purpose of his visit, Miss West invited the worker into her home, and indeed she did cut out clippings from newspapers. There were bundles everywhere, but all rather neatly arranged. This was somewhat eccentric; but it might be viewed as a good way to keep up with the news in a rapidly changing world; more important, it was essentially harmless. She was well informed on current events and seemed to take an active interest in them. The thought of a fire hazard occurred to the worker, but he realized that he didn't know whether Miss West's bundles of clippings were any more or less hazardous than the magazines piled in his own basement. But the neighbor's impression of hoarding was incorrect in the worker's opinion, for no other sign of hoarding was evident.

Miss West spoke of her dead sister during the course of the conversation. The worker sensitively and deftly drew her out. In fact, there were times when the worker was not sure whether Miss West was speaking about a living or a dead person; the meaning this person held for Miss West was immense. She had nursed many members of her family through their final illnesses and her sister was the last survivor of her family, save for Miss West. Speaking to dead persons is, in textbooks, a sign of mental disorganization, of delusions or hallucinations. But, in the context of this situation, the worker doubted the seriousness of this impression. He did not deny the experience of listening to her talk to or of a dead person in a personal way, but he was aware of his part in bringing on this conversation.

Miss West proudly showed the worker around her tidy home. She was thin but in no apparent physical way feeble. The worker poked and peeked and found very little food in her cupboards. When asked about this, she mentioned the high price of foods and that she was "saving for a rainy day." Obviously her sense of need for spending money on food—or, more correctly, for stockpiling food—was different from that of her neighbors. Pictures around the house suggested that Miss West weighed more in earlier times. No, she hadn't noticed that she had lost much weight recently. Her clothes hung somewhat loosely. The worker knows that malnutrition is serious, especially when it interferes with other forms of adaptation. What is the reality in this situation? Is Miss West's need for food less than a middle-aged person, and is she realistic in her conservation of her money? How do we make sense of a set of such events? Is Miss West starving herself without realizing that it is **now**, for her, a "rainy day"?

FROM EVENTS TO CONCEPTS

Concepts are formed by abstracting and generalizing from events. In developing concepts, it helps to group events in sets and to observe the patterns and sequences among them. As we observe the commonalities, we remove them from the time and place of the particular events which gave rise to them. The end product of this process is the generalized abstraction we called the concept. But what events are we to use, and what patterns and sequences are we to observe among them? I can only offer a rule of thumb: Account for as much of the behavior as possible, and deal with what is obviously present. There will be time for looking for missing evidence and for constructing underlying notions, but, right now, what is present?—An elderly lady watering her lawn; a lady willing to talk with a stranger; a person willing to invite him into her home to discuss the question of whether a social agency could be of assistance to her; one who appears to be managing her own household, even if with some eccentric behavior patterns.

What patterns among these events speak to the worker? (Sometimes patterns speak to us very quietly, so listen carefully.) Miss West is doing many things, lots of physical activities: watering the lawn, tending the house, cutting voluminous clippings. We can give these diverse events a conceptual label that brings them together; let's call these examples of her **physical functioning**. Given the context of possible service to an older person, it makes sense to consider a concept that labels economically and familiarly a variety of events which, on their own, might be hard to pull together into a meaningful package. The concept of physical functioning may lead to a literature from a variety of helping professions. Those same words, "physical functioning," may also indicate a variable; the worker can collect objective information about Miss West's current level of functioning as a baseline measure of whether the services he performs have a beneficial or harmful effect on this same aspect of the client's life at the conclusion of the intervention. Because these uses of concepts are important, it is wise to choose carefully among the many ways the same events may be abstracted and generalized.

Other impressions give rise to other potential concepts. The worker noted a number of events which he might group under the label "funny behaviors," like talkativeness, cutting numerous newspaper clippings, and speaking with feeling so intense that there is confusion as to whether her sister is living or dead. Is this a useful concept? For the practitioner, the ultimate criterion of whether a concept is well constructed and well chosen is whether it helps to produce a successful resolution in client problems. We are a good distance from making this determination (see Chapter 17), but because we will test our concepts and propositions, we should tentatively retain this idea about "funny behavior".

Another rule of thumb in developing concepts is that once you have a concept that seems to be a reasonable beginning, look for others at the same level of abstraction in the sense of their affecting and being affected by the same sorts of conceptualizations. For example, physical functioning is a functional concept rather than a concept describing structure or development. Are there other relevant functional concepts that will serve to reduce the mass of details to a manageable size?

The worker might have considered these: **cognitive functioning**, involving such events in Miss West's life as a slight memory loss, or a confusion concerning her sister, or her active, intelligent knowledge about current events. Some positive, some negative, but all aspects of cognitive functioning. Another concept might be **affective functioning** for which Miss West's intensive feelings about her sister and her overfriendliness toward strangers would be examples. Pursuing this line of thinking could lead to other ideas such as spiritual functioning and economic functioning. Where does one stop? Another rule of thumb: Stop when the evidence runs out. We don't have too much information on these last-named topics at this point, but concept formation is a continuing enterprise and these or other concepts may prove to be important later.

It also may become important to make finer conceptual distinctions. While Miss West is subject only to minor memory loss, there may be major elements of confusion which would lead to problems in living different from memory loss problems. However, the larger category of cognitive functioning may not only be conceptually subdivided as necessary but may also call attention to aspects of the concept for which there are currently no events—like a capacity for problem solving which has not yet occurred in the presence of the worker.

If the worker begins to formulate a large number of concepts, he may wish to condense further this information about the client by identifying a construct abstracted and generalized from his concepts. Constructs like **personal competence** or **personal functioning** would encompass all three of the concepts relevant to Miss West. So would the construct of behavior, but we can easily recognize that that would be too general, signifying everything and therefore nothing.

Now our worker talks about the case with his supervisor. He is able to communicate a large number of impressions succinctly by using the concepts he has developed; they communicate his ideas clearly and meaningfully. But the supervisor asks: What about the home situation? And the neighborhood? And the worker realizes that he has overlooked many impressions. Without labels, impressions of events are liable to escape memory—and attention. The worker ponders and comes up with two other concepts: One could meaningfully speak of Miss West's **physical environment** and characterize it by such events as her home, the slippery rugs on the floor, the sturdy banister on the stairs; and Miss West's **social environment**, represented by her neighbors, the absence of relatives, and the teenage hot-rodders who come racing down her street on hot summer nights. These two environmental concepts form a cluster which might be labeled by a higher-order construct such as **environmental protectiveness**.

Lo and behold! We have developed a person and an environment construct, thus performing what social work has long claimed to do—to look at the person in his or her environmental context. We have not described a whole person —no finite sets of concepts can—but we have indicated some of the significant features of a person, and a worker had jolly well better be aware of these kinds of facets if he is to make sense of the situation. Moreover, we have begun to put these sets of concepts into a system of propositions, an individualized theory about the client and her situation. Such a theory is what we will eventually use to help solve problems.

VALUES

After a short time with Miss West, the worker picked up the central message of their relationship, that Miss West wanted to remain in her own home until she died. This took precedence over all other concerns—survival itself, health problems, social-psychological dysfunctions, discomforts, and other sorts of dissatisfactions. She was no stranger to these concerns, but the satisfaction of living as she wished took priority over survival and other problems.

And yet her neighbors were genuinely worried about her. They had tried all the means available to them to help her and still were left with the dread that she would be harmed or would harm herself unless given more assistance. Their concern for her well-being must be taken into account.

The social worker was fully cognizant of the code of professional ethics supporting the self-determining independence of the client, but he was under great pressure not to make a mistake in judgment of her capabilities for self-care. Imagine the headlines in a newspaper that an old lady, presumably under the watchful attention of agency X, had been allowed to live in such conditions that when she had a minor accident, it resulted in her tragic death. . . .

The society of which Miss West was a part was deeply involved in programs for the aged but resources were not unlimited, and many specific care agencies were seeking their share. Who should decide?

Conflicts in values are often a part of the paradox of the helping professions. Any action we take is, ipso facto, a resolution of these value conflicts, whether we intend them to be so or not. Scientific practice involves bringing these value judgments more openly into the weighing of decisions. Probable alternatives resulting from different actions can be rated by the persons involved for desirability and feasibility. These values added to the other parts of the decision-making process will be tested in action just as are the other steps. Patterns among the person's actual behaviors are the operational statement of the desirable for him, i.e., of his values.

FROM CONCEPTS TO PROPOSITIONS

Propositions are statements connecting two or more concepts. Which concepts should we join together in Miss West's case? From a systems point of view, it is conceivable to view each factor as affecting every other factor; however, from the perspective of a worker seeking to intervene in the situation, some combinations seem to be more plausible than others. Let me suggest a rule of thumb: Begin by considering what factors influence the goals in question. Consider the initial concern of the neighbors, connecting Miss West's condition and her survival. Using the concepts and constructs developed previously, we might connect personal competence with an important goal, "survival." We might say "Personal competence is exhibited by the fact that a person continues to survive," a proposition analogous to a nominal level of measurement. At an ordinal level, we might say "The greater the competence, the greater the chance of survival." At the interval level, we might express the proposition in this way: "If the person has so many degrees of personal competence (or certain types of competences), then his chance for survival is likely to be at a certain probability level." At the ratio level, the analogous proposition might state that X number of units of competence will produce Y number of units of chances for survival.

Each of these four ways of expressing the connection among the concepts requires certain information from the events in question and permits certain actions to be taken because of the form of the proposition. The first (nominal) proposition merely asks that we be able to distinguish personal competence and survival and permits us to do so; this does not excite the imagination, perhaps, but it is a necessary place to begin. The second (ordinal) proposition requires that we be able to distinguish more or less of personal competence and survival, using a valid and reliable instrument (questionnaire, physiological measures, worker's judgments); this level of proposition permits us to see the organization existing between these two factors and to test our expectation about this relationship.

The third (interval) proposition requires that we specify the units involved in operationalizing the concepts so that we can test a more precise hypothesis, that having certain degrees or types of those units will result in improved chances for survival at a determinable level of probability. As a crude example, if a meals-on-wheels service were to deliver a hot lunch and a cold supper to Miss West, then we can expect the probability of malnutrition to decrease and survival thereby to increase. The fourth (ratio) proposition requires specifying units having an absolute zero point. For example, Palmore and Stone (1973) have empirically constructed a longevity quotient (LQ) which is the observed number of years of survival (after an initial interview), divided by the actuarially expected number of years based on the person's age, sex, and race. A major predictor of longevity was physical mobility. For unimpaired persons, the LQ was 1.05, meaning that such persons exceeded the actuarial prediction, while persons with difficulty in walking had an LQ of .88, and those in wheelchairs or bedbound had an LQ of .64. Such ratios require data having an absolute zero point, such as years lived; they permit exact estimates of life chances, given certain conditions. With both the third and fourth types of propositions, the practitioner can formulate statements of cost/benefit analyses.

FROM PROPOSITIONS TO THEORIES

Theory has been briefly described as a system of interrelated propositions. Take the ordinal level of proposition about Miss West developed previously—this is the most likely form in which practitioners in the field will state their individualized theories—"The greater the personal competence, the greater the chance of survival". Add another proposition, using concepts at the same level of abstraction, such as: "The more environmental protection, the greater the chance of survival." These two propositions share a common (goal) concept, but how are the constructs of personal competence and environmental protection related?

One can formulate logical combinations that might be useful to the helping professional: (1) If competence deteriorates and environmental protection either remains the same or decreases, then chances for survival will decrease. (2) If competence is improved and if environmental protection either stays the same or improves, then chances for survival will increase. (3) If competence deteriorates and environmental protection improves, then chances for survival will increase. This system of propositions informs the practitioner of the various options and risks in dealing with Miss West (and other clients, of course). They direct attention to major factors that might be points of intervention—personal competence or the environment. If organic deficits make improvements in personal competence impossible, then several environmental options remain open, such as the social or the physical environment. And if the physical environment is chosen for initial action, then the questions arise of whether to continue to use Miss West's present home situation (with prosthetic additions to make it safer) or to use another location (such as a nursing home). In each case, one attempts to identify the probability that a specified action will lead to the desired goal. Logically, all three propositions above should do this; it becomes an empirical question as to how well each would do, and how feasible each option is.

FROM THEORY TO EVALUATION

There are two major paths from a worker-generated theory to evaluation. The first is a **group design** where, for example, a number of persons from the same population-at-risk are divided into experimental and control groups in a test of a certain treatment. Indeed, Miss West was a participant in such a study (Blenkner, Bloom, and Nielsen, 1971), one of many participants. The results deriving from such control-group designs relate to the pattern of typical results, even though these results may not be reflective of Miss West's particular situation.

The other path from theory to evaluation is an **individual design** where, for example, a number of events in the same person's life are analyzed into desired or undesired zones of behavior, before and after a degree of intervention. The comparison is then made between these time periods for the same individual, with the resultant presumed to be due to the effects of the intervention on the specific case.

Each path has its strengths and weaknesses, and both would be appreciably strengthened with their combined use. But even if both were combined, there is no certainty in scientific outcomes, because the practitioner, just as the researcher, must be aware of alternative explanations. Campbell and Stanley (1963, pp. 5, 6) point out several types of rival explanations when one's hypotheses are supported. I will attempt to translate their research explanations into illustrations from practice:

1. **History**. Events in addition to the intervention occur between measurement points. For example, Miss West's income may become higher after service, owing to a change in the social security laws—not to the worker's efforts.
2. **Maturation**. Events change as a part of life development, not the intervention activities, such as Miss West's transient confusions appearing and disappearing.
3. **Effects of Testing** (Effects of Client Experience). Repeated experiences with the same test (or with helping professionals) tend to produce changes in the scores received (or relationships formed). If Miss West had had a bad experience with a previous worker who tried to relocate her in a nursing home, it is likely that the current worker would have had a much harder time, through no fault of his own.
4. **Instrumentation**. Changes in the perception or judgment of the worker, for example, when he is overloaded with work as contrasted to when he is not, will likely mean differences in client behavior not attributable to the client herself.
5. **Statistical Regression**. Judgments initially made from extreme observations, such as when the client comes to the attention of the agency in a time of crisis, are likely to be more moderate during the second measurement period simply because such moderate behaviors are more likely to occur.
6. **Biases in Selection**. Depending on how cases are assigned to workers, there may be an effect on the workers' overall averages that is distinct from their individual effectiveness.

These are some of the rival explanations Campbell and Stanley present, which each worker should consider after his action hypotheses appear to have been supported.

FROM THEORY TO STRATEGY

It is now time for the practitioner to look with great care at the theory presumed to guide his behavior. Which parts are identifiable and accessible to the worker and controllable by him at a reasonable cost and in a suitable ethical context? Constructs, like personal competence, are difficult to translate into strategies because they are so distant from the events which gave rise to the concepts which in turn provided the basis for constructs. Concepts, like physical functioning, offer a number of means of identification so that the other factors —controllability and the others—may be determined. The worker might simply identify whether Miss West was unimpaired in her physical mobility, had difficulty in walking, or was restricted to a wheelchair or bedbound. This one aspect of physical functioning is itself a predictor of longevity, as Palmore and Stone (1973) point out. More complex operational statements of physical functioning combine several aspects, such as the index of daily activities developed by Katz, Downs, Cash, and Grotz (1970). This standardized procedure requires trained personnel to administer it; one obtains precise measurements of independent functioning in eating, dressing, bathing, and other basic physical activities. Precision is bought at the double price of extensive work to develop such procedures and of intrusion on the privacy of clients in revealing this information. Many helping professionals may be excessively sensitive to the later consideration on ethical grounds, for in the helping context, such precise questions are just as useful in promoting social functioning as medical questions are in promoting physical health. By knowing the factual level of physical functioning, the worker may offer such alternatives as home aides or more intensive care in institutions. Without precise information, the worker is shooting in the dark.

Once the referents of our concepts are identified, we must ask whether we have access to them and whether we have control over them—or at least influence concerning their functioning. If malnutrition seems to be a problem and Miss West doesn't appear to be eating properly, our conceptual analysis should distinguish at least three stages: purchasing the food, preparing the food, and consuming the food. Our careful observations and measurements should supply information on which of the three stages is the key problem. If the key problem were getting out to buy foods, then the worker might have sought out a grocery store that delivered. If the problem were in the cooking of the food, then a meals-on-wheels that delivered prepared foods might be the answer. If getting food from the plate into her mouth were a problem—and it would be likely that the other two would also be problems if this were the case—then the worker would have to consider ways of having someone present to feed Miss West, like a home aide, a neighbor whose services might be purchased, or possibly institutional placement. The worker's control over these events depends in part on their availability and on their acceptability to Miss West.

Another concern is the durability of such solutions beyond the time the worker is present in the situation. Would a neighbor always be dependable? Would money hold out? Creating an effective strategy from an abstract theory is to orchestrate a large number of events. Money paid to a person who helps in preparing food is money not available for other needs. The several functions of the theory are helpful in developing an overall view of a situation. The theory first delimited the scope of events, thus classifying the factors that the worker had to consider. The theory described these groups of events, summarizing the problems and the strengths succinctly. It also led to some tentative explanations of the problems, such as deterioration in certain aspects of personal functioning leading to problems like malnutrition. By considering the logical possibilities among the concepts, the worker had a sense of integration about the problems, how the concepts were linked, one leading to another. This same network of propositions generated some new ways of looking at the case, some new points of intervention so as to affect positive changes. By having an integrated network of concepts, it is likely that the worker did not overlook any major part of the problem situation. By making further conceptual distinctions in areas where problems were apparent, the worker was given even more detailed direction on where to look and possibly what interventions were feasible. In this fashion, abstractions become vitally practical.

SUMMARY

We began with one old lady whose style of life was worrisome to her neighbors. We progressed through the tools of a philosophy of scientific practice from the raw events to concepts and then to propositions, and then to a theory. And, finally, we attempted to translate a portion of the theory into a strategy for action. Of course we could only illustrate some of the concepts, propositions, theory, and strategy in this type of chapter; the reader would have to complete the sketch begun here. But even as we discussed personal competence and environmental protection as related to survival, did we ever leave Miss West out of our considerations? I hope it was clear that the limits of our abstracting and generalizing were set at the point from which we could always see Miss West as the beneficiary of our theorizing. The logical relations of personal competence and environmental protection gave rise to specific strategies of intervention that could be tested for feasibility and desirability in Miss West's case. Conceptualization is indeed abstract but not absent from the arena of action for the helping professional.

CHAPTER 15

Analysis of a Philosophy of Scientific Practice: Strategy Generated from the Literature

As with the inductive and deductive phases of problem solving, so too the helping professional must move back and forth between generating his own strategy and drawing from the scientific and professional literature the information needed in constructing designs for action. Where and how the worker looks for this information will depend on his orientation to knowledge (cf. Coan, 1968), but this chapter will seek to present some of the difficulties he will encounter and some of the possible solutions he might try.

USING RESEARCH FINDINGS: FROM A SPECIFIC STUDY

The October, 1971, issue of **Social Casework** carried a report of a project on protective services to older persons (Blenkner, Bloom, and Nielsen, 1971). This study of noninstitutionalized older persons who had come to the attention of health and welfare agencies involved a control-group design in which persons were randomly allocated to an experimental service program and to a standard treatment (control) group. The basic question was whether the experimental treatment more than the standard treatment could positively affect the lives and circumstances of these persons who were admitted to the study because they appeared to need protective services. They exhibited behaviors indicating mental incapacity for adequate care of self and interests without serious harm to self or others and because they had no other relative or friend able and willing to assume the kind and degree of support needed to control the situation.

The report discusses the background of the issue of protective services for older persons, questions of prevalence, and of past efforts in dealing with this social problem. Then the study itself is described, the sample, the research and service designs, and the findings. The details of the findings cover each of the major outcome variables about the lives and circumstances of the participants of the study—survival, mental and physical functioning, protection from the physical and the social environments, affective states, and discussion of collateral stress. The report concludes with a discussion of the entire study and its implications.

This is a conventional pattern of presentation in professional journals. How is the practitioner in his agency setting to use such a report in his practice? Let us assume that the worker has a client like Miss West (who was, in fact, a participant in this project). A first question often asked is How well does my client fit the type of person being reported on in this study? The report indicates the median age of study participants was 78, with the following characteristics predominant: female, white, native born, widowed, grammar school education, living in a private house, with a monthly income (median) of $102 stemming from Social Security. Let us continue to suppose that the worker's client fits all of these characteristics—or many—or most—or some—or none. How close a fit is necessary before data can be considered applicable? A difference in any one of these major factors will mean a significant difference in the life situation and experiences of the client. And yet, are we to ignore these data because we are working with a 65-year-old man . . . who shows signs of mental incapacity to care for himself and his interests? Obviously not; we must use the best available information, even if the fit between client and study is not exact. We must identify **outcome variables** that are common to our client and the study; if survival, mental and physical functioning, and the other variables listed above are relevant to our client, then to some degree the study data will be relevant. The discrepancy in fit between predominant demographic characteristics of the study and our client becomes a measure of caution in using the results full strength as an empirical weight in determining risk for our client. But how much any one discrepancy in such demographic characteristics means in terms of our client is not clear at all.

A second question for the practitioner who would use a given piece of research in his own practice is how much the worker has access to the types of interventions described in the study. If services are described that are beyond the range of the available then the worker is left to improvise. The workers in the Blenkner study had access to financial assistance, medical evaluation, legal and psychiatric consultation, fiduciary and guardianship services, home aide services, nursing consultation and evaluation, and placement in a protective setting. The difference in the service component means another caution in using research results in one's own practice.

A third question for the worker who is considering an article from the literature in relation to his client concerns the goals sought and the effectiveness achieved in reaching them. The results from the Blenkner study in which highly experienced workers were provided with rich ancillary services as needed should give us pause to reflect. Competence, both mental and physical, deteriorated on all measures for both groups, but differences that existed favored the controls—especially in death rates. Protection, physical and social, improved in both samples, with differences significantly favoring the experimental group. In the affective area, there were mixed results; concerning reduction of stress on others, the evidence significantly favored the experimental group. How can the individual practitioner profit from these results?

The most direct answer is that to model future practice on the experimental service package is most likely to produce similar results, including some that are not desirable. Does the article help to sort out which parts of treatment were responsible for the undesirable outcomes? In part it does, suggesting that premature institutionalization may account for the higher death rates among the experimental group participants together with the point that, contrary to expectations, earlier institutionalization did not prove to be protective.

Do these data suggest that older persons in need of protective services should not be institutionalized? They most certainly do not; they simply point out the correlation between certain events—institutionalization and mortality—within a network of circumstances which should raise a flag to any future quick decision to institutionalize an older person supposedly for his own good. But does this report tell us which events are predictive of various untoward outcomes? Especially in relation to any one client, the answer is no. The worker is left to speculate on the critical factors in his own client's situation.

There is still another consideration in the worker's use of information from a given research report. The Blenkner study is replete with various statistical notations, from median age to Weibull analyses. Many helping professionals have been schooled in statistics at some point in their careers but more likely in how to plug numbers into formulas, rather than in how to **use** the results in making practice decisions. There are few books written from the point of view of sophisticated consumership of research information for practice. It is unlikely that workers will use available information unless they understand the language in which it is presented. Thus, we find ourselves in another paradox, that even when good research is available, many cannot use it in its present form. The long-range answer is better education of workers; the short-range answer might be the creation of a new role in the helping professions, a facilitator, one who is conversant with research and with practice and who assists professionals (in each area) to understand each other's problems and language.

USING RESEARCH FINDINGS: REVIEWS OF THE LITERATURE

We encountered a number of problems facing a practitioner who wished to use the results of one research project with his client; we will find additional problems when this practitioner reads a review article—but, also, some major sources of support. Let's take Kasl's (1972) illuminating review article on physical and mental health effects of involuntary relocation and institutionalization of the elderly. Over 100 citations are given. It is not practical to assume that even the most diligent worker could study all of these within the context of normal agency practice. But what is presented in a review article is the author's estimation of the topic covered. This may vary in thoroughness in locating and reporting relevant articles, accuracy in presenting major findings and trends among research reports, and critical assessment of research design. Chances are that reviews of the literature in major journals present coverage greater than most practitioners could afford to devote to such a search. So we are placed in the position of depending on the competence of colleagues in other fields. This may be uncomfortable for some but it is practical for most.

Kasl begins by pointing out that even with his reasonably thorough search of the literature on relocation of the elderly, very little is known for certain. Other topics have taken precedence over pure relocation effects moreover, most of the studies are cross-sectional rather than longitudinal, thus permitting many competing explanations for the results that are available. Should we throw up our hands in despair? No, as practitioners with a client, we had better use these data as much as possible.

Turning to the evidence, Kasl notes the widespread generality of the findings that high mortality is associated with institutionalization (eight studies are cited, which should greatly strengthen our confidence in the common empirical findings). How this is to be interpreted is another question; are predominantly ill and dying people admitted who subsequently die, or are there adverse effects of the institutional environment, or both? Or is it a matter of having a choice about relocation that is associated with low mortality rates? Or is it the person's mental and psychological state that leads to certain outcomes after relocation? Kasl discusses a variety of studies dealing with these and other issues. The worker has to sort out those that seem to be relevant to his client's situation; this is difficult to do from brief critical statements, but it is not impossible.

Kasl does what readers are typically required to do for themselves: The research findings are combined into hypotheses for further research. I quote these in detail as they are useful in their own right and as models of reconstructions readers can derive from the professional literature:

"Relocation and/or institutionalization will have adverse effects on the physical and psychological well-being of the elderly if: (a) it increases the physical distance from **friends, kin,** and **age peers,** as well as from various **services and facilities;** (b) it interferes with their engaging in their usual **leisure** and **social activities;** (c) it represents a deterioration in the quality of their dwelling unit and their neighborhood along valued dimensions (e.g., **independence, privacy, safety, security, convenience, familiarity**). If one extrapolates further from the studies cited in this and the previous sections, it may be suggested that the following characteristics of the elderly may be particularly indicative of an adverse effect of relocation and/or institutionalization: being **male, older,** and in **poor health; living alone** and having **few contacts** with friends and kin; in poor **financial** circumstances and of **lower social class;** having lived in the **old neighborhood** a long time; of **low morale** and **life satisfaction, reacting to move with depression,** giving up, and hopelessness-helplessness.

"... A move which is **voluntary** and desired and which provides a striking **improvement in the living conditions** [produces consequences which] may be all positive. Carp's study of Victoria Plaza clearly demonstrates the beneficial effects of such a move in many different areas: life satisfaction and morale, evaluation of health, frequency of social contacts, activities and their enjoyment" (p. 381, bold face added).

Kasl's summary begins to formulate hypotheses deriving from his review of the literature. We will discuss these hypotheses shortly, but first note that we must assume that the studies are of equal quality in design and execution, an assumption almost certain to be in error. We also assume that this reduction of information does not do violence to the results, another very tenuous assumption. What we do in using summaries of reviews of literature is to trust the author to pick out the key studies and to identify the major trends on significant variables in hopes that we also have access to these same factors.

I propose that a worker might read a review article with an eye to framing a number of hypotheses which are presumed to be of equal quality and relevance to the client in question. These hypotheses would have the following general form: the more of some factor (or the presence of some quality), the greater the risk of some action. In the present case, this hypothesis would suggest, for example, that the greater the physical distance between Miss West and her friends, the greater the risk of negative outcomes stemming from relocation. With appropriate variations for wording, one could come up with as many hypotheses as there are key concepts in the review of relevance to the client. These hypotheses represent a summary of the best available information (for better or worse). The practitioner would then assess his client's situation to predict whether there is evidence in favor of the hypothesis, or against it, or whether information is lacking or irrelevant. Using the two paragraphs quoted from Kasl, let me suggest how this might be done. First, I will list independent variables or characteristics shown in research to be related to adverse effects on older persons who are relocated. Then using a +, —, and 0 for favorable, unfavorable, or indeterminant predictions, respectively, let us see how the individualization of the empirical findings in Miss West's situation stands.

1. Friends (—)/ kin (0)/ age peers (+)→ resultant (0)
2. Services and facilities (+)
3. Usual leisure time and social activities (—)
4. Independence/privacy (—)
5. Safety/security (+)
6. Convenience/familiarity (—)
7. Male (+) (i.e., not being male reduces Miss West's risk)
8. Older age (—)
9. Poor health (+)
10. Live alone (—)
11. Few contacts with friends/kin (+)
12. Poor financial circumstances (—)
13. Lower social-class standing (+)
14. Long-time resident of neighborhood (—)
15. Low morale/life satisfaction (+)
16. Reacting to idea of move with depression, etc. (—)

By my count, there are eight reasons which appear to be negative or adverse to Miss West's relocating and seven in favor of her relocating, with one situation in which factors appear to balance each other out. Thus, using the research findings in this way gives us a very crude indicator of courses of action. In this case, there is less chance of harming Miss West by leaving her in her own home than by relocating her in an institution, given this interpretation of summarized research findings.

It might be possible to add weights to each factor, that is, how important each is in Miss West's life. From previous discussion of this case, we learned that independence and living in a familiar home were two chief goals of Miss West, and so this would add to our empirical decision. But what if these value weights went against our empirical decision? We have not solved our dilemma, but perhaps we have raised it to a new and agonizing level of consciousness through explication of all the factors involved. . . .

USING PRACTICE WISDOM

Constructing a strategy from articles describing service programs and practices involves difficulties of another kind. Even though the attempt is made to account for what was done in a particular instance, it is rare that this account is abstracted and generalized for a conceptualized view of the practice wisdom as applicable to new contexts.

Consider the paper by Wasser (1971), a sagacious caseworker dealing with protective services to mentally impaired, aged persons. At one point in the paper, she deals with intervention with involuntary clients; persons needing protective services rarely seek out such aid voluntarily. Wasser points out that while there are social and professional bases for such service, there is no legal basis yet, as there is in the protection of children. The worker must take responsibility for entering a protective situation uninvited, but, Wasser points out, an important insight arising from her experience is that in order to develop a taste for service, the client must taste it. Once a worker politely but firmly insists on entry into a protective situation over the objections of the aged client, the worker is likely to find that the client eventually agrees to voluntary cooperation, although some continue to resist help to the bitter end. (In view of the outcome of research on survival which Blenkner reported, perhaps these resistive clients were right.)

These are strong words, given the social worker's code of ethics regarding the value of client self-determination, although Wasser has also pointed out that we may hide behind this value statement to mask our irresponsible inactivity. But granting the validity of Wasser's discussion on work with the involuntary client within the context of experience from which she speaks, how is the worker on a new case to use this practice wisdom?

I spoke earlier of three types of hypotheses (Chapter 11): the action hypothesis concerning an immediate communication with the client; the directional hypothesis that tests whether a sequence of events conforms to some intermediary goals; and the outcome hypothesis which deals with verification of the end goals we seek. I would now suggest that the use of practice wisdom be restricted to action or directional hypotheses, while more objective data and systematic theory might guide any of the three types of hypotheses. This means, in effect, that we cannot put as much weight upon our reconstructions of practice wisdom until these reconstructions have received the conventional scientific tests. Yet we can continue to use much of this practice wisdom in an active or directional way. The action hypothesis and, to a lesser extent, the directional hypothesis, receive more rapid feedback on their accuracy and utility than the outcome hypothesis. In this way, idiosyncratic experiences which take the form of practice wisdom can be eliminated without great harm.

With reference to Wasser's suggestion to develop a taste for service by having the client taste it, let us consider this as a directional hypothesis. Let us further assume that Miss West has been resisting any encroachment on her life, although the worker has established that she is definitely malnourished. With a combination of reality-oriented pleas and threats, the worker arranges to have a home aide come in three times a week for four weeks to help Miss West purchase and prepare foods so as to work toward a solution of the malnutrition problem. If at the end of this period of time Miss West still doesn't want to have the service, the worker will withdraw it.

The risks facing the worker are many. He has no idea whether Miss West will become a converted voluntary client or will continue to resist to the bitter end, since there is no basis for making these probability estimates in most discussions of practice wisdom. He doesn't know whether Miss West will haul him into court for invasion of privacy. He really doesn't know whether he is doing the right thing by leaving her in her own home if her mental condition worsens. But if the best available information is a literary expression of the experiences of others with similar cases, then the worker is basing his course of action on more than his own very limited experience and, by using a directional hypothesis only, he is testing it in a limited period. Thus, the worker has to compromise, and it isn't easy. But the more knowingly he clarifies his decisions and puts them to an objective test, the better his practice will be for it.

USING THEORIES FROM THE LITERATURE

There is, in principle, little difference between using a theory one has generated and a theory one has found in the literature, insofar as direct translation of propositions into strategy statements is concerned. There are considerable differences in the sophistication and refinements one can find in some theories reported in books and journal articles, polished by their authors over many occasions before they see life in print. This is to be contrasted to the ad hoc theory generated by the worker in the field. However, the latter is much more closely related to the specific client, and its assumptions are better understood than those appearing explicitly or implicitly in writings.

The major task of using theories from the literature is to find them (Chapter 20), to know how to understand them, and, finally, to translate them into direct strategy statements (discussed in the preceding chapters of this book). After all this has been done, the worker has earned the right to call himself a partner with the original author in theory construction and application.

SUMMARY

In some ways, this has been a pessimistic chapter in that there are many difficulties in using research from the literature in developing practice strategies. Many workers lack competence in understanding research and statistical conventions, and, likewise, these conventions have made little attempt to communicate findings for consumption by practitioners. Yet, there are some very crude rules of thumb that can be suggested by which workers can make reasonable use of these materials, although they depend on the knowledge and skills of colleagues in other disciplines. Statements of practice wisdom have different types of difficulties attached to their translation into strategies, but, again, some rules of thumb may be offered. In the long run, better education for practitioners and for researchers may provide the meeting ground for knowledge providers and knowledge users. In the short run, a new role of facilitator may be needed to bridge the gap between scientist and practitioner, although eventually each person must become his own interpreter of theory, research, and practice.

Part IV

TOOLS FOR A SCIENTIFIC
HELPING PROFESSION

CHAPTER 16

Creativity: Productive Rule Breaking

Heretofore, I have been at great pains to present rules, laws, and principles. But now I propose rule breaking in the name of a better solution to a problem. I call such rule breaking "creativity in social work" as contrasted to conventional ways of dealing with problems. There is nothing wrong with conventional wisdom, I must emphasize; today's conventions were yesterday's creations. However, tomorrow's problems are something else again. And new solutions must be found. When new solutions are proposed, they almost inevitably break new ground—that's why they are new. Any pioneer is in for surprises, risks. What can we know about this risk-taking called creativity in social work? Before we begin the discussion, let me reintroduce the notion of paradox, for teaching rule breaking (in the name of a better solution) is somewhat paradoxical to a profession endeavoring to teach rules. . . .

Creativity is a fascinating concept to consider. Variously described by many authors, creativity can be given a working definition as behavior which produces a novel outcome that is socially useful. The outcome may be production of a product (inventing a new medicine, for example), or a process (being aware of the aseptic procedure for delivering medicines subcutaneously), or even definition of a problem (why do people get infections even when the physical operation seems to have been successfully performed?).

If this be creativity, then we can ask where does it come from and how can it be encouraged to appear more often? I suggest that creativity, like any behavior, comes from information that feeds it. I further suggest that there are three classes of information to be considered: (1) experience—the direct apprehension of events; (2) knowledge—indirect apprehension of events; the experience of someone else's experience; and (3) projections—extrapolations from experience or knowledge.

All information may be categorized into these three mutually exclusive areas for artists as well as for scientists and helping professionals. I further assert that creativity is rarely to be found in the first two categories because, if it is someone else's experience, then it isn't novel; and experiences themselves tend to have more to do with commonplace events. Accidently walking into a novel situation is a possible experience, but it might better be classified as an accidental projection (discussed below) since one usually has to project from the commonplace to the novel, as when Fleming saw something beyond the moldy culture dish in his eventual discovery of penicillin.

Projections may be classified along a continuum based on the degree of awareness of the experience and/or knowledge from which one's extrapolations are made. When one's awareness is low, when extrapolations are essentially unfounded and merely set off by an accidental feature of the environment, then I would label this type of projection an "accident." When one's awareness of the experiences and knowledge involved in making the projection is at its maximum, and one planfully involves the elements of one's experiences, then I would label this type of projection "inference." The area between I would label "intuition."

If ever there was a Pandora's Box, the concept of intuition is it. Sarbin, Taft, and Bailey (1960) discuss the various definitions and conceptions of intuition. In particular, they characterize **stereotypes** of the major components of the term as involving the occurrence of knowing something that is achieved through an inexplicable and unanalyzable method (thus making it mysterious) which carries the conviction of truth, certainty, complete credibility, and which occurs immediately—without the intervention of a thought process that one is aware of.

It is my opinion that intuition, as Sarbin, Taft, and Bailey describe the **stereotype**, represents a disease which I call **clinical omniscience**. It strikes nearly every practitioner, some earlier, some later, such as when a client's difficulties resemble some previous experiences. When this occurs, the practitioner has the overwhelming feeling that he has been here before, that he knows the answer. The feeling, being a feeling, is not subjected to testing as a cognitive proposition normally would be. And so you have, veritably, a mystical experience in the social agency! However, for every St. Francis there is a Savonarola; we must ask by what fruits will we know the **true** intuition (or inference)? (By "true," I mean successful in its effects on clients.)

I believe that there is a place for intuition defined more simply as projection, that is, extrapolation, from the known to the unknown, without a high-level awareness of the basis of the projection—but also not from a low level of such awareness. All extrapolations, as all scientific propositions whatsoever, must be tested in reality, for their fruits. The essential point is, by which means of projection—accident, intuition, or inference—is creativity more likely to occur?

My hypothesis is that for the helping professional, a higher potentiality for creative solutions occurs as one moves from accidents, through intuition, to inference. Let me explain why this may be so. There are several dimensions for the analysis of the types of information. Let me present these in tabular form (Table 16-1):

Table 16-1

Dimensions of Analysis for Three Types of Information

Types of Information	Applicability to the Same or Different Situation	Iatrogenic Potential: The Degree of Risk of Doing Harm
A. Experience	Strictly speaking, an experience is applicable only to an identical situation; or else one would be projecting from the known to the unknown. (See C below.)	The degree of risk is known and presumed low—one would not seek to repeat a disastrous experience.
B. Knowledge	Limited to same situations as contained in one's fund of knowledge, however wide that may be.	The degree of risk is medium, due to loss or distortion in the communication process.
C. Projections	By definition, projections go from the known to the unknown.	The overall degree of risk is high. See separate categories below.
1. Accidents	Applicability is limited by the accidental features of the environment that set off the projection.	A very high degree of risk, as there are no controls on the sources of information or on the various forms of bias which influence the direction an accident may lead to.
2. Intuition	Applicability is limited by the amount of knowledge base one has, by the openness (flexibility) to events one experiences, and by the **personal** values or biases (like compassion).	A high degree of risk is present due to many sources of personal biases uncorrected by external value standards.
3. Inference	Applicability is limited by the amount of knowledge	A medium degree of risk present, due to the many

Table 16-1—Continued

Types of Information	Applicability to the Same or Different Situation	Iatrogenic Potential: The Degree of Risk of Doing Harm
	base one has, by the openness (flexibility) to events one experiences, and by the **professional** values or biases (like "compassionate objectivity").	sources of professional bias; however, such biases are in part self-correcting by reference to external value standards which are under scrutiny by many eyes.

First, note that there is no perfect solution to the type of information one may use. Applicability and degree of risk progress in a paradoxical manner. In a sense, the more applicable to different situations, the more risky the form of knowledge. Experience is least risky, but highly limited. Knowledge is more broadly applicable but with a higher degree of risk owing to the incompleteness of communication. Projections are widely applicable to different situations but are limited in several ways, which also present the basis for some degree of risk involved in using projections. Of them all, by the way I define these terms, inference appears to be most applicable and least harmful. Therefore, it becomes the most preferable type of information among projections, when one is faced with a problem about which little is known.

Note also that creativity can occur in any of the forms of projection, but my hypothesis is that it is more likely to occur for practitioners if careful planning is made with known information. This approach is similar to the view of Sarbin, Taft, and Bailey (1960). A contrary hypothesis would probably suggest that creativity would likely be low with accidental projections and planned (merely mechanical) inferences, while intuitions would be the greatest source of creative solutions. Perhaps; but this is a matter of empirical test, after many other issues are carefully defined and operationally controlled. My hypothesis is more heuristically valuable for the state which I envision the helping professions to enter in the future. We are encouraged to educate creative social workers who can effectively adapt new solutions to novel currently unknown events. To train for pure intuition is to abnegate our educational responsibility. To inform the student that he is henceforth responsible for creative solutions to his client's problems is to provide a healthy expectation which all reasonably intelligent persons may hope to attain to some degree. This is particularly important because we cannot give sufficient knowledge to meet all exigencies students will encounter; we provide training in problem solving which is to project the best of currently available information to novel problem situations.

Wertheimer (the great Gestalt psychologist) is quoted as saying that creative thinking is the process of destroying one gestalt in favor of a better one (Gerard, 1952). It is paradoxical again to combine creating with destroying, a theme as old as the phoenix and found in philosophies both east and west. Let us pursue this further.

This is not the place to describe in detail the theories and research on creativity (see, for example, Stein and Heinze, 1960), except to remind the reader of the psychodynamic position which suggests that the unconscious is the ultimate source of all that is creative, and that the creative person undergoes regression in service of the ego in order to tap this fertile source. But the creative person, as contrasted with the madman, returns to reality and reworks these elements taken from the unconscious into the socially useful product. A learning theory approach (Mednick, 1962) suggests that creativity is the socially useful combining of remotely associated events.

Interestingly, these usually antithetical approaches agree on the combining of events in reaching creative solutions. To be sure, the psychodynamic approach places all the exciting action in the hidden unconscious while the behaviorists hide the creative act in the statistically improbable combination of events, but both agree in suggesting to the would-be creative worker that he or she be **open** to events which the client is communicating, to be open to the **combinations** that "simply occur by intuition," as well as to those which are planfully made to occur, in arriving at creative theories and strategies. Thus, the crux of the matter of creativity in the helping professions appears to lie in the perceiving of events and in the forming of sets and systems of events. These appear to be the raw materials for creative professional helping. What makes for creative perception of events? And for creative formations of sets and systems of events? I don't know of any better rule of thumb than to **keep trying** to find creative combinations of events and to be well-enough **informed** to recognize an innovative solution when you make one. Another rule is to study the creative solutions of others, from the practice wisdom communication circuit especially. Most creative solutions of individual practitioners rarely find their way into the professional literature, unfortunately.

By the way, if knowledge or experience will provide the **appropriate** guide for your professional actions, don't feel you have to come up with a "creative" solution since it is more likely that you can't improve on a good workable solution, or the effort involved may not be practical in light of other obligations you face. But when do you break rules?

You are justified in breaking rules when the probabilities of your creative professional actions greatly exceed those of your convention-determined professional actions in affecting a successful solution to a problem. This involves the regular determination of probabilities for strategy statements combined with the determination of probabilities for value statements. As usual, risks abound. If your risk works, then a broken rule becomes a new creative rule. If it doesn't work, back to the drawing board. (See also, chapter 15.)

One can minimize the possible negative effects of creative solutions that don't work by using them as a part of the action hypotheses. Make on-site creative leaps; test them immediately in action, and move along in the direction of those that give you appropriate feedback. Build up evidence to a larger creative solution from smaller ones.

For instance, Carkhuff's (1972) approach to training for the helping relationship involves several stages of communication, going from active listening to making tentative therapeutic thrusts beyond the information the client has given, based on the conceptual knowledge and experience of the helper. Active listening and responding to the feelings and content which the client communicates become the interchangeable base, when the worker's responses are accurately and perceptively interchangeable with the feelings and ideas of the client. Once this base is established (and it is continually being reestablished), then the worker is able to add to or go beyond the events that the client has communicated. These therapeutic communications help the client to put some remote events together or some common events together in a new way, leading to a creative solution to the problem. Such additive suggestions are given tentatively, in the context of the rapport the worker has attained with the interchangeable feeling/content base. If the client accepts the suggestions from these on-site hypotheses, then a larger creative solution is built from each new addition. Thus, by providing the client with both security and challenge, the worker moves the helping process to a creative outcome.

Examples of Creative Clinical Efforts

Accident

Consider the situation of a worker who was trying to involve a shy deaf-and-dumb teenager in social activities with his normal peers. Appropriate activities were very limited, but, by accident, the worker noticed the blinking lights of the neighborhood movie theater which he had passed dozens of times previously. There was a foreign film with **subtitles**, a perfect solution for starting a group of teenagers, including the client, out on the same footing. It is my guess that many such small accidental creative acts mark the everyday work of social workers.

Intuition

Theodore Reik (1948) is a sensitive and creative psychiatrist who reports case materials in which he uses his "inner ear." One such session begins as follows:

"After a sentence about the uneventful day, the patient fell into a long silence. She assured me that nothing was in her thoughts. Silence from me. After many minutes she complained about a toothache. She told me that she had been to the dentist yesterday. He had given her an injection and then had pulled a wisdom tooth. The spot was hurting again. New and longer silence. She pointed to the bookcase in the corner and said, 'There's a book standing on its head.' Without the slightest hesitation and in a reproachful voice I said, 'But why did you not tell me that you had had an abortion?' " (p. 263, 264).

Reik's discussion of this case leads one to believe that he was not aware of combining elements of information and calculating what inference might be made from them, as he arrived at this creative (and exactly truthful) statement. Yet, the background of the case was such that the elements were nearly all present: The woman had had an affair with a married doctor (gynecologist) who refused to leave Nazi Germany with her. Whether the upside-down book-fetus analogy was intended by the patient or the pulled tooth–abortion analogy, is a moot point. The fact of the matter is that Reik correctly saw a connection and made an intuitive statement which was correct. (No one records how many intuitive statements fall flat.) My contention is that there was considerable information available to Reik's conscious mind, including the theory of symbolic analogies which in this case proved to have startling predictive accuracy.

Inference

Stuart (1970) presents the fascinating case of Bob, a 10-year-old boy who had been labeled a "passive-aggressive character disorder" case and who was eating only ten foods and was reading below his grade level at school. His parents, concerned about his behavior, had had eighteen months of special education and therapy aimed at his emotional blocks to eating and reading appropriately. He was removed from this treatment because the parents were unhappy with his lack of progress.

Considering the food problem, let us follow the therapist's analysis and plans. First, the foods Bob ate were fresh fish, chocolate milk, popcorn, toast, fried potatoes, peanut butter, mushrooms, pizza, steak, and pancakes. The therapist noted that each of them was brown in color. Bob was also known to be very interested in artwork and he spent long hours building model cars (behavior hardly befitting a "severe characterological problem with features of anger, passive-aggressive qualities," Stuart notes, p. 146). With a creative

Excerpt from LISTENING WITH THE THIRD EAR by T. Reik is reprinted by permission of Farrar, Straus & Co. © 1949 by Farrar, Straus & Co.

stroke, the therapist arranged a color-coded menu in which Bob was to choose a new food each day which was not the same color as the two main-dish foods. If Bob had steak and potatoes (brown and white), he had to chose a red (like tomatoes) or a green (like peas) or a purple (beets) . . . in order that Bob would have enough energy to watch his favorite TV programs or work on models. Documented changes in food habits show Bob eating 35 foods within the treatment period of four weeks; these were maintained after a year's follow-up.

Is this case of Bob one which can be described as creative because of inferential projection or because of intuitive projection? There is no hard-and-fast line, but I would suggest that this falls closer to inference because of the awareful planning that Stuart used both in deriving an interventive strategy from his theoretical orientation (behavior modification—the use of positive reinforcements for socially desired behaviors) and in locating the individualizing aspects of the case, namely, that Bob liked colors in his artwork.

Nowhere in any theory does it say to create color-coded menus for persons with eating problems, but practice theories (strategies) urge the use of indi-vidualizing of theoretical propositions and findings from research. The creative act is the combining of general theoretical propositions with individual prop-ositions derived from the client's problem situation. And this is what helping professionals are directed to do all the time. In a word, helping professionally is a continually creative act—or should be.

Environmental Influences on Creativity in the Helping Professions

A sensible question for the helping professions is how to stimulate the production of creative help. In a major program of research and conceptualiza-tion concerning productive climates for scientists, Pelz (1972; Pelz and Andrews, 1966) has offered another paradoxical situation: Scientists were found to be most effective in creative problem solving when they experienced high levels of **security**—"that is, some condition or conditions which serve to protect the scientist from demands of his technical environment"—and **challenge**—"that is, some condition or conditions which serve to expose the scientist to demands of his environment" (Pelz, 1972, pp. 2, 3). In conceptualizing how these two concepts are related, Pelz (1972) suggests a number of interrelated subconcepts which he applies to institutions of higher learning (from the research organiza-tions in government, industry, and the university from whence his original research came). By extension, these are equally provocative for the specialized institutions of higher learning related to the helping professions.

Pelz first suggests several personal-quality concepts: (1) competence (intellectual abilities and technical training); (2) curiosity (the capacity to detect problems and to enjoy trying to solve them; a form of challenge); and (3) self-confidence (the individual's conviction that he can solve the problems that he undertakes; a form of security). These three concepts are interactive and reinforce each other.

Pelz then suggests several environmental concepts: (1) resources (money, equipment, access to colleagues and specialists; a form of security); (2) achievement (the solving of professional problems); (3) reporting visibility; and (4) recognition (a form of security), leading to exposure to new problems (a form of challenge).

Linking both the personal and the environmental concepts is another term, involvement (or enthusiasm or commitment), the sense of being absorbed in one's work. Involvement is fed by the personal qualities of curiosity and self-confidence but also by environmental recognition and exposure to new problems.

Reviewing this system of concepts, Pelz is suggesting that the personal concepts of competence, curiosity, self-confidence, and involvement with one's work, plus the environmental resources available, lead to achievement—creative problem solving which then results in reporting visibility of one's achievements, recognition, and the exposure to new problems which stimulate curiosity and involvement, thus reactivating the entire system. Pelz makes a number of stimulating suggestions derived from his other research, for a creative environment at institutions of higher learning, but I would like to raise the question of how an individual worker might attempt to make his or her own work more creative.

Achievement, recognition, and exposure to new, challenging problems are the environmental factors stimulating the personal qualities of competence, self-confidence, and curiosity (respectively). An individual worker cannot easily control these factors, although an agency executive can do much about these factors. But note that Pelz gives equal weight to competence, self-confidence, and curiosity, whereas many schools and agencies tend to regard competence alone. Curiosity may be stimulated by raising questions of what is not known in order to seek information and solutions about it. This should be a routine procedure in the helping professions, defining the nature and scope of the problems and seeking information about them.

Self-confidence may be developed through achievement, but Pelz notes that when one supervisor alone had the major voice in deciding a technical person's assignments, his performance was poor. Whereas when the technical person shared decision making jointly with his superior or jointly with his colleagues, his peformance was substantially better (Pelz, 1972, pp. 10, 11). Translating this to the context of the helping professions, we can borrow Pelz' term of "multiple channels of decision and evaluation" to suggest that the worker should have some say as to the types of problems he wants to work with; also, evaluation of an assignment should be based on multiple procedures, such as the objective procedure discussed in Chapter 17, subjective ratings by clients and supervisors—as well as self-ratings, with discussions of discrepancies. Another source of self-confidence would come from fellow professionals in conferences and through publication of creative practice wisdom. Pelz suggests that early publication or presentation is a potent factor in self-confidence but one that is currently underplayed. (The journals rightly stress empirically founded presentations, but there should be a professional vehicle for articulated practice wisdom, perhaps presentations by practitioners, and some reaction sections by others attempting to formulate conceptualizations of these innovative experiences.)

Concerning competence itself, Pelz raises some questions whether competence is really being taught effectively, as higher education seems to stress teaching rather than learning by putting the responsibility of transmitting standard-sized packages of knowledge on the instructor rather than on the learner. Pelz mentions some individual-sized self-paced modules of learning which require active rather than passive learning. The focus is on learning how to learn, how to be flexible in the face of unknown problems. Students take the initiative and are motivated by seeing the relevance for actual complex problems, and yet there are multiple channels of decision making and evaluation. Creative students are likely to be creative workers.

The Paradox of Creativity in the Helping Professions

While our culture and our times value the creative person in the general sense, it is well to recognize that not all cultures and times have valued creative rule-breaking. More to the point, not all subgroups within our own professional helping culture value these activities which are intrinsically in opposition to the structures which others—often our superiors—have built through their creative processes. Creativity has associated with it a certain degree of tension not only in the production but in its reception by one's peers and clients. The creative person is the one who not only manages to stick by his insight but who is able to produce evidence for it.

SUMMARY: Rules for Rule-Breaking

1. No rule is forever; be open to better formulations of tradition.
2. Not everything new is better; be willing to test the effectiveness of new and old, but also be willing to entertain **anything** in your mind's eye, so long as you are willing to look their consequences in the eye.

3. Assume that full individualization of any specific client will demand creative solutions; be willing to look for them and to take the risks involved in finding them.
4. Creativity demands adequate information as its basis, but be creative in locating adequate information.
5. Creativity involves combinations of available information in ways that project to some new outcome presumed to be desirable for the client (and society); be willing to trace out the most likely outcomes, not just for the immediate but also in the future; not just for the client, but also for society; not just the expected but also the unanticipated.
6. Creativity is part of life, part of the system of events that acts—or can be caused to act—on the client and his situation; be willing to kill a creative idea that has the probability of doing more harm (to the system of events which surround the client) than good (for the client alone).
7. Creativity comes more than once and wears many guises; expect many aspects of helping to require creative solutions.
8. Creativity grows with practice; be willing to admit your own creative gestures and be observant as you increase them in practice.

CHAPTER 17

Worker Accountability:
A Problem-Oriented Evaluation Procedure

Repeatedly there has been implied the primitive fear that if we name what we know the magic will disappear from it, that if we eat of the tree of knowledge, the Eden of intuitive arts will be lost to us.
—H. H. Perlman (Social Work, 1964, 9:3, 54)

Doing social work without systematic evaluation throughout the entire process is like driving a car with your eyes closed—you're going places but you don't know for certain where you are or what you did that got you there, to say nothing of being a hazard while you're in motion. A major goal of social work has often been described as helping the client—individual, group, or community—toward effective social functioning. The client counts on the helping professional for preventive assistance, direct treatment intervention, and/or maintenance of functioning. All aspects of social work—education, practice, research, administration—are vehicles to this end. If this is what really counts in social work, why don't we count it?

Evaluation, in the most general sense, refers to a planned comparison between an ideal reference point (a goal) and the current state of affairs regarding an event. Evaluation in the helping professions entails attaching symbols to events in order to reach decisions. Usually these symbols are words. We often say words to the effect that "he's getting along better" or "he's getting along much better." These evaluative phrases do communicate, albeit vaguely. We are here concerned with attaching numbers to events in order to reach decisions more precisely. By assuming that events behave as if they possessed the properties of the numbers, we can calculate in numbers in order to generate information about events. This information is then used to help make decisions. However, it is never numbers alone that make decisions; it is rather how the helping professional uses this information.

This chapter has three central tasks. First, it will present a frame of reference for evaluation in the context of practice. As introduced in Chapter 9, evaluation is the third component of scientific practice, along with professional action and information. (Chapter 21 will present the integration of these three major elements.) Second, a procedure will be suggested to attach numbers to events in order to gain the precision which measurement systems afford. Third, the topic of how helping decisions may be made more scientifically by the use of such measurement information will be discussed.

EVALUATION: THE THIRD COMPONENT OF SCIENTIFIC PRACTICE

Six aspects of evaluation in scientific practice will be illustrated in this chapter (see Fig. 17-1). The first aspect is the verbal attempts of the client to describe the problems and of the worker to understand what he means. A large number of problems may be communicated, intentionally or not. In this stage of evaluation, the worker tries to gain some perspective on the size of the problems, their character and interrelationships, so that when she focuses on objective measurements of these problems, her efforts may be proportional within the system of problems and circumstances.

The second aspect is the collection of objective and precise information **before** intervention, so as to establish a baseline of comparison as the worker moves into the intervention phase. The third aspect of evaluation is the continued collection of the same data during intervention. The fourth aspect of evaluation is the analysis of the data regarding the intervention **process**—that is, to reflect the on-going course of events in comparison with strategy expectations and to use this as feedback information to correct practice as needed—and regarding the **product** of intervention—that is, in terms of the overall outcome of intervention.

The fifth aspect of evaluation is a follow-up beyond the intervention period,

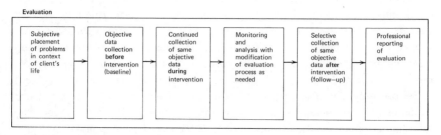

Figure 17-1—Schematic diagram of six aspects of evaluation in scientific practice.

using selective data comparable to the earlier data collection to learn whether the adaptive changes of the service period are being maintained without the worker's assistance. The sixth aspect is the professional reporting of the evaluation either to the agency records for accountability purposes or to the professional literature as a contribution to the growth of scientific practice.

A PROBLEM-ORIENTED EVALUATION PROCEDURE

It is important to note that evaluation is called for where choices among alternatives in professional services are presumed to make a difference in the functioning of the client. Where there is no viable choice, where treatment is mere custody, there would be little need to evaluate. Knowing the rate and direction of change of problem events in the life of the client can influence the quantity and quality of professional intervention. Continuing evaluation thus implies continuing hope of affecting treatment favorably. In a word, evaluation is a continual process essential to scientific problem solving and hence essential to every act of the helping professional.

Evaluation can be a pain in the neck, too. It may divert time, energy, or money from the pressing needs of clients. Worst of all, evaluation may tell us more than we want to know about how well the client is doing as a result of our service or the total impact of a service program or agency. However, pressure for evaluation—accountability—comes mainly from society, which requests more **evidence** than our goodwill or our untested assumptions about how successful we are; or from those who say just the opposite, that the helping professions are so weak and social science so puny that scientific criteria of successful outcomes would be prematurely applied to our work.

The present discussion is focused on evaluation of the helping professional's work with his client. This is a very limited part of research on the helping professions (see, for example, Bergin and Strupp, 1972), yet it is a vital topic, for its purpose is to enable the individual practitioner to evaluate his services as part of his on-going practice. Full-scale control-group design research must also be done, but these complex projects give little feedback to the day-to-day problems of the vast majority of helping professionals. The measurement procedure suggested below is one attempt to become more nearly objective in assessing the effects of our practice on clients (see also Davidson and Costello, 1969; Stuart, 1971; Revusky, 1967; Kiresuk and Sherman, 1968). Any such procedure simplified for general use necessarily makes certain assumptions in its construction and represents a crude approximation of the kinds of measurements the helping professions so badly need.

And what shall we evaluate? If we are to evaluate whether we have been successful as helping professionals, then minimally we must be able to specify clearly how the client's problems or aspirations have been affected by our efforts. The evaluation procedure suggested below does not assume any specific theory is to be used to guide practice, but it does require that the problematic events in the client's life be clearly identified and monitored throughout the course of the service. We may construct and use any **concepts** we wish in theorizing about the case, but we must help resolve the client's **problems**, namely, the **events** in himself or his situation defined as problematic. It is action against these clearly specified events which is to be evaluated, however these events are gathered together under the rubric of one concept or another. We may choose our theories wisely or unwisely—that is another story; for now, we deal in evaluation of an individual practitioner's efforts.

The Problem-Oriented Evaluation Procedure in a Nutshell

Evaluation will involve asking how many, with what pattern, or to what degree these problematic events occur or potentialities remain unfulfilled, before and after our intervention. Each of these and other questions can be approximately measured so that we can begin to tell whether our intervention was related to more or less of the problem event.

In brief, the problem-oriented evaluation procedure—which I will call PEP for short—seeks to do the following:

1. To identify the preintervention nature and level of the problem
2. To monitor the same events during the intervention period (regardless of what theoretically guided practice is used)
3. To compare the number of problematic events during the intervention period with the proportion of those events beyond a typical range of occurrence during the preintervention period, by reference to Tables 17-1, 17-2, and 17-3 in order to ascertain whether or not significant changes have occurred
4. To evaluate whether the changes conform to intervention plans or not, so as to decide whether to do more or less of the intervention in order to reach the goals in the case

Case Examples of a Problem-oriented Evaluation Procedure

In this section, a number of cases will be presented to illustrate how the PEP might be applied in a variety of situations. These are actual (but disguised) cases conducted by first-year social work students. I am emphasizing the evaluation procedure rather than the practice methods for purposes of this chapter.

Alan Antipathy—An "Acting Out" Problem in School (Treatment of One Person)

Alan's teacher referred him to the school social worker because he was, in her words, an "acting out" problem. When pressed by the social worker, the teacher clarified what she meant: (1) Alan hit other children; (2) he made inappropriate noises which disrupted the class; and (3) he talked back to the teacher. These are all the problems with which the teacher wanted assistance— if there were other problems, presumably the teacher felt she could handle them —and so these are the events we will want to deal with in practice.

Step 1. **The preintervention nature and level of Alan's problems.** In discussing the nature of the specific problems involved in acting out, the teacher said that each was about equally problematic and that they were interrelated—one tended to lead to the others. In determining which problematic events to observe and to count, the worker and the teacher decided to record any instance of any of these three events as one unit of problem behavior. (Under other conditions, it might have been useful to observe each event separately.) When plotted in Figure 17-2, the clear picture of Alan's acting out emerges. It becomes possible to say not merely that Alan was worse on the sixth day, but, more precisely, there were five counted instances in which Alan acted out (hit, made noise, or talked back), as opposed to his more typical pattern of acting out behaviors that occurred two, three, or four times for most of the other days.

Notice some basic characteristics of the graph in Figure 17-2. The horizontal line is divided into equal time units relevant to the situation at hand. The vertical line is divided into units of problem behaviors—numbers in this case, although it could be rates or percentages of problem occurrences as well. And,

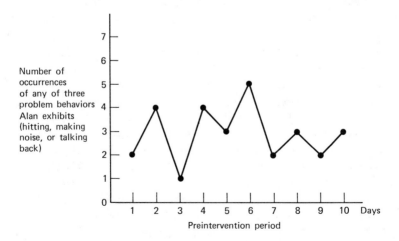

Figure 17-2—Tracking Alan's acting out behaviors during the preintervention period.

finally, note that the problem behavior was clearly specified as to how it would be recognized, regardless of what concepts were used to guide the observations in the first place.

After ten days, the teacher states that the graph portrays a fairly typical picture of Alan's behaviors. We can end the preintervention period of collecting baseline information when we are confident that a relatively **typical** and **stable** pattern of behaviors has been observed. If there were external factors influencing Alan at this time, if there were great fluctuations in behavior, or if circumstances required more evidence before taking action, one could extend the preintervention period. But taking this ten-day period, let us now identify the nature of the problem.

The procedure is simple; we are trying to identify what is typical in a set of problem behaviors.

a. Count the **number of time units** on the horizontal line. (This is ten in Alan's case. Do **not** count the number of individual acts: two the first day, four the next. . . .)

b. Next, we identify the typical range of problem events where typical range refers to a statistical pattern like the middle two-thirds of a normal curve— plus and minus one standard deviation from the mean. To find the middle two-thirds, divide the number of time units by three and multiply the divided by two. (For Alan, this would be 10 divided by 3, which is 3.3; and then 3.3 times 2, which is 6.6.)

c. Draw lines enclosing the nearest approximation to this **middle** range of problem behaviors. The nearest whole number to 6.6 is 7, but as is often the case there is no way to enclose seven events representing a typical middle range in Alan's case. Figure 17-3 represents one solution, the reasons for which will become clearer shortly. We **must** leave at least one event above and below the typical range in order to calculate proportions needed in Step 3.

d. Indicate the nature of the three zones thus distinguished. The middle range of problem behaviors is represented by the nearest approximation to two-thirds of the stable baseline distribution of problem occurrences; this is what the teacher expects as typical problem behavior from Alan. The desired behavior zone includes at least one event from the preintervention period and represents the zone in which the goals of intervention appear. In Alan's case, this zone includes one and zero occurrences. Even if the teacher's goal is to have zero occurrences of problem behavior, we must include the entire zone in our calculations because we must start from where the client is in evaluation as well as in practice. The extremely undesired behavior zone includes those behaviors worse than typical. Because it is

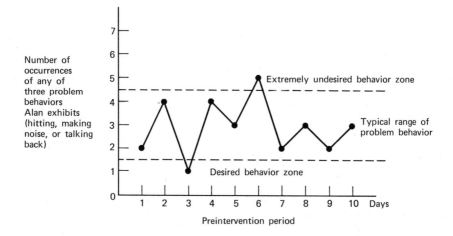

Figure 17-3—Tracking Alan's acting out behaviors during the preintervention period, with the typical range of problem behaviors indicated, along with a desired behavior zone and an extremely undesired behavior zone.

possible that the intervention may be harmful, we must be able to indicate when matters have become significantly worse. When there is a choice in approximating the middle range of behaviors, as in Alan's case where we might include either the six occurrences of 2s and 3s or the eight occurrences of 2s, 3s, and 4s—both being one unit away from the approximate middle range of seven occurrences—we must let the nature of the problems determine our choice. In Alan's case, the question is where to draw the line in distinguishing extremely undesired behaviors, whether to include 4s and 5s (and over), or just 5s (and over). In this case, the problem is how many cases of extremely undesired behavior would be needed to demonstrate significant deterioration, a topic discussed later.

Step 2. **Monitoring during intervention.** Now the worker is ready to intervene. She knows that a stable problem behavior is present. Perhaps she has sat in the classroom for a period of time and acted as a reliability check on the teacher's count of Alan's acting out behavior. She makes her plans, using the best available information from the literature, and the intervention begins. The teacher continues her cooperation by counting problem behaviors as before. In Alan's case, the actual intervention plan involved verbally reinforcing appropriate behavior and putting a star on a publicly displayed chart for all students (including Alan) who earned it each day by their appropriate behavior. The results of this intervention program are tracked in Figure 17-4.

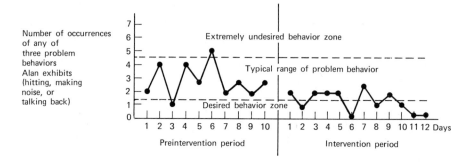

Figure 17-4—Comparing Alan's acting out behaviors during the preintervention period with those of the intervention period.

Step 3. Comparison of preintervention and intervention period events. Now the question arises: How statistically likely is a set of events that occurred during the intervention period to have occurred by chance alone? This question is one form of the statistician's null hypothesis, comparing what might have happened by chance with an alternative hypothesis, that is, that the worker's intervention affected the events in a planned way. (This is a one-directional hypothesis, assuming a positive outcome; we must be prepared to test for a negative outcome, using a two-directional test, as will be discussed below.) This question is answered by the following procedure:

a. On how many occasions during the preintervention period was the client's behavior in the desired zone? (For Alan, it was 1 time out of 10, or a proportion of .10 which is the number of desired instances divided by the total number of occurrences during the preintervention period.) Look at Table 17-1 and locate the left-hand column labeled **Proportion,** which stands for the proportion of observations of the type considered during the preintervention period. The proportions are listed in steps of .05, with several common fractions also included for convenience.

b. How many time units are in the intervention under consideration? Locate **Number** which stands for the total number of observational units during the intervention period. The numbers run by 2s up to 20 and by 4s up to 100. Figure 17-4 shows twelve time units in the intervention period with Alan. Note that the intervention period begins at day one, not at day eleven continuing from the preintervention period.

c. Enter the body of Table 17-1 at the intersection of the proportion of occurrences during preintervention and the total number of time units in the intervention period. (In Alan's case, these numbers are .10 and 12, respectively, and the cell entry is 4.) The table shows the number of occurrences of a specific type—in this case, the number of desired occurrences of fewer-than-typical acting out behaviors—during the intervention period that are necessary to represent a significant increase at the .05 level over the proportion of such occurrences during the preintervention period. Actually the cell entry means 4 or more—5, 6, 7, 8, 9, 10, 11, or 12—any one of which would be a significant increase beyond the .05 level of significance. Figure 17-4 reports six out of twelve occurrences of acting out behaviors were below Alan's typical pattern and thus the pattern of events showed a statistically significant improvement.

Step 4.   Evaluation of results. The intervention plan was designed to reduce acting out behaviors by systematic use of positive reinforcements. This pattern of reduced acting out behaviors did occur after the initiation of the intervention plan, and, by using the statistical procedure in connection with Table 17-1, we are able to say that such an event could have occurred by chance less than five times in one hundred. Evaluation of results involves an **inference**, that within the context of the client-worker situation and the conceptualized network of events that constitute the individualized plan of intervention, the occurrence of the desired pattern of events leads to support for the **hypothesis** that the worker's efforts were the likely **cause**. There is no necessary connection between a statistically significant event and causation, but it is by inference, within the context of a theory, that we can entertain such a hypothesis. We continue to use this causal inference in the development of other hypotheses to be tested in practice. We also look for other possible events which might have influenced the outcome and which, if found, would challenge our inference of worker causation (cf. Campbell and Stanley, 1963 and also Chapter 15 of this book). We might, as was done in the work with Joan, the shy kindergartner who had experienced severe burns (Chapter 8), remove the planned intervention and observe the outcome under these conditions. If acting out behavior were to reappear, it would lend further support to the causal hypothesis and give further direction to next interventions.

Thus, evaluation of practice is always an inference based on empirical events, and it involves a degree of risk. The risk is minimized by tying the hypothesized causal links closely to practice and testing the outcomes of events frequently. The statistical procedure may be used to monitor the intervention—to continue current plans if satisfactory progress is being maintained or to change into a new phase or plan when the conditions call for it. These conditions might be when a plan is not working sufficiently well or when it is working well but has reached a plateau in its capacity to change events. These will be illustrated with later examples.

If the results should show only a trend in the right direction rather than statistical significance, the worker is free to use this information any way he chooses. Statistics provide an indication of the degree of risk he undertakes if he continues the intervention plan unchanged. By continuing to collect data, the worker will learn how far behind he is falling from the **possibility** of significant improvement. At some point society will require an accounting in tangible terms; both quality services and quantitative evaluation are being demanded of the modern helping professional.

Mr. and Mrs. Brandywine—An Alcoholic Husband and a Bored Nagging Wife
(Treatment of a Couple with Problems Contingent upon the One's Reaction to the Other)

This case is complicated by the fact that the couple didn't want to discuss their problems or to be involved in a treatment process to any large degree. They did define the immediate problems they both felt were causing the greatest amount of distress, namely, the husband's drinking, the wife's nagging, and the wife's feelings of boredom. Mr. and Mrs. Brandywine recognized that these problems were interrelated, and so they were persuaded to keep track of all of them so that they could demonstrate to themselves whether or not they had dealt with their problems. Unfortunately, Mr. Brandywine entered the hospital with acute appendicitis and was therefore out of the home for a large portion of time so that only a count of Mrs. Brandywine's feelings of boredom is presented (Figure 17-5), although it still reflects her life in interaction with her children and her husband.

In Figure 17-5, there are twenty-one days in the preintervention period; 3 into 21 is 7 and 2 times 7 is 14. The best approximation to fourteen middle-range occurrences is indicated in Figure 17-5, and the proportion of occurrences in the desired zone (few feelings of boredom) is 4/21 or .19. Note that there is no .19 listed in Table 17-1. Likewise, note in Figure 17-6 that the intervention

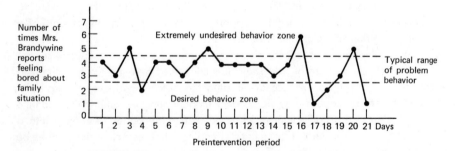

Figure 17-5—Tracking of Mrs. Brandywine's reported feelings of boredom regarding her family situation during the preintervention period.

period consisted of twenty-seven days; there is no number 27 listed in Table 17-1 either. To have listed all proportions and all numbers would have resulted in very long tables; instead we must interpolate using a conservative rule (one which operates against the worker attaining an easy statistical significance): **Use the next higher proportion and the next higher number.** Let us see why this is a conservative rule. Look at the cell entries at the intersections of proportion .20 and fraction 1/6 and the numbers 24 and 28—where Mrs. Brandywine's figures fall. Had we used the lower proportion (fraction, in this case) or the lower number, the cell entry would have been a lower number and hence it would be easier to attain statistical significance. Thus by using the next higher proportion and the next higher number, we make it most difficult for a worker to attain statistical significance, the most conservative interpolation rule we might devise.

Figure 17-6 shows the patterns of feelings of boredom Mrs. Brandywine reported during the intervention period. A plan was devised for getting her to interact more with friends and neighbors, after analysis showed that feelings of boredom were associated with being alone. (By adding contextual notations to the graph in Figure 17-5, the worker was able to identify the antecedent and consequent conditions that were associated with feelings of boredom. This analysis was the basis of the strategy which the worker used.) Figure 17-6 shows that Mrs. Brandywine reported occasions of feeling bored seventeen out of twenty-seven times below the typical range of these problematic feelings set in the preintervention period. Reference to Table 17-1, using modified proportions and numbers as indicated by the interpolation rule given above, shows that there is significant change at the .05 level. Ten occasions were needed, while seventeen were reported.

In fact, the difference between what was expected for significance at the .05 level and what was observed is so great that we wonder whether the results are even more significant, that is, whether results such as this could not have occurred by chance alone in one time in a hundred (.01) or one

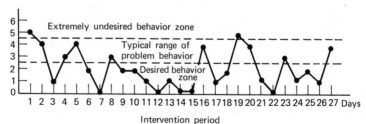

Figure 17-6—Tracking of Mrs. Brandywine's reported feelings of boredom regarding her family situation during the intervention period (compare with Figure 17-5 preintervention period).

time in a thousand (.001). Tables 17-2 and 17-3 are designed exactly as Table 17-1, except that the former provide information at these more stringent levels of significance. Using the same proportion and number as before (.20 and 28), we observe the cell entries in Tables 17-2 and 17-3 as 12 and 14, respectively. Our observed seventeen is larger than these numbers, indicating that the worker can claim statistical significance at greater than the .001 level.

The practical importance of having three levels of statistical significance—.05, .01, and .001—is to strengthen the claim that the observed change in the direction planned by the worker is less and less likely to have happened by chance alone. This provides stronger evidence for the inference of method efficacy. (However, as discussed in Chapter 12, there are some risks of setting the confidence level too stringently.)

As in many client situations, there are multiple problems at work in the lives of the Brandywines. There are two options regarding evaluation of multiple problems: either to take each problem singly or to suspend judgment until all problems have been attacked and then make a combined judgment. Say, for example, that the worker also dealt with the nagging and the drinking problems, and attained significant results with the former but not the latter. Two out of three problems would thereby have been significantly improved, and on one no significant change. This permits a kind of batting average to be constructed across clients in general, or with particular types of problems. For example, at this point the worker is batting .667—the proportion of significant positive improvement in client problems. Or the worker is batting 1.000 on feelings of boredom and nagging types of problems, and .000 with drinking problems, of which there have been one instance of each case. Of course, both types of accounting may be kept.

The case of Mrs. Brandywine also brings up some problems in getting clients to participate in counting their own behaviors as part of an accurate analysis of the problem and an important part of evaluation. The task of counting cannot be made too cumbersome, lest client and worker get discouraged, but without some basic information, both client and worker are running in the dark. Participation by the clients in the data collection may have a side benefit of giving them a responsible role in their own help. Awareness of the causal factors may itself produce changes in these factors, as the client records them day after day. Sometimes naturally occurring counts of events are available to the worker, such as the gradebook of the teacher, the family calendar of events, the spaces in a contraceptive pill dispenser, etc. Other times, the worker's ingenuity is tapped to discover the unique measurement opportunities for a client situation. But if an event occurs, then it occurs in some amount or form, and if it occurs in some amount or form then it can be counted.

Carla Cacophony and Her Parents and Siblings—Measurement Within a Family Problem Situation (Multiproblem Evaluation)

Carla is an attractive 13-year-old girl with average intelligence, but she is doing very poorly in school in part because she never does her homework. Her mother came to the family agency requesting assistance because Carla was making life hellish at home. She was reported to be causing arguments with everyone in the family, her parents, her older sister Carol (who soon left for college and was effectively out of the picture), and her older brother Calvin. Carla would throw temper tantrums, embarrassing her parents in public places. She also had few friends and frequently verbalized how dumb and ugly she was.

In trying to get some perspective on the problems in this family situation, the worker helped the parents to decide to work first on the arguments provoked by Carla and second on her homework difficulties. These were two major sources of trouble, and so simultaneous records were kept on their presence. These records were simply charts placed on the refrigerator door where the parents would indicate publicly how much of each event occurred, with a high degree of reliability and validity. See Figures 17-7 and 17-8 for the preintervention data.

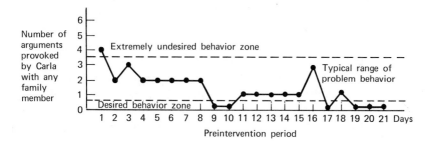

Figure 17-7—Tracking of Carla's arguments with members of her family during preintervention period.

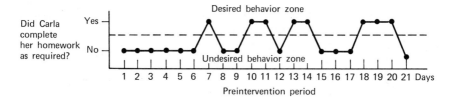

Figure 17-8—Tracking of Carla's completion of homework during preintervention period.

Inspection of Figures 17-7 and 17-8 **together** reinforces the hunch that these two problems are interrelated: periods of relatively few arguments are associated with periods of homework completed. Thus, graphing of relevant factors may serve as a stimulus to thinking about the conceptualization of problems.

Another nonobvious and perhaps nontrivial observation from the graphs is the indication of a trend toward decreasing numbers of arguments and increasing numbers of homework assignments completed during the preintervention period. It may be that the few conversations with the worker and/or the presence of a public chart indicating the occurrence of defined problems may be therapeutic in their own right. This kind of contamination of the measurement procedure is not a problem in evaluation for the helping professions for two reasons. First, this is what the clients desire as a goal and it may be happening merely through their heightened awareness of the situation, but, second, the larger proportion of desired behaviors in the preintervention period makes it more difficult for a worker to achieve statistical significance within the evaluation procedure.

There might occur another type of problem with upward or downward trend data such that what looks like no change may be quite important. For instance, a client who is becoming increasingly ill may be maintained at the statistically typical range by professional efforts. While the PEP procedure would likely show no significant improvement, the very fact that the client did not continue to get worse must be taken into account. This is a genuine problem with the procedure which could be managed with additional mathematical procedures, but I have chosen to accept as an equal risk maintaining a client in the face of upward or downward trends, since in the long run these conditions would tend to balance out on showing success or nonsuccess in client movement. Thus, my suggestion is to use the PEP even with data showing trends upward or downward because of the long-run balancing out and because of the simplicity of the method.

Notice that the homework event of Figure 17-8 is treated as a dichotomy. The user should feel free to fit the spirit of the evaluation procedure to the nature of the events in question. The use of the trichotomy with its specification of the typical range of problem behaviors, is an artificial device to identify how much change toward improvement may be considered significant, namely, that much change which is significantly different from the typical. But dichotomies and, as we shall see, even predetermined goals (and predetermined proportions) can be selected when the situation calls for them. Likewise, it is appropriate to begin with a dichotomy in the preintervention and to move to a trichotomy in the intervention period as one becomes able to make finer distinctions.

Returning again to Carla and her family, the worker created a family-oriented behavior modification plan that involved each member in an inter-contingent manner. A contract was drawn up and signed by all members of the family, specifying the goals and the specific actions and reinforcements that were involved for each. The data resulting from this program are presented in Figures 17-9 and 17-10. Family arguments are reduced significantly (at the .05 level), but notice what happens to Carla's homework.

During the preintervention period Carla was none too good about doing her homework, completing it only eight times in twenty-one occasions for a proportion of .38. But, during the intervention period, she completed her homework only once in twenty-one times, which raises the question of whether there was significant deterioration present. Could such poor results have appeared by chance alone, or was the intervention the major factor? Helping professionals do not like to think about iatrogenic illness, that is, illness caused by treatment, but as Stuart (1970) has pointed out, such events can be documented and must be faced squarely.

To locate the significance of deterioration, we must look at the proportion of **undesired** behaviors—in this case, the proportion of times Carla did not do

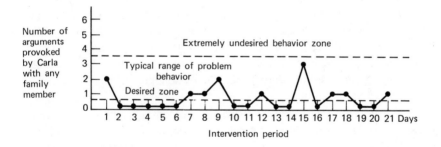

Figure 17-9—Tracking of Carla's arguments with members of her family during the intervention period.

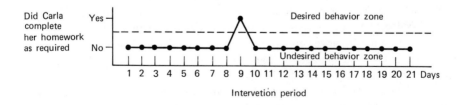

Figure 17-10—Tracking of Carla's completion of homework during the intervention period.

her homework during the preintervention period. This is thirteen times out of twenty-one, or .62. (Of course the combined proportions of desired behavior at .38 and the undesired behavior at .62 must total 1.00. If the situation were one in which events were trichotomized, then the proportion would be that of the extremely undesired behaviors as compared with both the typical range and the desired behaviors combined.) For a significant increase in **undesired** behaviors during the intervention period, the interpolated proportion (.65) and number (24) require a cell entry of 20. Since Carla in fact had twenty such undesired events, we must indicate that there was a significant deterioration at the .10 level during this period. Tables 17-1, 17-2, and 17-3 are designed for tests of positive change, as this is the direction of the helping hypothesis, that events will get better. Strictly speaking, the helping professional should use a two-directional hypothesis, that the effects of intervention may be either beneficial or harmful. The same tables can be used to test such hypotheses, only that the level of significance such as .05 is then viewed on both ends of the distribution requiring us to combine them (.05 positive end to .05 negative end is .10), when the hypothesis says that either significant improvement or significant deterioration may occur.

In general, the procedure to locate significance of deterioration is simply to look at the proportion of undesired behaviors (rather than the usual procedure of looking at the proportion of desired behaviors) and find the cell entry of how many of these undesired behaviors occurring in the intervention period would constitute a significant increase in undesired behavior. One would be wise to consider the deterioration test whenever there was a lower proportion of desired events during the intervention period than in the preintervention phase.

Several important points may be made with reference to the case of Carla and her family. First, it should be noted that the worker did obtain a significant positive change in the reduction of family arguments. But **statistical significance** is not the objective of evaluation in the helping professions; it must be combined with **practical significance** which concerns attainment of the goals of the case. In the Cacophony family, one goal was to reduce family arguments to a very low level; the data in Figure 17-9 shows only a first successful step in the right direction. The next stage of intervention may continue to move toward the practice goal through means of more or different methods, but in order to test for significant movement in the second intervention period, the worker would use the first intervention period as a new baseline for comparison by constructing new ranges of typical behaviors and desired and undesired zones. This achieves a step-function for successive approximations of the practice goal. At each step, the worker has to improve the results over the succeeding step to achieve new significance.

The worker must also deal with the facts of significant deterioration (from Figure 17-10). The worker was collecting the data each day and was able to see the family process in operation, almost the reversal of the preintervention pattern where now an absence of family arguments is associated with no homework completed. The worker obviously chose to place a higher value on solving the family argument issue, while letting the homework slide during this intervention phase, before he changed the contract in the next intervention period. The worker may also have had empirical, theoretical, or practice wisdom information that supported his emphasis on resolution of family conflicts before attacking homework problems. Whether the decision was a wise one or not, the worker made it with precise information from his evaluation procedure, fully knowing the risks he was taking. Only the long-term disposition of the case can reveal whether this made a difference in the overall results and then only by inference. (A more complex design would have been needed to single out one factor's influence. See Browning and Stover, 1971.)

Don Doppelganger—An 11-Year-Old Boy Institutionalized for Severe Emotional Disturbance (Measurement in an Institutional Setting)

In this situation, the worker had to practice by instigational means (working with the resident staff) and had to use indirect measurement (collecting data by phone). Don had lived in this private mental hospital for the previous two years, the culmination of a long line of institutional placements. All the staff agreed that Don's most serious problem was loud, obnoxious behavior, which included yelling, throwing things, swearing, stomping, all extreme and inappropriate to given situations.

During the preintervention period, the staff were asked to count the number of times Don was loud and obnoxious and to record the time of each occurrence so that the amount of time between each problematic event could be determined. It happened that Don had an inappropriate outburst about every 7 minutes in the classroom and every 15 minutes in his dormitory. The intervention plan called for stretching the amount of time between outbursts, thus in effect reducing the outbursts and increasing self-control. A timer was carried around set for 10-minute periods in the classroom and 20-minute periods in the dormitory (until bedtime); if Don lasted a period of time without an outburst, he received a token which was redeemable for certain goods and activities which he especially enjoyed. Later intervention periods increased the length of time in which no outbursts were to be recorded in order to get the reinforcements. The various staff people were enlisted and trained to count the outbursts and to bestow the token reinforcers. Figure 17-11 shows the combined preintervention and intervention periods. The very brief preintervention period reflected a crisis situation. In desperation the director of the hospital was going

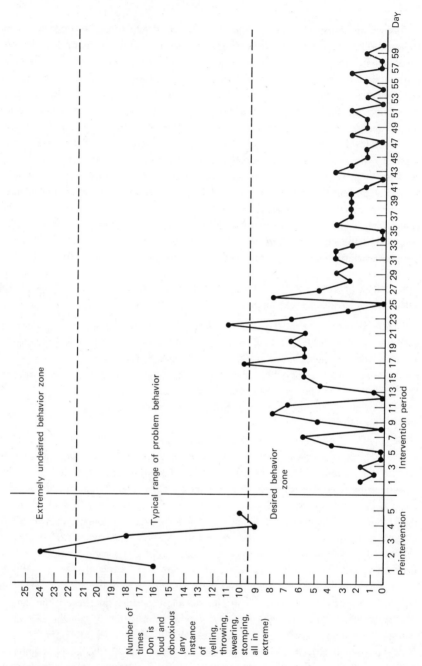

Figure 17-11—Tracking Don's loud and obnoxious behavior during both preintervention and intervention periods.

to send Don to the state hospital. The student worker requested a chance to work with him, and she was given only a short period of time.

By inspection of Figure 17-11, we can observe that the intervention was remarkably successful, both in statistical and practical terms. With 58 out of 60 occasions in the intervention period in the desired behavior zone, Table 17-3 indicates that the requirements for a .001 level of significance have been far exceeded. But there are several other points that can be made in reference to these data. Recall that the worker was monitoring these events by phone most of the time. Notice the peaks on the sixth and the tenth days. Investigating the sudden appearance of the peaks, the worker discovered that Don had stolen some tokens and wasn't working for his reinforcement of appropriate behavior. A change of tokens returned Don's behavior to acceptable levels.

But then, again, in the next week, another peak emerged. The student worker studied the intervention plan in action the next time she was at the hospital and discovered that the housing staff were not clear on the distribution of tokens and were unintentionally subverting the therapeutic regimen. By careful detective work using statistical information, the student worker was able to correct the intervention plan and attain remarkable success with a boy the professional staff had considered hopeless.

Having graphic tangible evidence of effectiveness convinced the administrators of this hospital to give Don another chance. Keeping the staff persons informed by means of the graph helped to motivate them to maintain the regimen. Monitoring of the results at a distance helped the worker to use her professional skills most effectively and economically, to identify nascent problems in the therapeutic design, and to resolve them before they caused serious trouble.

Toward a Scientific Selection of the Length of Intervention

Looking again at Figure 17-11, we can ask another question of the data: How long should a worker continue one strategy plan? Or, put another way, when is the earliest occasion on which statistical and practical significance converge, indicating that the worker should consider terminating this phase of intervention or adding new ones to move the client further? Because of the seriousness of Don's problems, the worker may have chosen to use the most stringent statistical significance level available, the .001 level. Given the proportion of events in the desired zone during preintervention, namely, .20, we can observe in Table 17-3 that the worker would have to continue at least six days even to begin to consider the question of significant results and that she would have to find all six occasions in the desired zone.

Figure 17-11 shows that this in fact occurred. Should the worker have considered changing her intervention plans at this point when statistical significance has been reached at the .001 level? There are several considerations. First, if the intervention period behaviors were stable at desired levels, with no alternative explanations other than intervention as presumed cause, then it would be appropriate to consider changing to another phase of intervention. (In Don's case, it might have been working on aspects of his behavior that might be directed toward living outside an institution.) Second, if there had been a long history of undesired behaviors, if the intervention period events were not stable, if other events happening concurrently could be influencing the client's behaviors, then the worker would be justified in continuing this phase of intervention even though it had achieved a high level of statistical significance. Third, even if the worker were not sure of being in control of the situation to the degree indicated statistically, she might take the risk of introducing a new phase of intervention on the grounds that the consistency of the data does indicate meaningful changes in problem behavior. Once client movement has started, it might be wise to try to keep that movement going. If the worker is premature in starting a new phase, the data will so inform her so that she may return to the previous plan and continue to consolidate these gains before moving on.

In general, Tables 17-1, 17-2, and 17-3 can provide some rational determination of changes in interventive plans, a use which will become increasingly important as **efficiency** of delivery of services becomes as important as **effectiveness** of outcome.

In principle, the PEP is applicable at all levels of social behavior, including the problems dealt with by community organizers, recreational workers, and others dealing with large groups or organizations. For example, it would be easy to collect the attendance records of a senior citizens club, a PTA, or other group, before and after some intervention, in order to assess its level of functioning (for example, as indicated by the number of persons attending). Likewise, the number of products arising from such organizations could be measured before and after intervention, such as the number of activity groups for older persons in operation or the number of petitions sent from the local PTA to the Board of Education on behalf of the school. Even the concrete successes might be counted, such as number of regular attenders at new activities at the senior citizens, or the money actually spent on the local school as a result of lobbying by the PTA.

However, there are complications in dealing with numbers of persons as a unit. If the attendance is larger after intervention, one should be certain that it isn't hostile audiences tearing down the structure. But vaguely defined goals at the larger group levels are not sufficient to deter measuring outcomes, anymore than the same vaguely defined goals at the individual level carry any weight on the scales of social justice and accountability.

Bootstrap Evaluation: What to Do When You Don't Have Data from a Preintervention Period

There will be occasions when a helping professional will not be able to obtain information before intervention. For example, in the case of Don Doppelganger, a crisis had burst and he was about to be expelled unless it was proven that his obnoxious behavior could be controlled. But even with a very brief baseline—with its attendant risks of not being an accurate reflection of preintervention behavior—the worker was able to use observations very effectively.

Even if no preintervention period information is obtainable at all—if the client or others refuse to cooperate in collecting such data—there is still a final recourse. In essence, the worker picks a proportion over which she would like to see some improvement. For example, say a client has been experiencing long periods of anxiety each day. One behavioral event desired in such a case would be to have the client experience increasing portions of the day without anxiety. We do not know, as no preintervention information was collected, what proportion of the preintervention period was free of anxiety, but, based on some value judgment, we might say that we would like to have the client free from anxiety at least a third of each day, as a begininng goal of service. Referring to Table 17-1, if our intervention period was fourteen days, then nine of those days would have to show at least one-third of the time free from anxiety in order to claim a success compared with our selected goal. Now, if in fact a preintervention period had a proportion of say .20, then the corresponding number of days needed to claim successful intervention would have been only six (as contrasted to nine days required with a proportion of .33).

Thus, the general effect of using a bootstrap operation, without collecting preintervention data, is often a weakening of the worker's claim to successful intervention. Correspondingly, the client is required to produce more in order to exhibit statistical significance and while higher aspiration levels may be themselves influential in producing change, a level too high may inhibit change. The judgment as to what goal to set—.33 or .50, or .99—is important although it has influences not clearly understood in the helping professions. Because of these reasons, it is strongly suggested that preintervention data be collected as often as possible as part of the clear construction of the case as well as for evaluation purposes; otherwise, bootstrap operations will tend to work against the professional and will have an unknown effect on the client.

Follow-Up Research on Individual Cases

One critical stage of problem solving (as discussed in Chapter 11) is the termination phase, when the goals of intervention are stably attained and when there is some assurance of continuity of this desired state of affairs after the helping professional leaves the scene. Follow-up evaluations are methods of assessing this continuity and can be handled by the individual practitioner in one of two basic ways.

Projecting the zones of the last measurement period into the follow-up period, a worker could collect a set of consecutive data. The number of such data would be whatever minimal number is necessary for the given proportion of desired behaviors in the preintervention period. (For example, with a proportion of .25, one would need to obtain a minimum of four observations for testing a significance level of .01 but would need a minimum of six observations for the .001 level.) One could, of course, collect more than this number of observations. Or the worker could collect samples of data on randomly scattered times after intervention closes, and treat them as an aggregate, as described above.

Follow-up data are possibly the strongest data the helping professions could assemble, as they indicate the long-term effect of intervention when the clients are presumably back in their natural environments. Unfortunately, the topic of follow-up studies by individual practitioners is practically unheard of in the professional literature.

Validity and Reliability of the PEP

A potential user of any measurement procedure should ask for certain critical information, such as the reliability and validity of the procedure. In the case of the problem-oriented evaluation procedure, the critical information on reliability and validity is—or can be—built into the data collection process itself. Let me illustrate with reference to the case of Don Doppelganger, the 11-year-old boy institutionalized for severe emotional disturbance. The staff of the institution all agreed about Don's more serious problems of yelling, throwing things, swearing, and stomping, carried on in extreme degree and inappropriate to given situations. What would it mean to collect reliability and validity information about this case?

The term reliability is taken to mean consistency of behavior throughout a series of measurements. Applying this psychometric definition to the practice situation, we can ask whether a client's behavioral problems are consistent over time. Earlier I spoke of stability of behavior during the preintervention period— so that a reliable picture of the client's problems might be obtained. We can also ask whether several qualified observers agree on the manifestations of the problem. With Don, the entire staff easily agreed that his obnoxious behaviors were clearly observable. To be sure, the worker might have asked several staff persons to observe Don **independently** during the same period of time and to compare their observations. The worker could have arrived at a statistic indicating degree of agreement among staff observers; this would have constituted reliability.

Validity is more complicated. In psychometrics, the validity of a test concerns "**what** the test measures and **how well** it does so" (Anastasi, 1968, p. 99). Sometimes the names of tests or the names of dimensions on tests are misleading; an "anomie" test does not measure anomie as such but rather presents scores on specific questions chosen to reflect a concept labeled "anomie." The "depression" scale of the MMPI does not measure depression as such but rather presents scores empirically predictive of persons known by other, independent means to be depressed. In the same way, theories and the practices of practitioners are not valid simply because their names—"ego-supportive casework" or "behavior modification"—label important events. How can we know the validity of practice?

Psychometricians suggest several types of validity. First, content validity asks whether the specific set of events (such as the preintervention sampling of problems) is representative of the total problem picture. It is relatively easy for Don's houseparents or the teachers who have known him reasonably well for two years to assent to the impression that a preintervention period sampling is representative of the total picture. If the sampling is representative, then the worker can move into the intervention period. If not, then a longer preintervention period would be necessary in order to be more representative.

Another type of validity refers to use of an evaluation. The administrator of the hospital at which Don was placed wanted to know whether Don was functioning sufficiently well to be kept at this hospital or whether he needed to be sent to the state institution—an admission, in this case, of failure to provide therapy for Don. There are two ways of making such judgments: How was Don doing in other spheres of life at the same time that the worker was intervening against selected obnoxious behaviors? And how would Don do in the future with reference to these obnoxious behaviors? To be more specific, the worker might have inquired about Don's concurrent work in his classes, or whether present interventive efforts would predict to a stable pattern of appropriate behaviors in the future. The data show a fairly stable pattern of appropriate behaviors (relative to Don's past record) going into the third month after intervention began, a strong picture of valid effects on the predictive criterion, although nothing was said about other concomitant behaviors like schoolwork.

The final type of validity commonly discussed by psychometricians is construct validity, which refers to the extent to which a test relates to the set or system of concepts, that is, whether empirical events behave in a manner consistent with a theoretical portrayal of events of that type. In the case of Don, perhaps the best we can do is to find an independent event predicted by a system of abstract concepts and to see whether the realities of Don's situation conform. Independent of the worker's efforts were the hospital administrator's actions regarding keeping or sending Don to another hospital. It is a logical consequence of successful intervention that Don be maintained in a treatment setting consonant with his chances of being helped. Thus, the decision to keep Don at the present treatment setting (perhaps a more likely place for effective treatment than the state hospital) is a type of independent confirmation of the validity of successful outcomes as measured by the PEP procedure itself.

So as not to give the impression that Don's situation was all sweetness and light, it must also be reported that at a middle stage of the intervention period, he became more demanding of the staff. "I want you to come here, now!" The staff found this behavior objectionable and included it as part of the behaviors to be extinguished, and it was, over time. However, the logical prediction of the theory guiding the treatment was that no new problem behaviors would appear—assuming that such assertiveness of a long-time institutionalized patient was pathologic. Since it was defined as problematic by the staff, we must conclude that the evaluation procedure showed the intervention to be limited, so far as events did not conform fully to the theoretical network of ideas.

In general, we have yet another example of the need to translate ideas from a scientific enterprise to a helping context. The translation is not one to one, but must be modified by the nature of the helping context. We are at the beginnings of this important effort.

Limitations

The problem-oriented evaluation procedure presented here is subject to many limitations. First, the assumptions that problems of clients may be conceptualized and dealt with in observable or reportable events may be a difficulty for some types of theories or approaches. If so, I think this is perhaps more a weakness of the theory than of the measurement procedure, but I recognize the limiting usage such restrictions might impose. Yet it cannot be stressed too strongly that a client's problems exist in terms of the problematic **events** in his life, not the abstract concepts of our theories. At some point in our theorizing about a case, we must come down to earth and say specifically and clearly what it is we are trying to affect in a positive way. If we cannot say this is how the client will behave when we have affected his "quasi-structural superego-oriented dynamic interactional alloplastic inhibition," then we should strongly consider dropping that concept from our working tools. This is no joke: If we cannot specify some of the basic concepts in a network of concepts with clear behavioral precision, then we are frauds. I say **some** basic concepts, for it may be that certain hypothetical constructs may be used to create a logical network of ideas which themselves cannot be directly operationalized, but no science can long sustain the use of such terms without progress toward behavioral precision. The critical test is this: Whenever you use a concept as descriptive of a client's problem or the goals of intervention, can you identify specific observable events with sufficient clarity that another worker, taking your place, would clearly and distinctly know what you were talking about from your case record? Not "communication breakdown," but at least the number of times mother and father contradict one another in disciplining child, by direct messages or by qualifying metacommunications—events on which observers could agree.

Second, there are a number of assumptions which are questionable from a strictly statistical point of view, such as an assumption of the preintervention period being a population of independent events against which intervention period events are tested as samples. It is likely that the preintervention period events are also samples, but this is a matter of debate and, in any case, I am again willing to compromise a degree of purity in statistical assumptions for practicality of usage.

In the third place, it is readily admitted that the PEP procedure is a simple-minded approach, a fairly weak statistical procedure relative to some; but I have not found as workable a procedure for helping professionals that required less in the way of demands on the worker and therefore would be more likely to be used in the cumulation of relatively objective data. Further, PEP is a beginning point, not an end in itself. The issues of values added to statistical results and of inferences made to caused patterns have been joined only; much more remains to be said—and done—on this point.

SUMMARY

The problem-oriented evaluation procedure suggested here for immediate and cumulative use by the individual practitioner may be summarized as follows:

1. Identify the preintervention nature and level of the problems by
   a. Counting the number of time units in which data were collected
   b. Finding the middle two-thirds of this number of time units (by dividing by three and multiplying the dividend by two)
   c. Enclosing the closest approximation to the middle two-thirds by dashed lines
   d. Indicating a zone of desired behaviors, extremely undesired behaviors, and a typical range of problem behaviors (or any other arrangement of desired and undesired behaviors, such as a dichotomy)

2. Monitor the same events during the intervention period
3. Compare the **number** of problematic events during the intervention period with the **proportion** of those events during the preintervention period by
   a. Finding the number of time units having events in the desired zone during the preintervention period and dividing this number by the total number of time units during the same period, which gives the proportion of those events
   b. Identifying the number of time units in the intervention period
   c. Choosing Tables 17-1, 17-2, or 17-3, depending on one's choice of level of significance relevant to the problem at hand
   d. Using the conservative interpolation rule when either proportions or numbers at hand are not found in the tables, by going to the next higher proportion and/or the next higher number
   e. Finding the intersection of the proportion of occurrences during the preintervention period and the total number of time units during the intervention period in the tables, the cell entry indicates the minimum number of occurrences of a specific type necessary to present a significant increase at the table level
4. Evaluation of statistical results in reference to practice goals
   a. A statistical result on a single problem indicates whether or not a significant change has occurred. The information may be used as a basis for deciding whether to continue or to discontinue the currently used mode of intervention or to move into another phase of intervention.
   b. The measured pattern of problematic behaviors must be compared with the projected pattern of behaviors defined by the goals of intervention in order to determine whether progress toward that goal is being made expeditiously or not. By considering the first intervention period as a comparison unit for a second intervention period, a step-function of measurements may be obtained, leading to measurement of successive approximations of the desired practice goal.
   c. Comparison of a single problem within the context of multiple problems may be handled either separately or as a combined batting avarage of the separate problems.

Table 17-1

Table Showing the Number of Observations of a Specified Type (e.g., a Desired Behavior) During the Intervention Period that Are Necessary to Represent a Significant Increase at the .05 Level Over the Proportion During the Preintervention Period.[a]

Proportion	4	6	8	10	12	14	16	18	20	24	28	32	36	40	44	48	52	56	60	64	68	72	76	80	84	88	92	96	100
.05	2	2	3	3	3	3	3	4	4	4	4	5	5	5	6	6	6	7	7	7	8	8	8	8	9	9	9	10	10
.10	3	3	3	4	4	4	5	5	5	6	7	7	8	8	9	9	10	10	11	12	12	13	13	14	14	15	15	16	16
1/8	3	3	4	4	5	5	5	6	6	7	8	8	9	10	10	11	12	12	13	14	14	15	15	16	17	17	18	19	19
.15	3	3	4	4	5	5	6	6	7	8	8	9	10	11	12	12	13	14	15	15	16	17	18	18	19	20	21	21	22
1/6	3	4	4	5	5	6	6	7	8	8	9	10	11	12	13	13	14	15	16	17	18	18	19	20	21	22	22	23	24
.20	3	4	5	5	6	6	7	8	9	9	10	11	12	13	14	15	16	17	18	19	20	21	22	23	24	25	26	27	28
.25	4	4	5	6	7	7	8	9	9	11	12	13	14	16	17	18	19	20	22	23	24	25	26	27	29	30	31	32	33
.30	4	5	6	6	7	8	9	10	10	12	13	15	16	18	19	21	22	24	25	26	28	29	30	32	33	35	36	38	39
1/3	4	5	6	7	8	9	9	10	11	13	14	16	18	19	21	22	24	26	27	29	30	32	33	35	36	38	39	41	42
.35	4	5	6	7	8	9	10	11	12	14	15	17	18	20	22	23	25	27	28	30	31	33	35	36	38	40	41	42	44
3/8	4	5	6	7	9	10	11	12	13	14	16	18	19	21	23	25	26	28	30	31	33	35	37	38	40	42	43	45	47
.40	4	5	6	8	9	10	11	12	13	15	16	18	20	22	24	26	28	29	31	33	35	37	38	40	42	44	46	47	49
.45	4	6	7	8	9	10	11	13	14	16	18	20	22	24	26	28	30	32	34	36	38	40	42	44	46	48	50	52	54
.50	—	6	7	9	10	11	12	13	15	17	19	22	24	26	28	31	33	35	37	40	42	44	46	48	51	53	55	57	59
.55	—	6	8	9	10	12	13	14	16	18	21	23	26	28	31	33	35	38	40	43	45	48	50	52	55	57	59	62	64
.60	—	6	8	9	11	12	14	15	17	19	22	25	27	30	33	35	38	41	43	46	48	51	54	56	59	61	64	66	69
5/8	—	—	8	10	11	13	14	16	17	20	23	26	28	31	34	37	39	42	45	47	50	53	55	58	61	63	66	69	71
.65	—	—	8	10	12	13	15	16	18	20	23	26	29	32	35	38	40	43	46	49	52	54	57	60	63	66	68	71	74
2/3	—	—	8	10	12	13	15	16	18	21	24	27	30	33	35	38	41	44	47	50	53	56	58	61	64	67	70	72	75
.70	—	—	—	10	12	13	15	17	18	21	25	28	31	34	37	40	43	46	49	52	55	58	61	64	67	70	73	75	78
.75	—	—	—	—	12	14	16	17	19	22	26	29	32	36	39	42	45	48	52	55	58	61	64	67	71	74	77	80	83
.80	—	—	—	—	—	14	16	18	20	23	27	30	34	37	41	44	47	51	54	57	61	64	68	71	74	78	81	84	87
5/6	—	—	—	—	—	—	—	18	20	24	27	31	35	38	42	45	49	52	56	59	63	66	70	73	77	80	83	87	90
.85	—	—	—	—	—	—	—	—	20	24	28	31	35	39	42	46	49	53	57	60	64	67	71	74	78	81	85	88	92
7/8	—	—	—	—	—	—	—	—	—	24	28	32	35	39	43	47	50	54	58	61	65	69	72	76	79	83	86	90	94
.90	—	—	—	—	—	—	—	—	—	—	—	32	36	40	44	47	51	55	59	63	66	70	74	77	81	84	88	91	95
.95	—	—	—	—	—	—	—	—	—	—	—	—	—	—	—	—	—	—	60	64	68	72	76	80	84	88	91	95	99

[a] Tables of the Cumulative Binomial Probability Distribution—By the staff of the Harvard Computational Laboratory, Harvard University Press, 1955. Table constructed under the direction of Dr. James Norton, Jr., Indiana University–Purdue University at Indianapolis, 1973.

Table 17-2

Table Showing the Number of Observations of a Specified Type (e.g., a Desired Behavior) During the Intervention Period that Are Necessary to Represent a Significant Increase at the .01 Level Over the Proportion During the Preintervention Period.[a]

Proportion	Number																												
	4	6	8	10	12	14	16	18	20	24	28	32	36	40	44	48	52	56	60	64	68	72	76	80	84	88	92	96	100
.05	3	3	3	4	4	4	4	5	5	5	6	6	6	7	7	7	8	8	8	9	9	9	10	10	10	11	11	11	12
.10	3	4	4	5	5	5	6	6	7	7	8	9	9	10	11	11	12	12	13	13	14	15	15	16	16	17	17	18	19
1/8	3	4	5	5	6	6	6	7	7	8	9	10	11	11	12	13	14	14	15	16	16	17	18	18	19	20	20	21	22
.15	4	4	5	5	6	7	7	8	8	9	10	11	12	13	14	14	15	16	17	18	18	19	20	21	22	22	23	24	25
1/6	4	4	5	6	6	7	8	8	9	10	11	12	13	14	14	15	16	17	18	19	20	21	22	23	23	24	25	26	27
.20	4	5	6	6	7	8	8	9	9	11	12	13	14	15	16	17	18	20	21	22	23	24	25	26	27	28	29	30	31
.25	4	5	6	7	8	9	9	10	11	12	14	15	16	18	19	20	22	23	24	25	27	28	29	30	32	33	34	35	36
.30	4	6	7	8	8	9	10	11	12	14	15	17	18	20	21	23	25	26	27	29	30	32	33	35	36	38	39	40	42
1/3	—	6	7	8	9	10	11	12	13	15	16	18	20	21	23	25	26	28	30	31	33	34	36	38	39	41	42	44	46
.35	—	6	7	8	9	10	11	12	13	15	17	19	20	22	24	26	27	29	31	32	33	36	37	39	41	42	44	46	47
3/8	—	6	7	8	9	11	12	13	14	16	18	19	21	23	25	27	29	31	32	34	36	38	39	41	43	45	46	48	50
.40	—	6	7	9	10	11	12	13	14	16	18	20	22	24	26	28	30	32	34	36	38	40	41	43	45	47	49	51	53
.45	—	6	8	9	10	12	13	14	15	17	20	22	24	26	28	31	33	35	37	39	41	43	45	47	49	51	54	56	58
.50	—	—	8	10	11	12	14	15	16	19	21	24	26	28	31	33	35	38	40	42	45	47	49	51	54	56	58	60	63
.55	—	—	8	10	11	13	14	16	17	20	22	25	28	30	33	35	38	40	43	45	48	50	53	55	58	60	63	65	67
.60	—	—	—	10	12	13	15	16	18	21	24	26	29	32	35	37	40	43	46	48	51	54	56	59	62	64	67	70	71
5/8	—	—	—	10	12	14	15	17	18	21	24	27	30	33	36	39	41	44	47	50	53	55	58	61	64	66	69	72	73
.65	—	—	—	—	12	14	15	17	19	22	25	28	31	34	37	40	43	45	48	51	54	57	60	63	65	68	71	74	75
2/3	—	—	—	—	12	14	16	17	19	22	25	28	31	34	37	40	43	46	49	52	55	58	61	64	67	70	73	75	78
.70	—	—	—	—	—	14	16	18	19	23	26	29	32	35	38	42	45	48	51	54	57	60	63	66	69	72	75	78	81
.75	—	—	—	—	—	—	—	18	20	23	27	30	34	37	40	44	47	50	53	57	60	63	66	70	73	76	79	82	86
.80	—	—	—	—	—	—	—	—	20	24	28	31	35	38	42	45	49	52	56	59	63	66	69	73	76	80	83	86	90
5/6	—	—	—	—	—	—	—	—	—	—	28	32	36	39	43	46	50	54	57	61	64	68	71	75	78	82	85	89	92
.85	—	—	—	—	—	—	—	—	—	—	—	32	36	40	43	47	51	54	58	61	65	69	72	76	79	83	87	90	94
7/8	—	—	—	—	—	—	—	—	—	—	—	—	36	—	44	48	51	55	59	62	66	70	74	77	81	85	88	92	96
.90	—	—	—	—	—	—	—	—	—	—	—	—	—	40	44	48	52	56	60	63	67	71	75	79	82	86	90	94	96
.95	—	—	—	—	—	—	—	—	—	—	—	—	—	—	—	—	—	—	—	—	—	—	—	—	—	—	92	96	100

[a] Tables of the Cumulative Binomial Probability Distribution—By the staff of the Harvard Computational Laboratory, Harvard University Press, 1955. Table constructed under the direction of Dr. James Norton, Jr., Indiana University–Purdue University at Indianapolis, 1973.

Table 17-3

Table Showing the Number of Observations of a Specified Type (e.g., a Desired Behavior) During the Intervention Period that Are Necessary to Represent a Significant Increase at the .001 Level Over the Proportion During the Preintervention Period.[a]

Proportion	Number 4	6	8	10	12	14	16	18	20	24	28	32	36	40	44	48	52	56	60	64	68	72	76	80	84	88	92	96	100
.05	3	4	4	5	5	5	5	6	6	6	7	7	8	8	9	9	10	10	10	11	11	11	12	12	12	13	13	14	14
.10	4	5	5	6	6	7	7	8	8	9	10	10	12	12	12	13	14	14	15	16	16	17	18	18	19	19	20	21	21
1/8	4	5	6	6	7	7	8	8	8	10	11	12	12	12	14	15	16	17	17	18	19	20	20	21	22	23	23	24	25
.15	4	5	6	6	8	8	9	9	10	11	12	13	14	15	16	17	18	18	19	20	21	22	23	24	25	25	26	27	28
1/6	4	5	6	7	8	8	9	10	10	11	12	14	15	16	17	18	19	20	21	22	23	24	25	25	26	27	28	29	30
.20	—	6	7	7	8	9	10	10	11	12	14	15	16	17	19	20	21	22	23	24	26	27	28	29	30	31	32	33	34
.25	—	6	7	8	9	10	11	11	12	14	16	17	19	20	21	23	24	26	27	28	30	30	32	34	35	36	37	39	40
.30	—	6	8	9	10	11	12	12	14	15	17	19	21	22	24	26	27	29	29	32	34	35	37	38	40	41	43	44	46
1/3	—	—	8	9	10	11	13	13	14	16	18	20	22	24	26	27	29	31	33	34	36	38	39	41	43	44	46	48	49
.35	—	—	8	9	10	12	13	14	15	17	19	21	23	25	26	28	30	32	34	35	37	39	41	42	44	46	48	49	51
3/8	—	—	8	9	11	12	13	14	15	17	20	22	24	26	28	30	31	33	35	37	39	41	43	45	46	48	50	52	54
.40	—	—	8	10	11	12	13	15	16	18	21	22	25	27	29	31	33	35	37	39	41	43	45	47	49	49	52	54	56
.45	—	—	—	10	12	13	14	16	17	19	22	24	26	29	31	33	35	38	40	42	44	46	49	51	53	55	57	59	61
.50	—	—	—	10	12	13	15	16	18	20	23	26	28	31	33	36	38	40	43	45	48	50	52	55	57	59	62	64	66
.55	—	—	—	—	12	14	16	17	18	21	24	27	30	32	35	38	40	43	46	48	51	53	56	59	61	64	66	69	71
.60	—	—	—	—	—	—	16	18	19	22	25	28	31	34	37	40	43	45	48	51	54	57	59	62	65	68	70	73	76
5/8	—	—	—	—	—	—	—	18	20	23	26	29	32	35	38	41	44	47	50	52	55	58	61	64	67	71	72	75	78
.65	—	—	—	—	—	—	—	18	20	23	26	29	33	36	39	42	45	49	51	54	57	60	63	66	69	71	74	77	80
2/3	—	—	—	—	—	—	—	—	20	23	27	30	33	—	39	42	46	49	52	55	58	61	64	67	70	73	76	79	82
.70	—	—	—	—	—	—	—	—	20	24	27	31	34	37	40	44	47	50	53	56	60	63	66	69	72	75	78	81	84
.75	—	—	—	—	—	—	—	—	—	—	28	32	35	39	42	45	49	52	55	59	62	65	69	72	75	79	82	85	89
.80	—	—	—	—	—	—	—	—	—	—	—	32	36	40	43	47	50	54	58	61	65	68	72	75	79	82	85	89	92
5/6	—	—	—	—	—	—	—	—	—	—	—	—	—	40	44	48	51	55	59	62	66	70	73	77	80	84	88	91	95
.85	—	—	—	—	—	—	—	—	—	—	—	—	—	40	44	48	52	56	59	63	67	70	74	78	81	85	89	92	96
7/8	—	—	—	—	—	—	—	—	—	—	—	—	—	—	—	—	—	—	—	64	68	71	75	79	83	86	90	94	97
.90	—	—	—	—	—	—	—	—	—	—	—	—	—	—	—	—	—	—	—	—	68	72	76	80	84	88	91	95	99
.95	—	—	—	—	—	—	—	—	—	—	—	—	—	—	—	—	—	—	—	—	—	—	—	—	—	—	—	—	—

[a] **Tables of the Cumulative Binomial Probability Distribution**—By the staff of the Harvard Computational Laboratory, Harvard University Press, 1955. Table constructed under the direction of Dr. James Norton, Jr., Indiana University–Purdue University at Indianapolis, 1973.

CHAPTER 18

Computers and the Helping Professions

Before we get into a discussion of computers and the roles they may play in social work, let me present an excerpt of a conversation between a patient and her therapist (Weizenbaum, 1966). The lines are numbered for discussion purposes later:

1. **Patient:** Men are all alike.
2. **Therapist:** In what way?
3. **Pt:** They're always bugging us about something or other.
4. **Th:** Can you think of a specific example?
5. **Pt:** Well, my boyfriend made me come here.
6. **Th:** Your boyfriend made you come here?
7. **Pt:** He says I'm depressed much of the time.
8. **Th:** I am sorry to hear you are depressed.
9. **Pt:** It's true. I am unhappy.
10. **Th:** Do you think coming here will help you not to be unhappy?
11. **Pt:** I need some help, that much seems certain.
12. **Th:** What would it mean to you if you got some help?
13. **Pt:** Perhaps I could learn to get along with my mother.
14. **Th:** Tell me more about your family.
15. **Pt:** My mother takes care of me.
16. **Th:** Who else in your family takes care of you?
17. **Pt:** My father.
18. **Th:** Your father?
19. **Pt:** You remind me of my father somewhat.
20. **Th:** What resemblances do you see?
21. **Pt:** You are not very aggressive but I think you don't want me to notice that.

22. **Th:** What makes you think I am not very aggressive?
23. **Pt:** You don't argue with me.
24. **Th:** Why do you think I don't argue with you?
25. **Pt:** You are afraid of me.
26. **Th:** Does it please you to believe that I am afraid of you?
27. **Pt:** My father is afraid of everybody.
28. **Th:** What else comes to mind when you think of your father?
20. **Pt:** Bullies.
30. **Th:** Does that have anything to do with the fact that your boyfriend made you come here?

I have frequently asked groups of social workers and students how they would rate this excerpt as a professional interview. Did the therapist attend to what to client was saying? Was the therapist aware of feeling and did he respond to it? Did the therapist grasp the cognitive picture as the client was describing it? Did the therapist come across as having nonpossessive warmth, accurate empathic understanding, and genuineness? Most people, upon hearing this excerpt, give the therapist average to good grades, and they are usually very surprised to learn that the therapist is a computer.

Obviously, this raises all sorts of questions, and these questions should be raised: depersonalization, mechanistic mind control, and . . . technological unemployment of helping professionals. Whether or not the computer lives up to its infamous or fantastic reputation by the year 2001, it behooves social workers to be aware of its potential and to take an active part in shaping that future.

How do you suppose that the computer was able to respond so reasonably and humanly and professionally to the patient? That is a long story (or series of stories; see Loehlin, 1968) and a complex one. The small portion which I am able to tell in this chapter has been selected to serve the practitioner who will not be likely to program computers, but who will be likely—and in the near future—to use the services of computers and computer personnel, for administrative purposes, for research, for retrieval of selective information, and, perhaps, for assistance in interventions.

To many citizens of the twentieth century, computers are still a mystery even though as devices that take data, apply ruleful processes to them, and supply the results of these operations, computers have been around for centuries. Though the mechanical and electronic forms have become infinitely more complex and rapid, the same basic functions occur in all computers. First, there is an input device to take in information. The information concerns events important to someone; these are translated into a form that the computer can understand, such as the punched cards whose pattern of holes permitted certain patterns of electrical impulses to enter the machine. (These cards were named after Dr. Herman Hollerith who designed them for aid in compiling the 1890 census, borrowing an idea developed by a French weaver, Joseph Jacquard, in 1801, for automating looms.)

The second major portion of computers has several elements. The first functional component is a memory unit in which information that has been put in is stored and to which the computer has constant access (like a human memory). A second functional component is the processing unit which deals with the set of instructions that controls what the computer is to do with the data at each stage of the process—this is called a control unit—and the actual manipulation of the bits of data—this is called the arithmetic unit. The set of instructions comes from a plan or program written by the programmer. Essentially, a program involves a set of symbols in a specified order which supplies the computer with all the needed information by which to do its operations. These operations, like adding or comparing one symbol with another, are built into the workings of the computer, just as people have genetic possibilities for performing certain acts.

What goes on inside the black box of the computer is not of direct concern to the helping professional, although it is a fascinating story (cf. Lehman and Bailey, 1968). Electrical impulses have the capacity to be in an on or off state. Notation developed that utilized these states to represent information about events. The binary mode has two digits, a one and a zero. Numeric and alphabetic symbols have been translated into patterns of binary digits, or bits. For example, here are some translations:

0 (zero) is translated as 000000
1 is 000001
2 is 000010
3 is 000011
A is 110001
B is 110010

Long strings of 1s and 0s can be handled by the computer at incredible speeds and great accuracy, enabling one to have access to large amounts of information in very short spaces of time.

The machine operator pushes the button to start the machine. The computer reads the first piece of information and performs the appropriate action; then it reads the second and does the appropriate thing, and so on until it is told to stop. Computers are basically very stupid, but they are loyal, trustworthy, reverent, and brave—as well as objective, flexible, and fast. They will churn out whatever they are told to do, including garbage if the programmer has made a mistake. It all depends on the person instructing the machine with program and raw data, given the natural capacities of the computer itself. (And this means whatever is praiseworthy or blameworthy must be attributed to the person controlling the computer.)

Because all this still may be foreign to the reader, I would like to present a homey personification of a program interacting with a computer. Each paragraph represents, more or less, a set of punched cards containing information that the computer goes through one at a time.

First, let me identify myself as a paying customer of yours.

Second, let me tell you to clear the decks so as to be ready to perform some arithmetic operations I call "obtaining mean scores" which you already know how to do. Look at such and such a location in your memory so as to exercise this natural talent of yours.

Third, I will now give you a set of symbols representing dollars given to people during the last month. I want you to keep them all in mind and when I am through, I want you to add them all up and divide this sum by the number of sets I give you.

Fourth, to make things interesting, I would like you also to remember which type of person got how much money, for example, how much money went to persons under 21 years of age or over 65 years; how much to married persons with children, to married persons without children. I will define each of these categories so you will know exactly which I mean.

Fifth, then, when you get the answers to these questions, I want you to compare them with the answers to the same questions I gave you last month and the twelve months previously, and give me information about trends in money expended. This is how I want you to do it. . . .

Sixth, here is the first set of symbols, now the second. . . . OK, that's all. Stop and do your calculations. Although I would like to ask you many more questions, I know from past experience that this will use up the money we have allocated to buy your services, so please print out all my answers neatly on a piece of paper and give them to me to think about (to justify my existence to the powers that be) (to attempt to improve the conditions of the downtrodden masses) (etc.)

And the computer, true to its nature, quickly calculates the means for the various subgroups requested and the totals, withdraws from its electronic memory previous answers, makes the comparisons in expenditure trends, and prints out the answers. It does not say anything about why we have welfare systems; it just tells the story like it is. The magnitude of this effort may not have dawned on you, but consider: If there were 1,000 welfare recipients on the average per month, each receiving varying amounts of money, some changing the categories to which they belong (by getting married or divorced, by aging, by death. . . .), it would have taken Bob Cratchit, working every day including Christmas, from Dickens' time to ours just to get one month's data calculated. Those were not the good old days. Computers will come to be increasingly used in a wide variety of housekeeping functions now typically performed by secretaries and social workers in welfare settings (cf. Vassey, 1968). And by thinking broadly as to what constitutes housekeeping functions, it may be possible that case records themselves might be put onto computer tapes rather than written and transcribed. . . . Please, no cheers. (See Kleinmuntz, 1969, instead.)

Computers are often used in research work, and social work students have been known to get in on some of the action: key punching, simple card sorts and counts, and maybe more. This is a topic that will be given increasing attention in the research area. The reader is referred to current books on research design utilizing computers such as Phillips, 1971.

Another use of computers will be discussed in the chapter on information resources and retrieval. This is an exciting new chapter in social work, and none too soon; the tidal wave of the information crisis is getting nearer and nearer the helping professional.

I would next like to consider briefly the possible role of the computer in social work practice. Consider the example of the development of a state-wide adoption system (Allen and Horniman, 1969). The problem is that this situation involves a large number of children in the charge of various agencies in the state who are to be placed for adoption. These children have, as a group, a fantastic number of individual characteristics which prospective adoptive families would like to know about. A working hypothesis might be that the more adequate the information about an adoptive child, the better the placement is likely to be, other things being equal. This means that adoptive families will have better information on which to base their decisions to adopt and will choose a child that most nearly fits their desires.

Basically, two sets of information are needed: one, descriptions of the children; the other, about the prospective adoptive parents and their wishes. Put them together and we increase the probability of the right child being connected with the right adoptive family. But what is "right"? This requires exact specification of characteristics and wishes or values. In the example about mean dollars spent on welfare, the units of analysis (dollars) were constant and known.

But "rightness" in adoption involves a series of value judgments, beginning by defining the characteristics (events) which are relevant to making that judgment. These would include, for example, age, sex, race, religion (of the biological parents), physical health (defined in a set of specific categories), psychological health (likewise carefully defined).

An adoptive family might specify that "right" for them is a baby under six months of age, a female, the same race as themselves, physically and mentally healthy; perhaps no mention is made of the religion of the biological parents. Classification of these choices is in principle no more complex than requesting an air flight on a particular airline, going to a particular place at a particular time, flying on a particular class of flight, and specifying the nonsmoking zone for seating. The waiting time for locating a child for a suitable adoption might be cut to a matter of minutes rather than months.

Of course, that is not all that is at stake in adoption. How likely is an adoptive family to be a good family? Characteristics from families and their experiences with adopting certain types of children might be able to generate predictors: This type of family is a poor risk given their characteristics, that type of family is an excellent risk given their characteristics. Should individual people be governed by abstract norms of behavior of people similar to themselves? This, again, is one form of the paradox of helping, that as professionals we are guided by abstractions. Not dominated by them, but guided. In a case where a risky family is identified, the worker would be more careful to analyze the situation before giving a child for adoption. But in cases where chances are very good, then there is little reason to overinvestigate.

The computerized adoption system has still other facets. Relatively large numbers of children have to be administered. There is constant motion and relocation among all manners of homes and institutions. To prevent some children from literally being lost to the authorities, the veritably infinite memory of the computer would be a valuable asset. For checking back on adopted children over time, the computer's memory again would be a valuable asset. For anticipating future trends such as changes in numbers or types of adoptive children and the consequent planning problems of where to put limited resources, computers would be valuable. For precision measurement in the evaluative studies of adoptive processes, computers would be most helpful. The technology exists today; is our social conscience far behind?

The computer may also be used to educate adoptive families. While it is able to individualize all adoptive children by their distinctive characteristics and also is able to make them all equally present to potential adoptive parents, the computer is powerless in the face of value judgments. Why is a child under six months wanted in contrast to an older child? Is this value decision based on available facts? The computer as potential reservoir of factual information may be called upon to bring vital information to the attention of adoptive families before they specify their choices—and thus limit themselves to certain adoptive children. Thus, we may dream about computers dealing with complex social networks which are doubtless currently administered, even with the best of intentions, at a lower level of effectiveness than what might be obtained. . . .

Now, let's return to the excerpt of the computer therapist. There are two separate points that might be made about this experimental situation in which an actual client would communicate with a computerized therapist: What about the effectiveness of the therapy and what of the educational value to beginning students to have not only the communication statements between therapist and client before them but also the communication principles on which the therapist's statements were based? Let's begin with the latter point, the educational value. (It's too early for data to have accrued on effectiveness of computers with clients.)

Look back to the first page of this chapter. The patient says (line 1) that men are all alike. The therapist responds (line 2) by asking in what way? A simple, reasonable interchange, but let's look at what might some day lie behind such communications. Logically speaking, the patient's statement is a universal statement. Psychologically, this might represent a working principle for the patient, a way she views the world of events in a consistent manner; all men bug. How should we respond to universal statements? I do not know what the author of the computer program had in mind by making his therapist respond as it did, but one might surmise that the principle could be this: Whenever a universal statement is made, ask for a specific example.

Had the statement been "Most men are alike," it would have been a reasonable principle to ask for the common feature of the set of "most men" that made them alike. Had the statement been "All men are different," a reasonable question would have been to ask on what aspects of humanity all men are different (since it is obvious that all men are alike in breathing air, etc.). To generalize, a higher-level principle would be that whenever a statement is made that involves "all," "most," "some," "no one," then an appropriate response is to ask for an example of the dimension on which this event is said to occur. Look also at lines 3 and 4; 11 and 12; 14, 15, and 16.

I am not saying (or denying) that this is the correct principle to derive from this example or that it is uniformly applicable in all interviewing situations, but I am suggesting that it is an illustration of a logical principle in therapeutic communication. Moreover, it may be possible to derive other logical principles and to test their effectiveness so that we may teach students to emulate successful therapists (at least in the form of their communications).

Look at other portions of the excerpt and see whether other logical principles might be inductively located. For example, when in line 5 the computer wasn't given enough information, it returned the response as a question to the patient;

the same occurs in lines 17 and 18, and possibly in lines 14, 15, and 16. Reflecting back content is an established technique, but with few rules about when it is to be most effectively applied. Perhaps the logical rule is to reflect back, at least during those times when there isn't enough information to move in another direction. Analysis of other effective therapists' techniques might generate other ideas about rules for reflecting, confronting, etc.

What about affect, reflecting back feeling, showing warmth, and such matters? Aren't computers weak on this? That depends on how you look at communications. The computer can say (line 8) that it empathizes with the client on her feeling depressed and is able to deal directly with feeling content (lines 21 through 30). But would a client feel that the computer was authentic in the sense that its messages and metacommunications about those messages were in congruence (or even that the computer had feelings or affective components of the messages it sent)? This seems to be an empirical question on which many biases are stirred. Do letters convey affective quality between the lines? If the computer were also a talking model such that the client could dial-a-therapist by phone whenever it was needed, would this kind of therapist be more liked than one who was seen only once a week or so? (With time-sharing on big computers, many clients could hold conversations with the same therapist at the same time, for all practical purposes like a chess grand master playing with a hundred challengers at one time.) The question of depersonalization is not all one-sided against the computer. . . .

Computer Simulation of a Complex Social Problem: Narcotics and the Community

One of the more important uses of the computer is to aid policy makers in the solutions of complex problems. By identifying the variables involved in the social problems and by stating their relationship to other variables, the entire complex pattern of interactions may be portrayed to a degree far beyond the construction of any one mind. The work of Levin, Hirsch, and Roberts (1972) involving a system simulation of a community area of some 180,000 persons dealing with narcotics is such an example. A computer simulation is an account of the system of events that is believed to have caused or to sustain some problem event, and it is derived, like all subjective explanations of how the world operates from facts, theories, and guesses. Each computer simulation using the best available information is complete at any one time but is always open to more information so that it becomes a flexible way of dealing with promising but tentative hunches which can be subjected to rapid logical testing.

Levin, Hirsch, and Roberts note that logical analysis can correct intuitive approaches which are counterproductive in dealing with complex problems like narcotics programs in a community. For example, many policy-makers agree that the social problems involving hard drugs consist of the number of addicts (too many), addict-related crime (too much), and the illegal presence of hard drugs (too great a quantity). One intuitive approach would involve eliminating the source of supply which, it is presumed, would lead to no addicts and hence no addict-related crimes. Analysis suggests, however, that even though this would be the long-run effect, the short-run effects would cause extremely high addict-related crimes, and it is doubtful whether society would be willing to put up with this solution. Thus, a logical analysis by computer simulation can reveal some likely events of one course of action which are not immediately apparent to intuition.

The computer simulation itself consists of the selection of variables whose effects on one another are assumed or known. For instance, a certain level of crime in an area causes outmigration of those who can afford to move and hence produces a drop in the socioeconomic level of the area, until only those who cannot afford to leave are left. Using the best available information—either the experiences of other communities or educated guessing—one can project the curve indicating the moving relationship between these two variables. The addition of other variables will modify this curve in the same sense that the elements of any system of interrelated events have interdependent effects upon each other. When a large number of variables are being studied in relationship to one another, this calls for the information storage and comparison capabilities which computers have but human minds do not. It is the human contribution to add creative combinations of variables, to recognize the implications of these projected consequences, and to make decisions congruent with them.

A policy-maker can call for computer simulations of different types and amounts of intervention plans which are presumed to have specified effects on events in reality. Things are not as they seem; some intuitive intervention schemes which will milk the public treasury masquerade as cream. For example, a methadone program may be introduced as a quick and cheap way of controlling a community narcotics problem (see Figure 18-1). Over the 300 months which this simulation projects, the following events are likely to occur: The socioeconomic level continues to drop while the total number of addicts increases sharply, although after 200 months a large portion of this population is made up of addicts on methadone. (On Figure 18-1, this would be represented by the difference between "total addicts" and "addicts on street.") The crime rate rises but it is predicted that it will level off after 250 months.

Now the same situation is again simulated but with a higher initial expenditure that is anathema to short-sighted political types; we add an educational program (designed to dissuade potential addicts from becoming addicted to

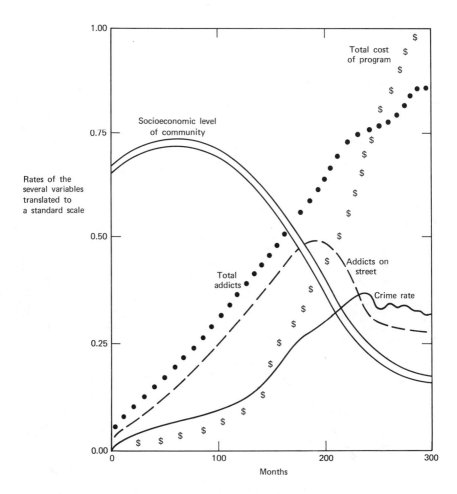

Figure 18-1—Computer simulation of police plus methadone programs used to combat drug problem (from Levin, Hirsch, and Roberts, 1972, p. 870).

hard drugs) and a community education program (to accelerate action in the community's definition of this state of affairs as a problem). Figure 18-2 shows the effects of these simulated factors. First, the community education program takes effect quickly, and the methadone program has its impact about 100 months earlier. The crime rate remains quite low. The net effects are a reduction of addicts on the street and a reduced need for police and other programs. The cost is not low, but the social value of these gains is certainly to be added to the decision-making process.

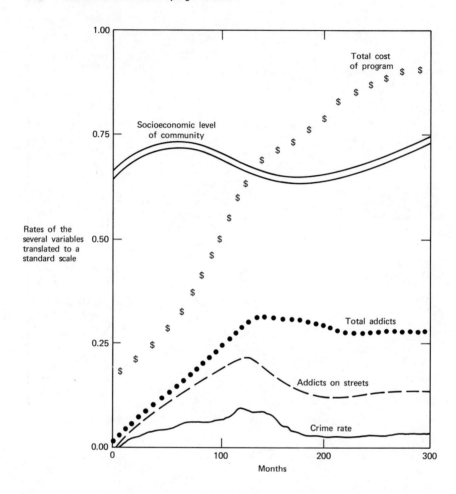

Figure 18-2—Computer simulation of police, methadone, education of potential addicts, and community awareness of drug problem programs used to combat drug problem (from Levin, Hirsch, and Roberts, 1972, p. 871).

The outcome of these still-preliminary simulations is so striking that the authors offer two broad recommendations applicable to a wide range of communities, and, I would add, to other types of problems as well:

"1. There is need for a balanced system of programs to cope with a community narcotics problem. A total program for dealing with the problem should include subprograms for rehabilitation, education, and policework directed at reducing the heroin supply. Intensive application of any one of these programs will not be nearly as effective as the balanced use of all of them.

"2. The community must perceive addiction at least in part as a social and medical problem in order for rehabilitation programs to be successfully implemented. Community education programs are required toward this end" (p. 868).

Thus, putting the best available information to work with modern technology has provided policy alternatives with predictable outcomes which are to be evaluated by decision-makers. The individualizing characteristics of different communities may easily be put into the computer run. . . .

SUMMARY

Whether with populations of events about persons (as in the illustration about state-wide adoption plans, or the previous example about identifying thyroid conditions) or with populations of persons and events (as in the instance of the projected narcotics program), the helping professions are becoming aware that the complexity of problems and interventions requires the capabilities which computers possess. With these new capabilities have come fears formerly expressed in science fiction, of the invasion of privacy or of unethical control of behavior. But every technological advance, whether it is atomic energy or the computer, offers as many chances to benefit mankind as to destroy it. The helping professions can shape this future only by knowing something of the nature of the future, from which there is no turning back.

Excerpts and modified diagrams from "Narcotics and the community: A systems simulation." AMERICAN JOURNAL OF PUBLIC HEALTH by G. Levin, G. Hirsch, & E. Roberts are reprinted by permission of the first author and the Editor. © 1972 by AMERICAN JOURNAL OF PUBLIC HEALTH.

CHAPTER 19

Instruments of Assessment for the Helping Professions

The most common instrument of counting throughout history has been man's fingers. When the ancient Egyptians realized that different men had differing lengths of fingers, they decided it was time to go to standard measuring instruments that would represent a standard finger's length, or whatever. The most advanced computers are still only an elaborate extension of man counting on his fingers. In the helping professions, we still are using our fingers per se. This chapter is but the simplest hint of possibilities when we discover how to use standard measuring instruments as extensions of ourselves. Indeed, it is more true of helping professions than of land surveyors or physicists that we must continue to remember always that measurement instruments are extensions of ourselves to be used as carefully and skillfully as we use ourselves as vehicles of intervention.

A full discussion of instruments and procedures for assessing individual, social, and physical events which are meaningful to human problems would be beyond the scope of this chapter, as there are literally thousands of such devices (see Anastasi, 1968; Bonjean, McLemore, and Hill, 1967; Buros, 1970; Cronbach, 1970; Lyerly and Abbott, 1966; Robinson and Shaver, 1969). Rather, I hope to give a rough perspective of this area, some examples of instruments currently available, and some leads for the future. Most of these measurement devices have been developed for research purposes. I want to limit this discussion to applied uses, in which values are a necessary consideration. Evaluation or assessment instruments are used by the practitioner only when their information will decidedly benefit the client's goal attainment, for example, as in data monitoring client changes. Data from these objective assessment devices would fit nicely into the problem-oriented evaluation procedure described in Chapter 17.

A FABLE

In order to give the reader an overview of the possibilities of assessment in relation to the helping professions, I offer the following fable (Bloom, 1973): Mr. Cliente del Futura is alerted by his physician that the time is ripe for an interdisciplinary health, education, and welfare care-team examination concerning his gerontological life phase. After an exploratory telephone conversation with Mr. del Futura, the H-E-W care team creates a demographic profile of their client—not "patient," for Mr. del Futura will be an active participant in his own life situation, including the various forms of care he may receive. These unchanging characteristics—date of birth, sex, race, educational and occupational history, place of birth, urban and rural experiences—locate Mr. del Futura on an integrated life table, one which shows the joint probabilities of his expected lifespan. These normative characterizations provide baseline predictors. Many factors may yet modify them as the individual characteristics of Mr. del Futura unfold. For example, longevity is one factor predicted by such life tables, and one tentative aim of the H-E-W care team is to equal or to exceed this life-table number in order to count the degree to which their services are successful (or unsuccessful). But sheer survival is only one goal among many, and it may not even be the most important goal at certain points in Mr. del Futura's life.

The laboratory-offices of the interdisciplinary H-E-W care team are in a most unlikely setting—an ordinary house in a suburban neighborhood near the client's own home. It has nonuniformed staff people and an efficiency apartment combination of kitchen, living room, bath, and recreation room as the examination rooms.

Seated in the living room, Mr. del Futura talks comfortably with the first staff person about his life—his goals and values, his satisfactions and discontents. This conversation is being tape recorded, with the staff person asking standardized questions or probing for more detail when necessary. Mr. del Futura is asked about his personal and social assets, strengths, and resources as well as his liabilities, weaknesses, and deficits. These are organized as part of a developmental picture of Mr. del Futura and his family and friends. Permission is sought and gained to have discussions with Mr. del Futura's relatives and neighbors, as well as private health caregivers as necessary, so that a rounded current and retrospective picture of the client within his milieu can be reconstructed. The client is at no time separated from his social and physical environment in this analysis and synthesis, for it may be just as important to intervene in these larger environments as it is to treat the specific client.

Mr. del Futura is videotaped as he walks about the living room and into the kitchen. From these pictures, various aspects of his gait and balance will be analyzed. His current capacities for routine activities are assessed and recorded, not only as a personal baseline for basic physical functioning but also as information about specific health care needs and as training materials for the direct service staff. The kitchen part of the examination has a number of familiar devices, handles to turn, doors to get opened, items to be retrieved from shelves. After the client's response to a problem is observed, the staff can suggest adaptive means of solving the problem. For instance, where arthritic hands cannot manage to grasp the tiny knobs on a cabinet door that is stuck, a cord loop will do quite well. Mr. del Futura is informed that all his turnings and pullings are being mechanically recorded and stored as part of his assessment package.

Mr. del Futura is invited to sample a smorgabord of preferred foods, both as a study of his nutritive interests and wisdom and his personal and ethnic variations on food and eating patterns. Mealtimes, as social situations, are assessed for their potential in the quality of Mr. del Futura's life, indicators of the meaning of social interaction and sociability. Questions are posed which assess the amount of control by others over his life functioning, an estimation of the institutionlike characteristics that are as relevant for the client's own home situation, as they are in the most Goffmanesque analysis of institutions (Goffman, 1961). Questions are posed concerning privacy, who oversees his comings and goings, and specific questions concerning control of his social, financial, and legal rights and possessions. Beginning estimates of household morale and cohesion are also being formed for later use as all the data are pulled together.

Later the client goes into the recreation room and the bathroom to try out some familiar—if out-of-place—devices. Perhaps there is a stationary bicycle; a balloon-blowing apparatus; steps to climb; a pinball-type machine in which Mr. del Futura has to match combinations of lights that appear on the board; a bathtub complete with steps, bars, chair—everything except water. (There might even be a swimming pool for the client to enjoy—as part of the assessment procedure.) The particular cluster of devices Mr. del Futura deals with depends on the tentative findings of the previous screening assessments. Some areas of functioning have aroused some suspicions and call for more detailed study.

In the bedroom, Mr. del Futura is allowed to relax as several physiological tests are conducted, including the administration of a microdata recording pill which assesses a number of internal functions and supplies the health care team with information about current biological functioning. All this information is likewise centrally recorded and combined with the other information gained previously. Discussions of sexual behavior are pursued, as are other intimate personal functionings. Attitudes, as well as knowledge, are assessed; perhaps this is one area in which reeducation might enrich his life.

Later, while Mr. del Futura chats with the assembled staff over a glass of juice to replenish the energy expended in the examination, the time-sharing computer is rapidly assembling the data, printing out tentative diagnoses and alternative courses of action. The client and staff together discuss the diagnoses and reassess the weightings on various goals, resources, and problematic conditions. For example, what values are to be assigned to living at home, given his condition, as contrasted to transferring to an institutional setting where the conditions could be more efficiently treated? How do these decisions bear on other members of his household and family? By discussing the implications of alternative plans of action, the client and staff arrive at a working plan of action.

The overall price of this diagnosis and treatment had been discussed in advance. Now, portions of the total bill are assigned to the separate subgoals. If the health care team can bring about the conditions and states described, then payment for those successes will be forthcoming, accidents excluded. Likewise, payment will be made if projected levels of education (continuing education, reeducation) are attained. Self-chosen goals and understanding the health team's suggested methods are, in combination, very motivating. Gerontological services are guaranteed within certain probability limits. The baseline data have been automatically recorded and stored and stand ready at all times for comparison on long-term outcomes or defined way-stations. The client and his family are provided with a type of actuarial support in health, education, and welfare which it is to their benefit to attain—with society deriving the benefits of a life fully and productively lived.

The assessment of client experiences indicates that Mr. del Futura is naive to care services and facilities—a testimony to the advanced state of the art of health technology. And so he returns (now or another day) to a library room and a television console which, by computer-assisted instruction, teaches him to be an effective client. Possibly these lessons can be repeated by cable television in the client's own home. Or it may be considered useful to involve the client in a discussion group with persons having related problems. In this way, Mr. del Futura can hear about a variety of alternative ways of dealing with such problems, but he can also give information about his approach that might be useful to others. Not only is the client involved in his own situation but he is also involved in helping others through the wisdom of his own experiences.

It may also be that Mr. del Futura needs continual monitoring of certain vital signs and types of functioning. Strategic placement of microelectronic devices will monitor these needed sources of information with a minimum of nuisance to the client. It is more likely that Mr. del Futura will need further assessment and monitoring of his social and physical environments as the vital arena in which his personal needs and resources are played.

The physical environment may require a prosthetic dimension, planned in connection with Mr. del Futura's diagnoses. Perhaps his problems with gait in combination with failing vision would require the relocation of furniture, the removal of throw rugs, the attachment of handrails on stairs, all of which will become a permanent part of the local environment in order to augment the client's strengths while taking into consideration, as far as possible, his limitations. Potential accidents can be minimized, and a sense of greater security in a functionally safe environment may add to the strengths of living in his familiar home. Where feasible, reconversions on types of housekeeping tasks in the name of reducing strain (such as replacing blinds with drapes) might be planned; a thorough conversion may be prohibitive and may prompt considerations regarding moving to a more physically commodious home.

Prosthetics are not so easily built into the social environment, for helping (and hindering) persons come and go. However, asking Mr. del Futura about persons with whom he would interact for various types of social contacts reveals a sociometric network which is exploitable in line with the goals of this case. For persons seen by the client to be his first line of friendship (and defense), the staff asks a set of (scaled) questions to reveal potential differences between a merely interested party and a person willing and able to give concrete assistance—a distinction not necessarily made by the client. This information is further qualified by ratings of the competence of collaterals to provide assistance as might be needed; this information yields a predictor of when societal defenses may be called upon to supplement or replace the natural defenses of kith and kin. This is not merely coming in to pick up the pieces when the primary groups fall apart, but rather to predict the optimal time to move in to prevent unnecessary and inimical stresses on the family and friends.

Indeed, Mr. del Futura is seen at home in order to do a reliability check on the laboratory assessment and to collect time-sampling data on social interaction patterns. Moving pictures of the neighborhood and the home are collected (film or audiovisual tapes) for analysis and comparison over time, for some parts of treatment may involve activation of community forces to repair environmental problems; visual demonstrations are powerful tools for persuasion of the clients themselves, and they can also be useful in court should protective action be needed.

It has become quite obvious that, although Mr. del Futura is our immediate client, he cannot be the only person for whom staff planning and involvement are necessary. Problematic matters of one person find repercussions on all members of the family and beyond. Direct discussion of the client's problems by the health-education-welfare team are paralleled in family discussions as the means to adapt collectively to current or future circumstances. These too require open dealing with goals that involve all members of the family. Procedures for rationally optimizing consensual goals are used to help the entire family plan to attain these objectives. At each new life stage, these group deliberations must be reconsidered in light of changing conditions.

With both the individual client and in group procedures, it is the role of the helping professional to provide systematic and objective information on the conditions and alternative means of dealing with them, but it is the role of the client, singly and collectively, to make the decisions. Issues of privacy are always difficult, more so when technological aids become privy to greater and greater amounts of information about citizens. Yet, like any machine, it depends on the persons behind the machine, for whatever good or evil the technology performs. Vigilance on behalf of one's own care requires vigilance over the caretakers, an active participation of objective knowledge and subjective values. As Mr. del Futura leaves, he is given half of a long random code identification number that will be required to gain access to his computerized health-education-and-welfare information—the other half belonging to the H-E-W care team. At each stage of gerontological life, Mr. del Futura (or his legal guardian if need be) must participate. New information or changes in client (and societal) values would require periodic reassessment of the total life-care plan. . . .

Reality

This long fictional anecdote brings together a number of assessment devices, but, more important, it embodies a philosophy of approaching evaluation in the gerontological phase of life, as illustrative of any type of client. First, values are established as goal points and treatment interventions as sequences of decision points based on normative and individual baselines. Second, evaluation procedures are moved away from paper-and-pencil questionnaires or simple interview data to nonobtrusive and nonreactive measures, naturalistic field settings utilizing the precision of the laboratory in the contexts in which the client lives his life. Systematic observer ratings utilize the multiple perspectives of the social systems in which the client is involved. Third, the treatment situation is one of mutual participation, mutual weighing of values and risks. The stress is on prevention over the long range of life rather than on attempted cures of acute illness. Incentives directed toward successful outcomes are provided for both therapist and client.

This is indeed a fable with a mission, because all the assessment procedures mentioned here are **currently** available (Bloom, to be published). It is the organization of these devices and their mode of delivery which is of the future.

A FRAMEWORK FOR EVALUATION DEVICES

What is it that we do when we evaluate an event in a client's life, using a constructed instrument rather than our own trained sense of observation? We seek a device which has undergone a standardization procedure in its development that assures us that the observations we make are real—are what other equally trained observers concerned with the same problem would also see under the same conditions. Unless we have objective measures as those presumably provided by assessment instruments, we have subjective observations which may stretch or shrink in the retelling and which therefore will not be helpful to the client in the long run. (I should add that we may train ourselves to be relatively objective instruments.)

Once we use an assessment device, we get evidence to inform us about an event. The score on the test reflects the sources of influence creating it. Test theory refers to a true factor and an error factor producing a test score. What is the meaning of truth here? I would suggest that we must defer to general behavioral theories to understand what we are measuring truly with our instruments of evaluation.

Behavior in general (both the overt motor acts and the covert but reliably reported inner states) and the specific behavioral responses comprising the problems of our clients are influenced by characteristics of the persons involved and by their environments. A person has both innate biological endowments (intelligence, energy level) and learned factors (attitudes, learned patterns of behavior), while the environment includes the social-interpersonal factors (family, friends of the client) set within the physical environment of objects arranged in space and time.

While few would dispute this general truism, I suggest that it be carried to its logical conclusion. I argue that it is premature for us to select certain factors as being more important than others. Or at least this should be treated as an empirical question rather than being dismissed. The following equation summarizes this point of view:

	Personal Factors		Environmental Factors	
Any behavior involved in the client's problem is influenced by	Innate demands and resources	Learned demands and resources	Social demands and resources	Physical demands and resources

This equation directs us to consider the **full** range of possible sources of influence on a given piece of behavior. The specific variables must be identified by the practitioner, presumably building on the work of others who have found certain variables to be more fruitful in explaining behavior than other variables. The theories by which the helping professions are guided have tended to focus strongly on one of these factors to the relative exclusion of the others—learned demands and resources (such as attitudes and socialized feelings). We do not have good theories that integrate biological and genetic understanding into social behavior; we do not have good theories that combine physical environment demands on understanding social behavior (though the work of Barker, 1968, is a most illuminating beginning). [Social psychological theories do make a beginning at connecting the personal and the social factors. (See Lindzey and Aronson, 1968.)] Yet, the helping professional should collect information when it is relevant to a case and attempt to build an **individualized** network of concepts embodying these factors.

APPROACHES TO DATA COLLECTION

Assuming agreement on the need to collect information on all of the vital areas of concern to a client, then how are we to collect this information? I would like to offer two approaches. The first stems from the question "Whose responses are used as the data?" One pole (labeled "subject-data") refers to the fact that information obtained from the person is directly used as information about himself. The other pole (labeled "observer-data") recognizes the fact that information obtained from a subject is interpreted by the observer or is compared with norms from previous research, and it is the observer's responses or the normative scores which are the data under consideration. Instruments like paper-and-pencil tests tend to blur this subject/observer-data distinction because such a test may be either subject-data or observer-data, depending on how it is used.

This distinction is based on the strengths and weaknesses of each type of data collection. The major strength of subject-data is getting the person's version of the situation, especially in subjective matters: "What are your feelings about . . . ?" "What's the connection between your actions in this situation and in that?" The weaknesses of subject-data are that the person may not be able to or want to tell the practitioner about the event in question, as the subject's responses will be highly influenced by his perception of what the practitioner will do with the information. Another basic problem is that the subject's frame of references may change over time.

The strengths of observer-data include what might be called **empirical leverage**—using small amounts of sampled behavior to project to larger patterns of basic or underlying behavior or to complex wholes. There is a very interesting dispute among clinicians as to whether the clinical judgment is more or less effective than ratings arrived at through instrument assessments (cf. Meehl, 1954; Sawyer, 1966). Whether the observer is overpowered by his own predispositions; whether he remains a constant judge over different clients, or with the same client over time; or whether his own characteristics become an essential part of the test data rather than those of the client—these are potential weaknesses of observer-data.

A second approach to data collection is another way of cutting the pie and is not independent of the first approach. The question here is "How intrusive is the mode of getting information on the information obtained?" The polar ends are labeled "intrusive-data," reflecting the fact that the client may be aware of either the purpose or the process of testing or both, while with nonreactive-data, the other polar end, such intrusiveness is at a minimum.

The strengths of intrusive-data are the high degree of objectivity and standardization that may be brought to bear in the varied settings in which such instruments may be used in practice, e.g., the agency office or the client's home. The same questions are repeated in nearly the same way across clients (and observers) and through time. Empirically constructed instruments present questions that may be far beyond the ability of individual practitioners to improvise. Yet, once constructed, such standardized tests are relatively impervious to change, insensitive to the personal states of the client, such as fatigue or boredom, and hide the need for individualized questions to pick up the unique aspects of this client's situation. Moreover, testy tests may be threatening or offensive to clients from whom cooperation is required in a world of persons who are increasingly hostile to being used as guinea pigs.

With nonreactive-data (Webb, Campbell, Schwartz, and Sechrest, 1966) there is a low degree of intrusion in the information-collection process, so that the obtaining of information does not itself influence the situation about which information is sought. However, nonreactive-data may not be under the control of the practitioner and are therefore subject to errors of others as well as to extraneous factors. I would hazard a guess that the nonreactive measures described by Webb, Campbell, Schwartz, and Sechrest (1966) will prove a gold mine for innovative helping professionals seeking more objective measures for their intervention effects.

ILLUSTRATIVE SHORT INSTRUMENTS FOR HELPING PROFESSIONALS

The assessment devices most likely to be used by helping professionals operating in the field will probably be brief instruments, rather than the long elaborate schedules [like the MMPI or the Cornell Medical Index, or the Psychiatric Status Schedule (Spitzer, Endicott, Heiss, and Cohen, 1970) used in special institutional settings]. This means that they should be maximally portable but still be reliable and valid. Brevity tends to operate against reliability and to some degree validity so that one must always be **cautious** in using short instruments.

Let's take as an example the situation of an old man whose "home" is a series of cheap hotel rooms in the center of a large city. Prior to our entering the scene, Mr. O'Brien had a heart attack, and now is about to be released from the hospital, back to his former existence. There are, of course, many ways to approach this man, including assisting in making his life meaningful and providing continuity of care after hospitalization. We would want to know something about him and his situation in order to suggest a plan of action. Typically, a worker would enter this situation, ask questions and make judgments; I am suggesting that by using more objective measurement procedures, our information will be more precise, and the worker will be in a better position to develop plans.

First, some basic questions. One important innate factor is a person's intelligence. How shall we estimate this? If Mr. O'Brien were of a very low intelligence, we would have to make far different plans than if he were in the normal intelligence range. An average worker would make some judgments based on conversations, but so many factors could mask Mr. O'Brien's innate capacities that making a judgment based on conversations alone would be very risky—and likely to be to the client's detriment. Now, intelligence testing is the jewel in the psychometrician's crown, but we will not get involved in the elaborate intelligence tests (see Anastasi, 1968; Cronbach, 1970). Instead, we might consider any of a number of short tests, such as the Rapid Approximate Intelligence Test (RAIT) (Wilson, 1967) which involves a series of mathematical computations, beginning 2 times 3, and then 2 times the succeeding successful answer (see Table 19-1). Such simple symbolic manipulations have been correlated with basic intelligence tests, such as the Wechsler Adult Intelligence Scale (WAIS), and while there is a risk in considering intelligence merely manipulation of symbols, it is one basic element. The following table is adapted from Wilson's article and indicates an 85 percent probability of matching given WAIS full-scale scores for each RAIT item level attained.

Table 19-1

The Rapid Approximate Intelligence Test Scores Showing Correspondence to the Full-Scale Wechsler Adult Intelligence Scale (Wilson, 1967)

RAIT item:	RAIT score and generalized clinical interpretations		85% probability of making a WAIS full-scale score less than:
Fails all	0		57
2 × 3	1	Suggestive of	64
2 × 6	2	intellectual	71
2 × 12	3	deficit	77
2 × 24	4	Dull normal	84
2 × 48	5	range	90
2 × 96	6		97
2 × 192	7	Normal	104
2 × 384	8	range	110
2 × 768	9		117
2 × 1536	10		124
2 × 3072	11	Superior	130
2 × 6144 (12,288)	12		137

There are numerous other short intelligence test procedures, but few as portable and easy to use as the arithmetic procedures. Every test should be carefully studied for its applicability to the given situation, as well as for the information it provides on reliability and validity. (See, for example, Dixon, 1965, who points out the instability of such brief arithmetic procedures.)

In addition to intelligence, a worker would want to have some idea about Mr. O'Brien's health. Again, the worker could observe and guess, but there are some good tools available which offer more objective estimates. Rosow and Breslau (1966) have developed a functional health scale for older persons, and report that studies have indicated that there is about 75 percent agreement between self-assessment and physician's reports on health (see Table 19-2). The Rosow and Breslau scale also has an empirical Guttman scaling, that is, the items can be arranged so that if a person answers affirmatively on the first or hardest item, he would be likely to answer affirmatively on all of the succeeding easier items. Likewise, wherever the first affirmative answer occurs, it is likely that the person will answer affirmatively from then on. The following is an adaptation of the Rosow and Breslau scale, 6 items taken from a matrix of 25 diversified items. The matrix is important, but in a field setting, the other types of questions a worker might ask would provide such a matrix for the 6 scaled items:

Table 19-2

Adaptation of a Functional Health Scale for the Aged (from Rosow and Breslau, 1966)

Items (arranged in descending order on a Guttman scale where acceptance of a higher item indicates acceptance of all lower items)	Healthy response indicated
1. Are you still healthy enough to do heavy work around the house, like shoveling snow or washing walls . . . without help?	Yes
2. Is there any physical condition, illness, or health problem that bothers you now?	No
3. (Response to this question:) "I am not limited in any of my activities."	Yes (I am not limited)
4. Walk half a mile (about 8 ordinary city blocks)	Yes
5. Walk up and down stairs to the second floor.	Yes
6. Go out to a movie, to church, or to a meeting, or to visit friends?	Yes

There are, needless to say, many types of health functioning scales, with great amounts of testing that have gone into their development. A few also have conceptual structures connected with them. For example, the Index of Independence in Activities of Daily Living (ADL) (Katz, Downs, Cash, & Grotz, 1970) is a six-item observer-rating procedure on actual functioning in several self-care areas—such as bathing, dressing, and feeding. It was noted that the pattern

Table from "A Guttman Health Scale for the Aged." JOURNAL OF GERONTOLOGY by I. Rosow & N. Breslau is reprinted by permission of the first author and the Editor. © 1966 by JOURNAL OF GERONTOLOGY.

of recovery from a disabling illness in older age parallels the development of functions in the child, but in reverse order; those that are most basic were the last to be lost and the first to be regained after severe illnesses.

Measures of intelligence and health presumably tap innate and biological factors to some degree. While the two illustrative procedures mentioned in these connections were observer-data type of approaches (as both compared answers to norms), they varied on intrusiveness. The intelligence test is probably more intrusive as a test than the health scale whose questions are fairly reasonable per se. The next illustrative measurement procedures concern the learned factors.

Mr. O'Brien appears to the worker to be unhappy over his lot. The worker might even say he was depressed. But how unhappy does a person have to be to be depressed? There is a brief depression scale which can be used (Zung, 1965). It involves a self-rating in terms of pervasive affect, and the physiological and psychological disturbances concomitant with it. There are twenty items with a scale from one to four indicating occurrence from none of the time to most or all of the time; items are balanced for positive and negative symptomatology. According to Zung, one can distinguish normal persons from various psychiatric validating groups such as depressed persons who are hospitalized or those on out-patient relationships. Each group has a characteristic range of scores which is distinguishable from other groups. Observe that such a self-rating scale has a subject-data aspect, even though it would be classified as observer-data because it is compared to norms. The fact that the client is also making statements about his problems offers points of departure for intervention as well.

Turning briefly to the social sphere, the worker might borrow a simple method used by Robertson and Banks (1970), a sociometric measure concerning the improvement of socialization among the elderly. In the context of a community project, Robertson and Banks surveyed older persons in certain areas and asked them to name as many senior citizens as they knew in the vicinity.

By repeating the survey at the conclusion of the project, they were able to offer indirect evidence that their outreach program had made older persons more aware of elderly and had thus raised the acquaintance level among them, one of the goals of the program. For our client, Mr. O'Brien, a variation might be to ask with whom he had spent time socially, or how many people he knew by name at a senior citizens' club, either being operational statements of improved sociability (assuming that is a goal in this case). The sociometric procedure is relatively nonobtrusive, although it still represents observer-data.

The physical environment presents a different kind of challenge, for it is not the bricks and mortar as such, but their impact on human inhabitants.

Simple measures that might be employed could include the census ratings for quality of dwelling—intact, deteriorating, or dilapidated. It might also involve measures of the persons-to-rooms ratio as an indication of the degree of crowdedness or privacy of the person's home environment. Measures of number of blocks to vital stores, accessibility to telephones, presence of handbars in the bathtub, all could represent safety measures as well. On each of these points, a worker might intervene in order to assist the client to obtain a better physical environment which would be more conducive to his overall contentment as well as his health. But pure cleanliness is not an absolute, as a worker would learn who tried to place Mr. O'Brien in an antiseptic institution rather than his fleabitten hotel rooms.

The last point returns us to the reality of practice. Objective measures are merely means to an end, which is quality service. One is prompted to ask, does the use of objective measures inhibit providing quality service, or does it reduce the genuine expression of human concern which the helping professions are to show? My response is that we can be no more deeply concerned about our clients than to get as accurate information as possible with as little disturbance as possible to the client in obtaining it. Neither accurate information nor personal concern for the client can be ignored. The question is, really, why have we ignored obtaining objective standardized information for so long?

ALL-PURPOSE MEASUREMENT PROCEDURE

If your clients do not have the specific problems for which standardized measurement scales or procedures have been developed, it may become necessary for you to improvise. What is needed is a type of all-purpose measurement procedure which can be used to count any of the important events in the life of the client. For this I recommend a modification of Cantril's (1965) self-anchoring ladder approach. The client is given to understand that for more effective service, you must know how he is doing just as a doctor takes a temperature with a thermometer to know about his client's state of health. Next, the client is asked to think of the highest state of a given event—say, getting along with his spouse. This is the top of the ladder, a ten on a ten-step interval procedure which the worker can draw to make it more graphic. The lowest state of the same event, that is, the worst time he has had getting along with his spouse, would be the bottom of the ladder, one on the same ten-step scale. Now, the worker asks for a current temperature of how well the client is getting along with his spouse. These readings may be recorded over time as a subjective report indicator of effectiveness of service. They are subject-data belonging directly to the client, and although they are intrusive in the sense of being known to be measurements, if taken in the spirit of a social thermometer, it could be perfectly acceptable to the client. Being self-aware of his own temperature may likewise be therapeutic.

SUMMARY

Everyday instruments of assessment for the average helping professional are still in the future. Yet a general sketch of the types of instruments we need can be suggested. A general behavioral theory was presented as a guideline for which specific tests could be chosen: Any behavior is influenced by the innate and learned aspects of a person, together with the social and physical influences acting upon him. Thus, instruments of assessment should pick out the salient influences and factors and provide information on these.

The objective and standardized information obtainable through many available research instruments is a most tantalizing goal for the helping professional, for whom any test must be used as carefully as an extension of himself as any other aspect of his professional behavior. Tests, of course, vary in their reliability and validity and must be carefully evaluated to determine if their use will add appreciably to the helping situation.

The strengths and weaknesses of subject-data or observer-data and of intrusive-data or nonreactive-data have to be weighed. Even without any formal instruments, the practitioner collects intrusive observer-data, namely, the act of interviewing itself. Since we use one instrument all the time—namely, ourselves—why not consider how this instrument can collect more nearly objective information?

CHAPTER 20

Information Science and the Helping Professions

Among all the other crises of our age, the information crisis passes almost unnoticed, although it strikes at the heart of the helping professions. Most paradoxical of its many facets is the dual fact of both overabundance and scarcity of information suitable for the practitioner. Consider: There were 120 million pages of scientific information published in 100,000 journals in 1970 alone, and the number of pages is estimated to double every 8.5 years; there are even 1300 abstracting services attempting to give some order to this avalanche of information (Schneider, 1971). However, the more that is known, the more difficult it is to locate any particular item of information.

Let's get closer to home. Assume that there are overall 10,000 books relevant to the field of social work. Assume that these books average 200 pages, with 30 lines to a page, 10 words to a line. This means 600 million words to be read by the average reader who reads about 250 words a minute, or 15,000 words an hour. It would take an average reader 40,000 hours to read these books related to social work. If one were to read at the rate of 12 hours a day, it would take one about 9 years—after which there would likely be another batch of materials at least equal to the size of the first to be read. Unwise is the solution seemingly adopted at some schools of providing reading lists which would have students read 54 hours a day in order to finish in the two allotted years. Is there any other solution? Or has the professional obligation to keep pace with the current literature (to say nothing of past classics) become an impossibility?

There is no question but that a student of the helping professions samples only a tiny portion of the available literature during his schooling and beyond. The question of dealing with the information crisis reduces largely to methods of effective sampling combined with selective storage and retrieval. New tools and procedures are becoming available to assist in this effort, and it is the task of this chapter to introduce some of these.

CONCEPTS VERSUS CONTAINERS

The first vital distinction to make is between the ideas (concepts) and the vehicles which contain or carry the ideas. The libraries of the future (Licklider, 1965) will be places or devices—maybe even pocket size ones at that—which will provide instantaneous dissemination of **ideas**, rather than mountains of containers to be scaled—the books and journals consisting of pages sewed together arranged on shelves in special buildings. This is not to say, as some have, that the printed page is dead but rather that it will come to a reader in a different way and with a different orientation. The delivery of information by computers is only in its infancy; it will be discussed briefly in passing. It is, rather, a new orientation to information which I would like to emphasize in this chapter.

As a transition to the libraries of the future, it is necessary for the contemporary information-user to become oriented to concepts rather than to containers of concepts. It has been the perspective of this book that the helping professional generates concepts from the flow of events which clients present to him. These concepts help the worker to organize the events in meaningful ways: defining patterns of problematic behaviors, goals, facilitative or hampering means, action plans, monitoring schemes—all in terms of concepts and networks of concepts and propositions. At the same time, theorists, researchers, and practitioners are communicating their ideas in professional media in the form of networks of concepts and propositions.

Therefore, location of relevant information involves the meshing of concept-information-needed with concept-information-provided. Characteristics of the information system, including users, become vital in this meshing (cf. Brittain, 1970). The more able a helping professional becomes in generating precise concepts concerning client problems and in locating precise concepts from the literature, the more relevant information he will have available to guide his work.

As an example of this meshing orientation, I would like to discuss the information retrieval system called **key word in context** (KWIC), in which the title of an article is rearranged around key terms appearing in that title so that a user may locate this article from any of the terms used. For example, let's say that you were interested in "decision making in multiproblem families." Among the places you would begin to look for information on this topic is a key word in context bibliography called the **International Bibliography of**

Research in Marriage and the Family, 1900—1964 (Aldous and Hill, 1967). Looking in the book under the term "decision making" you would see the following portion of "sentences":

.
.
.

OGIC FAMILIES.#	DECISION MAKING	IN NORMAL AND PATHOL FERRAJ-63-DNP
OCESS.# SOME ASPECTS OF	DECISION MAKING	IN THE FAMILY GROWTH WESTC-61-ABM
F METHODS USED TO STUDY	DECISION MAKING	IN THE FAMILY.# A SU SCHLB-62-SMV

.
.
.

Notice that DECISION MAKING is set off in the middle of these sentences as the word around which the title has been rearranged. The last part of each sentence is the citation information; a user would turn to the reference section of this book and find under FERRAJ-63-DNP, for example, the following:

Ferreira,AJ   Archs. Gen. Psychiat.,1963,8,68—73

together with the title of the article which you can read from the rearranged sentence above: "Decision making in normal and pathologic families." The DNP are the first letters of the significant words in the title. The sentence starts at the # sign; sometimes a few words or letters must be left out because of space limits, but this usually isn't problematic. If you had begun information seeking under the key words "normal" or "pathological" or "families" you would have found the same article FERRAJ-63-DNP, thus giving you a four-fold chance of getting the information this article presumably holds. It is this multiplication of potential for locating information which is the heart of many retrieval systems.

But the context of an information search is also important. If you had started with the term "family" you would have had pages of titles to look through before you came to the Ferreira article which, let us suppose, is just the kind of title you need. By putting your concept into a propositional context, such as "decision making in multiproblem families," you would have provided yourself with more precise entry points in that you might assume that "decision making" and "multiproblem" had fewer titles than "family." The point is to find information dealing with the **intersection** of the key concepts you are seeking. Notice that the Ferreira article has concepts close to the three in our information search and, therefore, may be presumed to be a good lead for the specific information we seek.

Another phenomenon occurs as the worker lays out his constructed network of ideas about the client's situation. Not only has the worker created an individualized theory about the client and his problem, but she has thereby individualized the information needed. There are some interesting parallels between such an individualized theory concerning a client and a flow diagram for a computer or a PERT diagram (an acronym for **P**rogram **E**valuation and **R**eview **T**echnique) (see Merten, 1966). These techniques present graphically the entire set of components of a program or task, arranged according to their relation to the goal and to other components of the task. If the worker had such a perspective on a case, then he could more easily see which terms were central to the progress of the case on which he needed information. PERT suggests the idea of a critical path, the series of activities and events that require the most time—and by extension to the practitioner, the most energy. Applied to the helping professions, there might be a critical path of concepts on which the worker needs information in a certain sequence as an aid to making decisions. Rather than being pressured by the moment, the worker would have a rough time sequence of probable future events and could be prepared in advance with information to guide the client among alternative actions.

I must stress that there is no substitute for direct exposure to information sources, even though the following guided tour of types of references may be of some value. Each library has its own characteristics which are to be mastered for effective use. I will present four major categories of information sources of which helping professionals should have intimate knowledge. Each of these categories has particular strengths and weaknesses that are relevant for the different situations in which a worker finds himself.

INFORMATION SOURCE: ABSTRACTS

Abstracts generally contain short nonevaluative summaries of the article in paragraph form so that they are readable in the conventional sense. **Abstracts for Social Workers**, for example, selects articles to be abstracted from some 200 journals, and produces over a 1000 abstracts a year. Such a quarterly journal can be read or scanned in a short time, making it possible to keep up with many special areas of social work thinking and research.

Consider the information problems of a worker who has been assigned a "multiproblem family." After some contact with the family, he determines that several major problems are present: There are economic problems involving limited income, problems on getting along with neighbors critical of the behavior of the children, problems on what to do with the children's discipline and school performance. Common to each problem is the difficulty the family has in making decisions. The worker wonders what is known about helping such families to be more effective in making decisions.

Looking at **Abstracts for Social Workers,** as illustrative of abstracts, we begin by noting that it is arranged by major headings indicated by a table of contents. We might find 50 abstracts under the headings of "family and child welfare" or "schools," but even this selection might be too much to read if the clients were waiting in the other room, so to speak. The other approach is to consult the subject index with the entry terms being the specific concepts on which we seek information. **Abstracts for Social Workers** also presents the context in which the concepts occur, similar to the way the worker defined the situation with the multiproblem family—decision making regarding economics, interpersonal relationships, and school matters. For example, here is a portion of the subject index of **Abstracts for Social Workers,** 1972, 8:1, p. 55:

"FAMILIES: black, jobs, and, 56; black, sociology of, 259; heavily indebted, agency program for, 151; influence of, on therapy outcome, 178; issues and problems faced by different types of, 260; maturation crises and parent-child interaction in, 155; primary extended kin relations of black couples, 250; retardates and life styles of, 107."

My thought process might have run as follows: First, I am dealing with a family. Hence, the first term "families" from the subject index. The context for my particular family is multiproblems involving economics, neighbors, delinquency, school problems. Taking the first one, economic contexts of family problems, I scan the context phrases under the key term to find those that are relevant— or which lead me to think of possible new connections. Say my family is not a minority family, so the first two articles (numbered 56 and 259 of this particular issue) would likely have emphases not relevant to my case directly, although I might think of parallels between the discrimination patterns of minority groups and those being experienced by this multiproblem family. However, rather than pursue every possible lead, I will first concentrate the main thrust of my information seeking. Reference 151 leads to the following abstract:

"151. LAUGHLIN, J.L. & BRESSLER, R.A. A family agency program for heavily indebted families. **Social Casework, 52(10):**617–26, 1971. Family Service Association of Nassau County, Mineola, N.Y.

As a result of a credit revolution, an increasing number of families are facing severe debt. Service to such families is provided almost exclusively by the Consumer Credit Counseling agencies that focus on relieving indebtedness.

Because such agencies are not equipped to alleviate the personal problems that often underlie the financial problems, a serious deficiency exists in their program. A family agency has developed a new approach to the problem by combining short-term therapy and debt counseling. Caseworkers provide short-term therapy and volunteers work with the family on repayment plans. A training program was developed that uses group process to teach volunteers the principles of credit counseling and human behavior. Case illustrations are given, and implications of family indebtedness for the social work field are discussed. (Author abstracts, edited.)"

Our concepts of concern led us to this abstract, but the network of concepts used by the authors is different from our immediate concern. We should not expect a carbon copy of our own problem case! But how, if at all, can we use this information we have identified by a two-step information-filtering process (concept and then context of that concept)? If we think that short-term therapy on basic problems can be combined with counseling on effective consumer behavior, then we will have crystallized a key practice idea from this abstract, although we note that no data are provided on the effectiveness of this plan. The case illustrations in the original article may provide more concrete ideas, although we are not immediately concerned with information on training programs for volunteers. Thus, we must read the abstract carefully to pick out what the original article may have for us in addition to the self-standing idea about combining therapy and credit counseling. Abstracts may provide both of these types of information: the immediately crystallizing ideas which help you to see how events in your case may be fitted together; and the procedural information, the concrete details located in the original article, which may provide more individualized information.

INFORMATION SOURCES: BIBLIOGRAPHY

Bibliographic lists of references often make up in length or specialized topic areas what they lack in conventional descriptions, although the annotated bibliographies are often equivalent to abstracts in meaningfulness. There are a variety of bibliographical organization principles which should be understood, such as the key word in context idea discussed earlier. Some bibliographies are simply lists of titles; others add some kind of classification system, detailed or gross. Still others provide some cross-referencing schemes, simple or involved; and yet others provide the annotations mentioned above. It is my opinion that bibliographic information sources vary directly in their utility to the helping professions as they give organized and descriptive information of their contents. But this is an observation which each user should experience for himself.

INFORMATION SOURCES: OTHER CURRENTLY AVAILABLE TOOLS

In addition to abstracts and bibliographies, there are a variety of other sources of information, some conventional and others perhaps new to the reader. Let's approach these tools as if we possessed different amounts of information.

If one were in a position of relative ignorance on a topic, it might be wise to approach the topic by seeking a broad orientation to the issues involved: What are the questions? One would seek some historical perspective (so as to avoid previously committed errors) and diversity in points of view (to prevent premature closure). For these purposes, tools like the **Encyclopedia of Social Work,** handbook review articles, and basic textbooks might be useful. One begins to sketch in broad questions, locating the networks of concepts that have been used to deal with the topic. Scientific dictionaries provide synonyms and common meanings. The Subject Heading book for the Library of Congress system of organizing books also presents networks of terms. Browsing through the card catalog or the book stacks is fun, but the cost in time and energy is disproportionately high to the fruitfulness of the information found dealing with a specific topic. This cost-benefit ratio should be kept in mind as one explores the structure, organization, selectivity, richness, currency, and other dimensions of the information tools one will be using throughout one's professional life.

If one were in a position of having a little knowledge on a topic but were uncertain of its quality or quantity, then the information search would be modified. Now, the perspective sought from broadly orienting sources is to test the adequacy of one's own knowledge base and to begin filling in missing pieces. It becomes possible to pass over the very general and historical in favor of focusing on specific and current information, which would involve some use of tools for precision information retrieval—the abstracts and the key word systems of various sorts.

If one were in the enviable position of having considerable knowledge on a topic, then one would move directly to the precision tools to find the best available information on specific answers for action hypotheses. Those who already have considerable knowledge gain the most from use of a precision tool because they can guess more accurately what the brief abstract actually contains. Knowing the work of certain authors and recognizing certain concepts enrich the sparse information of a key word system.

It takes practice to use information tools effectively. Yet, because of the comprehensive and current nature of many serial abstracts, one can move directly through the mountain of available information to the specific concepts one needs. Time cannot be better spent by the busy helping professional than in learning how to use precision information tools effectively.

Of immense importance to the future dissemination of information in the helping professions are the experiences of the medical, educational, and social welfare efforts at computer-based information services. The MEDLINE system, an active interchange between the requester of medically related information and a computerized data base of more than a half million articles, is a powerful tool for information retrieval. A user can frame a question—the key concepts in the context of his client's problem, type it into a field terminal, have the computer clarify the question if necessary, and then get the answer presented on a television-like screen or given on a printout. MEDLINE is an evolving product of the National Library of Medicine, 8600 Rockville Pike, Bethesda, Maryland, 20014.

ERIC (Educational Resources Information Center) is a nation-wide information system for educational materials. Consisting of a network of specialized-content clearinghouses at universities around the country, each clearinghouse also has access to the entire system of information. This enterprise involves a combination of monthly research abstracts (**Research in Education**) as well as the computer-based system. Central ERIC is the United States Office of Education, 400 Maryland Avenue, SW, Washington, D.C., 20202.

The information center of the National Conference on Social Welfare has pioneered in applying documentation techniques to the social welfare field, using a variety of methods for different information-delivery tasks (Hoffer, 1973). Reduction in the size of information containers through microfilm and microfiche is one such approach. The use of hand-sort punch cards for social welfare publications is another approach for moving a relatively small number of information containers around more rapidly.

The School of Social Service at Indiana University–Purdue University at Indianapolis has developed a prototype model of an intensively abstracted computer-based information system (Bloom, 1973b). This system was developed to assist helping professionals to acquire self-contained packages of information from which they not only gain concepts but will also receive an estimate of the risk involved in using information. Thus the intensive abstract includes some descriptive characteristics of the study abstracted, as well as the key concepts arranged in context—essentially an independent and dependent variable arrangement, where applicable—and the research or practice experience bearing on that proposition. This is necessarily a small, specialized-library approach specifically geared to the helping professions; it is used in combination with didactic training in the use of such tools. Future research will determine whether such a conception of the information needs of practitioners is best served in this fashion (cf. Brittain, 1970).

A major recent addition to information retrieval is the **Social Science Citation Index** (Institute for Scientific Information, 1973), which contains information from about 1,800 journals related to the social sciences. There are several components of this system. Let me present one example of a worker seeking information on school desegregation planning for a community. The first step would be to consult the key term retrieval system (called the "Permuterm Subject Index," PSI), in which every significant word in a title is paired with every other significant word, generating a very large number of such pairs—two million annually. There are some 27 pairs of terms with the concept DESEGREGATION, with each pair having citations listed in which both members of the pair appear in the title, thus improving our chances of locating a relevant article. An author's index may reveal additional articles by an author found through the PSI. A citation index may also be consulted to find the work of other persons who have used a given author's article, thus locating a network of related materials in which the given article may have been extended, tested, and updated. Thus, in one information retrieval system, the practitioner can do a large number of operations for assembling citations to the complete network of available information.

INFORMATION SOURCE: DOING YOUR OWN THING

The wondrous but expensive world of computerized dissemination of information is not likely to be available to most helping professionals for some time to come. In the meantime, it is necessary to devise procedures within the means of all practitioners for developing and maintaining a growing fund of information that has sensitive access to it, as needed. It is the task of this brief section to make some suggestions along these lines, as a survival kit against the information flood.

First, an overview source of information about the field at large is very helpful. Social workers have the easily accessible **Abstracts for Social Workers**. **Psychological Abstracts** delivers more than 10,000 abstracts annually, covering a wide variety of topics. There are other more specialized abstracts (listed in Table 20-2) dealing with limited topic areas, for example, **Adult Development and Aging Abstracts**. Persons working with older clients would doubly benefit from subscribing to the specialized JOURNAL OF GERONTOLOGY because at the end of each issue is an updating of Shock's immense **Classified Bibliography of Gerontology and Geriatrics** (1951, 1957, and 1963). These obvious suggestions are very passive ways of keeping up to date. Let's move on to more active information storage and retrieval on a personalized basis.

Broadhurst (1962) has suggested a method to develop a simple card collection of personalized information. Two types of cards are used. One card **(concept card)** contains the key term (and synonyms), plus the articles containing information about that concept listed in some code below (see Figure 20-1). The other type of card contains the full **citation,** plus whatever quotations or comments one wants to keep as reminders. The article identification may itself be useful. I use a system in which the year, journal, and page numbers are combined as a distinct identification system. For example, 73 SW 15–32 would represent 1973 **Social Work** pages 15 to 32. Where each journal issue begins at page one, it is necessary to add the issue number as well: 71SCW2:45–56. As new information becomes available, it would be added to a **new** citation card, as well as to the **existing** set of concept cards. It becomes possible, using this simple procedure, not to lose sight of any large portion of the literature one has gained during the course of professional education.

There is a sense in which a helping professional **is** his accumulation of information, theoretical, empirical, and practical. A personalized information system would be one way to formulate these experiences in terms of concepts and contexts, and thus, it might be a way through which he might offer his practice wisdom as a contribution to the professional literature. Thus, what

CONCEPT CARD

"Day Care"		
Theoretical or analytical articles	Articles having research data	Articles on practice or demonstrations
72SW5:36–46	69SCW527–33 73SSR266–77	69SCW527–33

CITATION CARDS

ID#: SSR 266–277
Author: Handler, E.
Title: Expectations of day-care parents
Source: SOCIAL SERVICE REVIEW, 1973 **47**:2, 266–277
Key Concepts in Article:
day care, client expectations

72 SW 5:36–46
Levenstein, S.
Day care: Gold coin or brass check?
SOCIAL WORK, 1972, **17**:5, 36–46
day care, child welfare, social welfare policy

69 SCW 527–533
Collins, A.H. and Watson, E.L.
Exploring the neighborhood family day-care system
SOCIAL CASEWORK, 1969, **50**:9, 527–533
day care, neighborhoods

Figure 20-1—Personalized information system (adapted from Broadhurst, 1962).

begins as an information storage and retrieval tool may become a source for sharing one's experiences in the helping profession.

AN EXPANDABLE INDEX TO GENERAL INFORMATION SOURCES FOR HELPING PROFESSIONALS

I would like to offer another do-it-yourself information system suitable for use by individuals, agencies, or libraries. It is expandable in the sense that users are invited to add to it as new materials come their way. Essentially it consists of two lists: One contains the key concepts by which a user would enter a library to seek information (Table 20-1). The other is a list of citations of abstracts, bibliographies, and other types of information resources (Table 20-2). The critical addition is the set of identification numbers of the various abstracts and bibliographies that are relevant to a given concept.

For example, if you were seeking information on the topic of ABORTION (which would include many subtopics like planned and unplanned pregnancies and psychological reactions to abortion), then looking in Table 20-1 would show the following:

ABORTION: 001-A, 046-B, 055-B, 067-B, 098-A, 136-B.

You are thus directed to the citation listings (Table 20-2) which are presumed relevant to this term. For instance, 001-A indicates **Abstracts for Social Workers,** an abstract; 046-B indicates a bibliography, **Abortion in Context: A Selected Bibliography.** The number with a -0 after it represents an information source other than an abstract or bibliography. Some general abstracts and bibliographies will appear frequently, of course, but there are a large number of specialized information sources as well, although not every term has an abstract to refer to. So the user must treat this index as a general entry point to locate further information on specific events.

The reader is invited to add to this working tool by writing in a new citation and giving it a distinctive number in Table 20-2. Then, after scanning the new information source to see what it contains, add that number to all the concept categories (Table 20-1) to which it applies.

SUMMARY

This chapter has introduced the A,B,Cs of information science relevant to the helping professions. A is for abstracts, the brief nonevaluative summaries of articles; B is for bibliographies, organized lists of references; C is for other current methods of information dissemination, some computer-based, others verging on obsolescence. D is for doing-it-yourself, putting together an individualized information storage and retrieval system that fits your own particular interests and needs in such a way that you do not lose information as time goes by. I also suggested that keeping up to date may be a basis for making your own contributions to the professional literature.

As so many times before in this book, **concept** proves to be central: in defining the client's problems, in understanding the theoretical and empirical ideas of professional colleagues, and, now, for connecting client's problems with the best available information. Thus, we return to the point from which we began this book.

Table 20-1

Key Concept List

This list provides identification numbers to general information sources (cited in Table 20-2) that are relevant to each given concept.

ABORTION: 001-A, 046-B, 055-B, 067-B, 098-A, 136-B
ABUSE; ALCOHOL & DRUGS: 001-A, 070-B, 079-B, 098-A, 122-B, 123-A
ABUSE, CHILD: 001-A
ADAPTATION: 017-A, 058-B, 098-A
ADDICTION (see Abuse, Alcohol & Drugs)
ADMINISTRATION, SOCIAL WORK: 001-A, 025-B, 029-B, 033-B, 060-B
ADOLESCENCE: 001-A, 026-B, 027-B, 058-B, 098-A
ADOPTION: 001-A, 024-B
ADULT DEVELOPMENT: 073-B, 098-A, 116-A
ADVOCACY: 001-A, 036-B
AFTERCARE: 001-A, 074-A & B, 133-B
AGED & AGING: 001-A, 008-0, 019-B, 035-B, 037-B, 058-B, 064-0, 098-A, 107-B, 114-B, 116-A, 119-B, 124-B, 125-B, 129-0
AGENCY ORGANIZATION: 001-A, 029-B, 060-B
AGGRESSION: 001-A, 058-B
AID TO FAMILIES WITH DEPENDENT CHILDREN (AFDC): 001-A, 033-B
ALCOHOL: 001-A, 005-B, 070-B, 090-A, 098-A, 123-A, 129-O, 143-B
ALIENATION: 001-A, 005-B, 075-B
ASSIMILATION: 072-B, 077-B
AUTISM: 011-B, 102-A, 128-A
BEHAVIOR DISORDERS: 001-A, 017-A, 098-A, 102-A, 116-A
BEHAVIOR MODIFICATION: 001-A, 010-B, 011-B, 037-B, 069-B, 098-A
BLACK AMERICANS: 001-A, 051-B, 072-B, 083-B, 093-B, 114-B, 144-B

Table 20-1 (continued)

BRIEF PSYCHOTHERAPY: 058-B
BUREAUCRACY: 001-A, 078-B
CASEWORK: 001-A, 013-0, 058-B, 060-B
CHICANOS: 001-A, 014-B, 015-B, 066-B, 072-B, 088-B, 114-B
CHILD DEVELOPMENT: 001-A, 016-A & B, 031-B, 040-A, 042-B, 058-B, 098-A, 118-B
CHILD GUIDANCE CLINIC: 001-A
CHILD REARING: 001-A, 031-B, 083-B, 102-A, 104-B
CHILD WELFARE & DEVELOPMENT: 001-A, 024-B, 026-B, 027-B, 030-B, 033-B, 042-B, 048-A, 064-0, 102-A
CHILD WELFARE RESEARCH: 076-0, 140-0
CHILDHOOD PSYCHOSIS: 001-A, 011-B, 026-B, 128-A
CHILDREN, EXCEPTIONAL & GIFTED: 001-A, 040-A, 052-A
CHILDREN, HANDICAPPED: 001-A, 006-B, 027-B, 039-B, 048-A, 052-A, 098-A
CIVIL RIGHTS: 001-A, 051-B, 082-B, 083-B, 093-B
COGNITIVE DEVELOPMENT: 016A & B, 073-B, 098-A, 102-A
COGNITIVE DISSONANCE: 098-A
COMMUNICATION: 001-A, 058-B, 098-A
COMMUNITY MENTAL HEALTH: 001-A, 056-B, 059-B, 071-B, 108-B, 117-B, 121-B, 133-B
COMMUNITY ORGANIZATION, DEVELOPMENT & PLANNING: 001-A, 013-0, 060-B, 078-B, 097-A, 100-A, 130-B, 111-A
COMPUTER: 001-A, 049-A, 098-A, 113-A & B
CONSUMERISM: 001-A, 092-B, 111-A
CONTRACEPTION (see Family Planning)
COPING: 017-A
CORRECTIONS: (see Crime & Delinquency; Courts)
COUNSELING: 001-A, 016-A & B, 028-B, 032-B, 058-B, 085-B, 096-B, 098-A
COURTS: LEGAL SYSTEM, CRIMINAL JUSTICE SYSTEM: 001-A, 063-A, 131-B
CRIME & DELINQUENCY: 001-A, 020-B, 041-A, 053-A, 058-B, 069-B, 070-B, 079-B, 098-A, 116-A, 131-B
CRISIS INTERVENTION: 001-A, 017-A, 018-A
DAY CARE: 001-A, 021-B, 033-B, 081-B
DEATH: 001-A, 037-B, 058-B, 118-B
DECISION MAKING: 001-A, 098-A, 135-B
DELINQUENCY: (see Crime & Delinquency; Courts)
DELIVERY OF SERVICES: 001-A, 087-0
DEPENDENCE, PSYCHOLOGICAL: 001-A, 058-B
DEPENDENCE, DRUGS: (see Abuse, Alcohol & Drugs)
DEPRESSION: 001-A, 037-B, 058-B, 098-A

Table 20-1 (continued)

DEVELOPMENT, PERSONAL: 102-A, 111-A

DEVELOPMENT, SOCIAL, URBAN, INTERNATIONAL: 111-A, 132-B

DISABLED: 001-A, 006-B, 039-B, 048-A, 050-B, 064-0, 085-B, 090-A, 114-B

DISADVANTAGED: 001-A, 009-B, 031-B, 042-B, 096-B, 097-A, 114-B

DISEASE: 001-A, 006-B

DIVORCE: 001-A, 032-B

DRUGS: 001-A, 090-A, 098-A, 099-A, 122-B, 123-A

ECONOMIC SECURITY: 001-A, 033-B, 035-B, 036-B, 065-A, 097-A, 119-B, 124-B, 125-B, 134-B

EDUCATION, ADULT: 001-A, 007-B, 073-B, 096-B, 117-B

EDUCATION, GENERAL: 001-A, 015-B, 016-A & B, 045-A, 061-B, 072-B, 083-B, 127-A

EDUCATION, SPECIAL: 001-A, 040-A, 050-B, 052-A, 069-B, 096-B

EFFECTIVENESS: (see Evaluation)

EMOTIONAL PROBLEMS: 026-B, 027-B, 039-B, 052-A

EMPLOYMENT: 001-A, 005-B, 065-A, 083-B, 090-A, 093-B, 114-B

ENCOUNTER GROUPS: 037-B

EPIDEMIOLOGY: 047-B, 054-B, 105-B, 122-B, 139-B

ETHNICITY & ETHNIC GROUPS: 001-A, 014-B, 015-B, 042-B, 072-B, 077-B

EVALUATION: 043-B, 044-B, 059-B, 071-B, 085-B, 102-A, 133-B

FAMILY & FAMILY SERVICES: 001-A, 004-B, 015-B, 021-B, 022-B, 023-B, 024-B, 026-B, 027-B, 030-B, 031-B, 032-B, 033-B, 036-B, 037-B, 058-B, 060-B, 076-0, 083-B, 093-B, 102-A, 103-B, 106-B, 111-A, 116-A, 140-0

FAMILY PLANNING: 001-A, 007-B, 046-B, 055-B, 067-B, 091-A, 095-B, 104-B, 126-A, 136-B

FOSTER CARE: 001-A, 027-B, 081-B

GERONTOLOGY & GERIATRICS: (see Aged & Aging)

GROUPS & GROUP WORK: 001-A, 012-B, 018-A, 034-B, 037-B, 060-B, 068-B, 072-B, 111-A, 116-A

GROUP THERAPY & TREATMENT: 001-A, 058-B, 098-A

HALFWAY HOUSE: 068-B

HEADSTART: 001-A

HEALTH, MEDICAL CARE: 001-A, 002-A, 015-B, 043-B, 050-B, 060-B, 071-B, 074-A & B, 089-A, 093-B, 105-B, 107-B, 111-A, 114-B, 118-B, 121-B, 124-B, 125-B, 132-B

HOMEMAKER SERVICES: 001-A, 019-B, 022-B

HOUSING & URBAN DEVELOPMENT: 001-A, 083-B, 093-B, 104-B, 114-B, 125-B, 132-B

HUMAN GROWTH & DEVELOPMENT: 031-B, 073-B, 098-A, 116-A, 138-B

ILLEGITIMACY: 001-A, 030-B

Table 20-1 (continued)

IMMIGRATION: 072-B, 077-B

INDIAN (AMERICAN):   001-A, 066-B, 096-B, 114-B

INSTITUTIONALIZATION: 008-0, 098-A

INTELLIGENCE: 001-A, 073-B, 098-A, 138-B

INTERGROUP RELATIONS: 057-B, 072-B, 082-B, 083-B

INTERVENTION: 103-B

LEARNING DISABILITY: 001-A, 039-B, 098-A

LEARNING THEORY: (see Behavior Modification)

LEGAL RIGHTS: 041-A, 094-B, 097-A, 137-B

LEGISLATION: 001-A, 046-B, 055-B, 063-A, 070-B, 079-B, 082-B, 116-A, 122-B, 125-B

MARRIAGE: 001-A, 004-B, 032-B, 106-B, 116-A, 129-0

MEDICAID: 002-A, 124-B

MENTAL HEALTH & MENTAL ILLNESS: 001-A, 008-0, 010-B, 018-A, 035-B, 044-B, 047-B, 050-B, 056-B, 058-B, 059-B, 069-B, 075-B, 085-B, 090-A, 094-B, 098-A, 102-A, 104-B, 108-B, 128-A, 129-0, 137-B, 139-B

MENTAL RETARDATION: 001-A, 006-B, 028-B, 050-B, 052-A, 069-B, 073-B, 080-A, 085-B, 090-A, 098-A, 129-0, 138-B

METROPOLITAN STUDIES: 115-A

MIGRATORY WORKERS: 001-A, 077-B, 096-B

MINORITY GROUPS: (see also specific minority groups) 001-A, 014-B, 015-B, 057-B, 062-B, 066-B, 072-B, 082-B, 083-B, 088-B, 093-B, 096-B, 097-A, 144-B

MOTIVATION: 001-A, 086-0, 090-A, 098-A

MULTIPROBLEM FAMILIES: 023-B, 103-B

MUNICIPAL-LEGAL PROBLEMS: 115-A

NARCOTICS: (see Abuse, Alcohol & Drugs)

NEIGHBORHOOD CENTERS: 001-A, 076-0, 140-0

NURSING HOMES: 001-A, 035-B

NUTRITION: 001-A, 098-A, 132-B

PARAPROFESSIONAL: 001-A, 038-B, 084-B, 108-B, 117-B

PARTICIPATION: 051-B, 078-B

PHYSICAL ILLNESS: 001-A, 064-0, 116-A

POLITICS: 001-A, 015-B, 063-A, 072-B, 083-B, 093-B, 111-A

POPULATION CONTROL: 001-A, 091-A, 095-B

POVERTY: 001-A, 009-B, 015-B, 042-B, 051-B, 082-B, 084-B, 097-A, 104-B, 114-B, 125-B

POWER: 015-B, 051-B, 057-B, 078-B

PREJUDICE: 001-A, 072-B

PREVENTION: 023-B, 054-B, 082-B, 105-B, 120-A

PROBLEM SOLVING: 073-B, 098-A

Table 20-1 (continued)

PROFESSIONAL, SOCIAL WORK: 001-A
PROTEST: 051-B
PSYCHIATRY: 001-A, 003-B, 016-A & B, 058-B, 059-B, 099-A
PSYCHOANALYTIC STUDIES: 058-B, 098-A, 102-A
PSYCHOLOGY: 001-A, 003-B, 016-A & B, 098-A
PSYCHOPATHOLOGY: 001-A, 058-B, 098-A, 102-A
PSYCHOTHERAPY: 001-A, 012-B, 058-B, 098-A, 112-B, 113-A & B, 116-A
PUBLIC ASSISTANCE: 001-A, 036-B, 065-A, 076-0, 084-B, 114-B, 119-B, 124-B,
    134-B, 140-0
PUBLIC HOUSING: 001-A
PUERTO RICANS: 001-A, 062-B, 072-B, 096-B, 114-B
QUALITY OF SERVICE: 043-B, 071-B
RACISM: (see Minority Groups)
REHABILITATION: 001-A, 006-B, 049-A, 050-B, 064-0, 068-B, 085-B, 086-0,
    090-A, 098-A, 107-A, 122-B, 133-B
REPRODUCTION: 095-B, 106-B, 116-A, 126-A
RESEARCH, GENERAL: 006-B, 008-0, 044-B, 045-A, 050-B, 056-B, 057-B,
    061-B, 064-0, 086-0, 089-A, 112-B, 116-A, 123-A, 126-A, 127-A
RESEARCH, SOCIAL WORK: 001-A, 004-B, 012-B, 013-0, 076-0, 110-0, 140-0
RETARDATION: (see Mental Retardation)
RETIREMENT: 001-A, 008-0, 035-B, 124-B
RIOTS: 001-A, 082-B, 093-B
ROLE: 001-A, 098-A
RURAL PROBLEMS: 001-A, 042-B, 104-B, 111-A
SCHIZOPHRENIA: 001-A, 011-B, 044-B, 058-B, 098-A, 128-A, 139-B
SCHOOL PHOBIA: 001-A, 039-B
SELF-CONCEPT: 068-B, 098-A
SELF-HELP: 068-B
SENSITIVITY GROUPS: 001-A, 037-B
SEX: 001-A, 046-B, 058-B, 094-B, 098-A, 106-B, 129-A, 137-B
SHELTERED WORKSHOP: 050-B, 085-B
SHORT-TERM TREATMENT: (see Brief Psychotherapy)
SIMULATION: 098-A, 113-A & B
SMALL GROUPS: (see Groups)
SOCIAL CHANGE: 001-A, 018-A, 104-B, 111-A
SOCIALIZATION: (see Development, Personal)
SOCIAL PLANNING: 001-A, 076-0, 100-A, 132-B, 140-0
SOCIAL POLICY: 001-A, 018-A, 097-A, 134-B
SOCIAL PROBLEMS: 078-B, 111-A
SOCIAL SECURITY: 001-A, 109-A, 119-B, 132-B
SOCIAL WORK: 001-A, 045-A, 060-B, 087-0, 110-0

Table 20-1 (continued)

SOCIAL WORK EDUCATION: 001-A, 014-B, 025-B, 038-B, 052-A, 091-A
STRESS: 001-A, 017-A, 018-A, 098-A
SUICIDE: 001-A, 037-B, 054-B, 120-A, 139-B
SUPERVISION: 001-A, 025-B, 029-B, 034-B, 038-B, 085-B
THERAPY: 001-A, 012-B, 028-B, 032-B, 034-B, 044-B, 050-B, 058-B, 068-B, 098-A, 099-A, 102-A, 112-B, 116-A
TOKEN ECONOMIES: 069-B
TRANSACTIONAL ANALYSIS: 037-B
URBAN AFFAIRS & CRISES: 082-B, 083-B, 100-A, 104-B, 115-A
URBAN DEVELOPMENT & PLANNING: 001-A, 100-A, 111-A, 115-A, 130-B, 132-B
VALUES: 001-A, 003-B, 078-B, 098-A
VIOLENCE: 001-A, 037-B, 082-B
VOLUNTEER: 001-A, 019-B, 108-B
WELFARE: (see Public Assistance)
WOMEN: 001-A

Table 20-2

Citation List

This list provides citations to recent abstracts, bibliographies, and other sources of information which are cross-referenced to the key concepts often used by helping professionals (Table 20-1). New citations can be added by giving a new number to them, and adding this number to all concepts in Table 20-1 covered by the citation.

001. ABSTRACTS FOR SOCIAL WORKERS
002. ABSTRACTS OF HOSPITAL MANAGEMENT STUDIES
003. Albert, E. M. & Kluckhohn, C. A SELECTED BIBLIOGRAPHY ON VALUES, ETHICS & ESTHETICS IN THE BEHAVIORAL SCIENCES AND PHILOSOPHY, 1920–1958. (1959)
004. Aldous, J. & Hill, R. INTERNATIONAL BIBLIOGRAPHY OF RESEARCH IN MARRIAGE AND THE FAMILY, 1900–1964. (University of Minnesota Press, 1967)
005. Bahr, H. M. DISAFFILIATED MAN: ESSAYS AND BIBLIOGRAPHY ON SKID ROW, VAGRANCY AND OUTSIDERS. (University of Toronto Press, 1970)
006. Bailey, Jr., J. P. & Muthard, J. E. RESEARCH AND DEMONSTRATION PROJECTS: A BIBLIOGRAPHY. (University of Florida, 1968)
007. Blake, R. R. FAMILY PLANNING EDUCATIONAL MATERIALS, AN ANNOTATED BIBLIOGRAPHY OF SELECTED ITEMS. (1969)

Table 20-2 (continued)

008. Blank, M. L. NIMH RESEARCH ON THE MENTAL HEALTH OF AGING. (DHEW Publication No. (HSM) 72-9133) (1972).

009. Booth, R. E., et al. CULTURALLY DISADVANTAGED: A BIBLIOGRAPHY AND KEY WORD-OUT-OF-CONTEXT (KWOC) INDEX. (Wayne State University Press, 1967)

010. Brown, D. G. BEHAVIOR MODIFICATION IN CHILD AND SCHOOL MENTAL HEALTH: AN ANNOTATED BIBLIOGRAPHY ON APPLICATIONS WITH PARENTS AND TEACHERS (DHEW Publication No. (HSM) 71-9043) (1971)

011. Bryson, C. Q. & Hingtgen, J. N. EARLY CHILDHOOD PHYCHOSIS: IN-FANTILE AUTISM, CHILDHOOD SCHIZOPHRENIA AND RELATED DIS-ORDERS, 1964–1969. (DHEW Publication No. (HSM) 71-9062) (1971) (Bibliography)

012. Casper, M. THE HELPING PERSON IN THE GROUP: A KWIC INDEX OF RELEVANT JOURNAL ARTICLES (in 2 volumes). (Syracuse University, 1967; 1969) (Bibliography)

013. Chaiklin, H. INVENTORY OF RESEARCH 1963–1965. (NASW. 7873/75-s) (1965)

014. Chicano Ad Hoc Committee, San Diego State College. CHICANOS: A STUDENT REPORT ON SOCIAL WORK EDUCATION. (1971) (Bibliography)

015. Council on Social Work Education: THE CHICANO COMMUNITY: A SELECTED BIBLIOGRAPHY FOR USE IN SOCIAL WORK EDUCATION. (1971)

016. CHILD DEVELOPMENT ABSTRACTS AND BIBLIOGRAPHY

017. Coelho, G. V., et. al. COPING AND ADAPTATION: A BEHAVIORAL SCIENCES BIBLIOGRAPHY. (PHS Publication No. 2087) (1970)

018. Coelho, G. V. MENTAL HEALTH AND SOCIAL CHANGE. (DHEW Publication No. (HSM) 72-9149) (1972) (Abstracts)

019. THE LIBRARY COUNSELOR: SOCIAL SERVICES TO THE AGING. 1965, 20:3. (Bibliography [a])

020. THE LIBRARY COUNSELOR: JUVENILE DELINQUENCY, 1955–1965. 1965, 20:4. (Bibliography [a])

021. THE LIBRARY COUNSELOR: DAY CARE FOR CHILDREN. 1966, 21:1. (Bibliography [a])

022. THE LIBRARY COUNSELOR: HOMEMAKER SERVICE: A BRIDGE TO THE FUTURE. 1966, 21:2. (Bibliography [a])

023. THE LIBRARY COUNSELOR: MULTIPROBLEM FAMILIES. 1966, 21:3 (Bibliography [a])

[a] THE LIBRARY COUNSELOR is from the Colorado State Department of Public Welfare, Social Service Library.

Table 20-2 (continued)

024. THE LIBRARY COUNSELOR: ADOPTION: THE CREATED FAMILY 1966, 21:4. (Bibliography [a])
025. THE LIBRARY COUNSELOR: SUPERVISION. 1967, 22:3. (Bibliography [a])
026. THE LIBRARY COUNSELOR: EMOTIONALLY DISTURBED CHILDREN. 1968, 23:1. (Bibliography [a])
027. THE LIBRARY COUNSELOR: A HOME AWAY FROM HOME—FOSTER FAMILY CARE FOR CHILDREN. 1968, 23:3. (Bibliography [a])
028. THE LIBRARY COUNSELOR: MENTAL RETARDATION. 1969, 24:1. (Bibliography [a])
029. THE LIBRARY COUNSELOR: ADMINISTRATION OF SOCIAL AGENCIES. 1969, 24:2. (Bibliography [a])
030. THE LIBRARY COUNSELOR: UNMARRIED PARENTS: THE INCOMPLETE FAMILY. 1969, 24:3. (Bibliography [a])
031. THE LIBRARY COUNSELOR: AS THE TWIG IS BENT . . . CHILD DEVELOPMENT AND BEHAVIOR. 1969, 24:4. (Bibliography [a])
032. THE LIBRARY COUNSELOR: MARRIAGE AND THE FAMILY. 1970, 25:1. (Bibliography [a])
033. THE LIBRARY COUNSELOR: "SUFFER THE LITTLE CHILDREN". . . CHILD WELFARE SERVICES. 1970, 25:2. (Bibliography [a])
034. THE LIBRARY COUNSELOR: SOCIAL GROUP WORK. 1970, 25:3. (Bibliography [a])
035. THE LIBRARY COUNSELOR: OLDER AMERICANS—THE UNWANTED GENERATION? 1970, 25:4. (Bibliography [a])
036. THE LIBRARY COUNSELOR: PUBLIC WELFARE AT THE CROSSROADS. 1971, 26:1. (Bibliography [a])
037. THE LIBRARY COUNSELOR: NEW APPROACHES TO UNDERSTANDING AND HELPING TROUBLED PEOPLE. 1973, 28:1. (Bibliography [a])
038. THE LIBRARY COUNSELOR: TRENDS IN SUPERVISION AND STAFF DEVELOPMENT, 1960–1972. 1973, 28:2. (Bibliography [a])
039. THE LIBRARY COUNSELOR: OPENING DOORS FOR PHYSICALLY HANDICAPPED AND EMOTIONALLY DISTURBED CHIDREN. 1973, 28:3. (Bibliography [a])
040. Council for Exceptional Children. THE GIFTED. (1969)
041. CRIME AND DELINQUENCY ABSTRACTS
042. Crymes, J., Fink, K., & Stull, E. INDEXED BIBLIOGRAPHY ON SOCIOLOGICAL ASPECTS OF POVERTY. (Ohio State University, 1970)
043. DeGeyndt, W. & Ross, K. B. EVALUATION OF HEALTH PROGRAMS: AN ANNOTATED BIBLIOGRAPHY. (University of Minnesota, no date)

[a] THE LIBRARY COUNSELOR is from the Colorado State Department of Public Welfare, Social Service Library.

Table 20-2 (continued)

044. Dent, J. K. A BIBLIOGRAPHIC INDEX OF EVALUATION IN MENTAL HEALTH. (PHS Publication No. 1545) (1966)
045. DISSERTATION ABSTRACTS
046. Dollen, C. ABORTION IN CONTEXT: A SELECTED BIBLIOGRAPHY. (Scarecrow Press, 1970)
047. Driver, E. D. THE SOCIOLOGY AND ANTHROPOLOGY OF MENTAL ILLNESS: A REFERENCE GUIDE. (University of Massachusetts, 1972) (Bibliography)
048. dsh ABSTRACTS (Deafness, Speech, and Hearing)
049. Dumas, N. S. MANAGEMENT AND PERSONNEL ABSTRACTS. (University of Florida, 1968)
050. Dumas, N. S. & Muthard, J. E. REHABILITATION RESEARCH AND DEMON-STRATION PROJECTS, 1955–1970. (University of Florida, 1970) (Bibliography)
051. Dunmore, C. POVERTY, PARTICIPATION, PROTEST, POWER AND BLACK AMERICANS: A SELECTED BIBLIOGRAPHY FOR USE IN SOCIAL WORK EDUCATION. (Council on Social Work Education, 1970)
052. EXCEPTIONAL CHILD EDUCATION ABSTRACTS
053. EXCERPTA CRIMINOLOGIA (Abstracts)
054. Farberow, N. L. BIBLIOGRAPHY ON SUICIDE AND SUICIDE PREVENTION. (PHS Publication No. 1979) (1969)
055. Floyd, M. K. ABORTION BIBLIOGRAPHY FOR 1970. (Whitston, 1972)
056. Golann, S. E. COORDINATE INDEX REFERENCE GUIDE TO COM-MUNITY MENTAL HEALTH. (Behavioral Publications, 1969) (Bibliography)
057. Glenn, N. D. SOCIAL STRATIFICATION: A RESEARCH BIBLIOGRAPHY. (Glendessary Press, 1970)
058. Grinstein, A. THE INDEX OF PSYCHOANALYTIC WRITINGS (Vols. 1–14, International Universities Press, 1956–1973)
059. Harvard Medical School. COMMUNITY MENTAL HEALTH AND SOCIAL PSYCHIATRY: A REFERENCE GUIDE. (1962) (Bibliography)
060. Hoffer, J. E. KWIC INDEX: PUBLICATIONS OF THE NATIONAL CON-FERENCE ON SOCIAL WELFARE, 1924–1962. (1964) (Bibliography)
061. Educational Testing Service. INDEX TO EDUCATIONAL TESTING SERV-ICE RESEARCH REPORTS. (1968) (Bibliography)
062. Institute of Puerto Rican Studies at Brooklyn College. THE PUERTO RICAN PEOPLE: A SELECTED BIBLIOGRAPHY FOR USE IN SOCIAL WORK ED-UCATION. (Council on Social Work Education, 1973)
063. INTERNATIONAL POLITICAL SCIENCE ABSTRACTS

Table 20-2 (continued)

064. Jackson, D. G. RESEARCH 1971: AN ANNOTATED LIST OF SRS RE-
SEARCH AND DEMONSTRATION GRANTS, 1955–1971. (DHEW, 1971)
065. JOURNAL OF ECONOMIC ABSTRACTS
066. Kaiser, E. "American Indians and Mexican-Americans: A Selected Bibliography," FREEDOMWAYS, 1969, 9:298–327.
067. Kasond, D. L. INTERNATIONAL FAMILY PLANNING, 1966–1968. (PHS
Publication No. 1917) (1969)
068. Katz, A. H., Husek, J., & MacDonald, C. J. SELF-HELP AND REHABILITA-
TION: AN ANNOTATED BIBLIOGRAPHY. (UCLA School of Public Health,
1967)
069. Kazdin, A. E. SELECTED DOCUMENTS IN PSYCHOLOGY: THE TOKEN
ECONOMY: AN ANNOTATED BIBLIOGRAPHY. (American Psychological
Association, 1971)
070. Keller, M. INTERNATIONAL BIBLIOGRAPHY OF STUDIES ON ALCOHOL.
(Rutgers University, 1966)
071. Krer, M. & Trantow, D. J. DEFINING, MEASURING, AND ASSESSING THE
QUALITY OF HEALTH SERVICES. (American Rehabilitation Foundation,
Minneapolis, 1968)
072. Kolm, R. BIBLIOGRAPHY OF ETHNICITY AND ETHNIC GROUPS. (DHEW
Publication No. (HSM) 73-9009)
073. Kuhlen, R. G., Monge, R. H., & Gardner, E. F. BIBLIOGRAPHY: LEARNING
AND COGNITIVE PERFORMANCE IN ADULTS. (Syracuse University, 1967)
074. LeRocco, A. PLANNING FOR HOSPITAL DISCHARGE: A BIBLIOGRAPHY
WITH ABSTRACTS AND RESEARCH REVIEWS. (United States Department
of Commerce, 1970) (PB 193 520)
075. Lystad, M. H. SOCIAL ASPECTS OF ALIENATION: AN ANNOTATED
BIBLIOGRAPHY. (PHS Publication No. 1978) (1969)
076. Maas, H. S. (Ed.) RESEARCH IN THE SOCIAL SERVICES: A FIVE-YEAR
REVIEW. (NASW, 1970)
077. Mangalam, J. J. HUMAN MIGRATION: A GUIDE TO MIGRATION LITERA-
TURE IN ENGLISH, 1955–1962. (University of Kentucky Press, 1968)
078. Mendes, R. H. P. BIBLIOGRAPHY ON COMMUNITY ORGANIZATION FOR
CITIZEN PARTICIPATION IN VOLUNTARY DEMOCRATIC ASSOCIATIONS.
(1965)
079. Menditto, J. DRUGS OF ADDICTION AND NON-ADDICTION, THEIR USE
AND ABUSE: A COMPREHENSIVE BIBLIOGRAPHY, 1960–1969. (Whitston,
1970) (A later supplement by Advena, J. C., 1971)
080. MENTAL RETARDATION ABSTRACTS

Table 20-2 (continued)

081. Merriam, A. H. A SELECTED BIBLIOGRAPHY ON DAY CARE SERVICES. (DHEW, 1965, 0-771-562)
082. Meyer, J. K. BIBLIOGRAPHY ON THE URBAN CRISIS. (PHS Publication No. 1948)
083. Miller, E. W. THE NEGRO IN AMERICA: A BIBLIOGRAPHY. (Harvard University Press, 1970)
084. Millman, L. I. & Chilman, C. S. POOR PEOPLE AT WORK: AN AN-NOTATED BIBLIOGRAPHY ON SEMI-PROFESSIONALS IN EDUCATION, HEALTH, AND WELFARE SERVICES. (DHEW, GPO 863 126)
085. Muthard, J. E., Dumas, N. S., & Bailey, J. P. A KWIC—KEY WORD IN CONTEXT—INDEX OF SELECTED REHABILITATION COUNSELING LIT-ERATURE. (University of Florida, 1968)
086. Muthard, J. E. & Dumas, N. S. SIX YEARS OF REHABILITATION RE-SEARCH: STUDIES OF PERSONNEL IN HEALTH RELATED PROFESSIONS, CLIENT MOTIVATION AND RESEARCH UTILIZATION. (University of Florida, 1969)
087. Muthard, J. E., Rogers, K. B., & Crocker, L. M. GUIDE TO INFORMATION CENTERS FOR WORKERS IN THE SOCIAL SERVICES. (University of Florida, 1971)
088. Navarro, E. G. ANNOTATED BIBLIOGRAPHY OF MATERIALS ON THE MEXICAN-AMERICAN. (University of Texas, 1969)
089. NURSING RESEARCH (Abstracts)
090. OCCUPATIONAL MENTAL HEALTH (Abstracts)
091. Oettinger, K. B. & Stansbury, J. D. POPULATION AND FAMILY PLAN-NING: ANALYTICAL ABSTRACTS FOR SOCIAL WORK EDUCATORS AND RELATED DISCIPLINES. (International Association of Schools of Social work, 1972)
092. Office of Consumer Affairs. CONSUMER EDUCATION BIBLIOGRAPHY. (1971)
093. Parker, D. THE NEGRO IN THE UNITED STATES. (1970)
094. Parker, W. HOMOSEXUALITY: A SELECTED BIBLIOGRAPHY OF OVER 3,000 ITEMS. (Scarecrow Press, 1971)
095. The Population Council. CURRENT PUBLICATIONS IN POPULATION/ FAMILY PLANNING. (Bibliography)
096. Potts, A. M. KNOWING AND EDUCATING THE DISADVANTAGED: AN ANNOTATED BIBLIOGRAPHY. (Adams State College, Alamosa, Colorado, 1965)
097. POVERTY AND HUMAN RESOURCES ABSTRACTS

Table 20-2 (continued)

098. PSYCHOLOGICAL ABSTRACTS
099. PSYCHOPHARMACOLOGY ABSTRACTS
100. QUARTERLY DIGEST OF URBAN AND REGIONAL RESEARCH (Abstracts)
101. REHABILITATION LITERATURE (Abstracts)
102. Rothgeb, C. L., Clemens, S., & Lloyd, E. M. (Eds.) THE PSYCHOANALYTIC STUDY OF THE CHILD, Vols. I-XXV. (DHEW Publication No. (HSM) 73-9007) (Abstracts)
103. Schlesinger, B. THE MULTIPROBLEM FAMILY, A REVIEW AND AN-NOTATED BIBLOGRAPHY. (University of Toronto Press, 1963)
104. Schlesinger, B. POVERTY IN CANADA AND THE UNITED STATES: OVER-VIEW AND ANNOTATED BIBLIOGRAPHY. (University of Toronto Press, 1966)
105. CURRENT BIBLIOGRAPHY OF EPIDEMIOLOGY: A GUIDE TO THE LITERA-TURE OF EPIDEMIOLOGY, PREVENTIVE MEDICINE, AND PUBLIC HEALTH.
106. Seruya, F. C., Losher, S. & Ellis, A. SEX AND SEX EDUCATION: A BIB-LIOGRAPHY. (Bowker, 1972)
107. Shock, N. W. A CLASSIFIED BIBLIOGRAPHY OF GERONTOLOGY AND GERIATRICS. (Stanford University Press, 1951, 1957, 1963, and in each issue of the JOURNAL OF GERONTOLOGY)
108. Sobey, F. VOLUNTEER SERVICES IN MENTAL HEALTH: AN ANNOTATED BIBLIOGRAPHY 1955–1969. (National Clearinghouse for Mental Health Information Publication No. 1002) (1969)
109. SOCIAL SECURITY ABSTRACTS
110. SOCIAL SERVICE REVIEW. (September issue reports doctoral dissertations in social work.)
111. SOCIOLOGICAL ABSTRACTS
112. Strupp, H. H. & Bergin, A. E. RESEARCH IN INDIVIDUAL PSYCHOTHER-APY. (PHS Publication No. 1944)
113. Taylor, K. COMPUTER APPLICATIONS IN PSYCHOTHERAPY. (PHS Pub-lication No. 1981) (1970) (Bibliography and Abstract)
114. Tompkins, D. L. C. POVERTY IN THE UNITED STATES DURING THE SIXTIES: A BIBLIOGRAPHY. (University of California, 1970)
115. URBAN AFFAIRS ABSTRACTS
116. U.S. Department of Health, Education and Welfare. ADULT DEVELOP-MENT AND AGING ABSTRACTS.
117. ANNOTATED BIBLIOGRAPHY ON IN-SERVICE TRAINING FOR ALLIED PROFESSIONALS AND NONPROFESSIONALS IN COMMUNITY MENTAL HEALTH. (PHS Publication No. 1901) (1969) (Bibliography)

Table 20-2 (continued)

118. ANNOTATED BIBLIOGRAPHY ON VITAL AND HEALTH STATISTICS. (PHS Publication No. 2094. Public Health Service Bibliography Series-82) (1970)
119. BASIC READINGS IN SOCIAL SECURITY. (SS Publication 76-70 (10-70) 1970)
120. BULLETIN OF SUICIDOLOGY. (DHEW Publication No. (HSM) 71-9053) (Abstracts)
121. THE COMMUNITY GENERAL HOSPITAL AS A MENTAL HEALTH RE-SOURCE. (PHS Publication No. 1484. Public Health Bibliography Series No. 66) (Bibliography)
122. DACAS: DRUG ABUSE CURRENT AWARENESS SYSTEM. (National Clearinghouse for Drug Abuse Information)
123. DRUG DEPENDENCE. (Abstracts)
124. MORE WORDS ON AGING: SUPPLEMENT—1971. (SRS, DHEW) (Bibliography)
125. POVERTY STUDIES IN THE SIXTIES: A SELECTED ANNOTATED BIBLIOG-RAPHY. (SS Publication 70-27 (4-70) 1970)
126. REPRODUCTION AND POPULATION RESEARCH ABSTRACTS
127. RESEARCH IN EDUCATION
128. SCHIZOPHRENIA BULLETIN. (Abstracts)
129. SELECTED SOURCES OF INEXPENSIVE MENTAL HEALTH MATERIALS: A DIRECTORY FOR MENTAL HEALTH EDUCATORS. (PHS Publication No. 1911) (1970)
130. URBAN AND REGIONAL INFORMATION SYSTEMS: SUPPORT FOR PLANNING IN METROPOLITAN AREAS. (HUD, 1968)
131. United States Department of Justice. DOCUMENT RETRIEVAL INDEX.
132. United Nations. SELECTED ANNOTATED BIBLIOGRAPHY ON SOCIAL ASPECTS OF DEVELOPMENT PLANNING. (1970)
133. Vacher, C. D. THE COMPREHENSIVE COMMUNITY MENTAL HEALTH CENTER. (PHS Publication No. 1980) (1969) (Bibliography)
134. Vogel, L. H. SOCIAL WELFARE POLICY: AN ANNOTATED BIBLIOGRAPHY OF SELECTED REFERENCES. (University of Chicago, 1973)
135. Wasserman, P. & Silander, R. S. DECISION-MAKING: AN ANNOTATED BIBLIOGRAPHY SUPPLEMENT, 1958–1963. (1964)
136. Watts, M. E. SELECTED REFERENCES FOR SOCIAL WORKERS ON FAMILY PLANNING. (PHS Publication No. 2154) (1971)
137. Weinberg, M. & Bell, A. P. HOMOSEXUALITY: AN ANNOTATED BIB-LIOGRAPHY. (Harper & Row, 1972)

Table 20-2 (continued)

138. Wright, L. BIBLIOGRAPHY ON HUMAN INTELLIGENCE. (PHS Publication No. 1839) (1969)
139. Zusman, J., Hannon, V., Locke, B. Z., & Geller, M. BIBLIOGRAPHY ON EPIDEMIOLOGY OF MENTAL DISORDERS. (DHEW. NCMHI Publication No. 5030) (1971)
140. Maas, H. S. (Ed.) FIVE FIELDS OF SOCIAL SERVICE: REVIEW OF RESEARCH. (NASW, 1966)
141. Havelock, R. G. KNOWLEDGE UTILIZATION AND DISSEMINATION: A BIBLIOGRAPHY. (Ann Arbor: Institute for Social Research, University of Michigan, 1968)
142. Kirkendall, L. A. & Adams, W. J. THE STUDENTS' GUIDE TO MARRIAGE AND FAMILY LIFE LITERATURE: AN AID TO INDIVIDUALIZED STUDY (5th Ed.) William C. Brown, 1971)
143. ALCOHOLISM TREATMENT & REHABILITATION. (DHEW Publication No. (HSM) 72-9136) (1972)
144. BIBLIOGRAPHY ON RACISM (DHEW Publication No. (HSM) 73-9012) (1972)
145.
146.
147.
148.
149.
150.
151.
152.
153.
154.
155.
156.
157.
158.
159.
160.
161.
162.
163.
164.

Part V

SUMMARY AND PROSPECTS

CHAPTER 21

Scientific Practice

A person with a problem tries to solve his own difficulties using a reasonable approximation of a process that has been labeled "problem solving." Indeed, the person might also seek **information** from various informal sources, and perhaps in a general way take soundings—what we might call **evaluation**— on the state of his difficulties before and after he tries one thing or another. And, as we said at the beginning of this book, it is only when the problem stubbornly resists solution that he may come to a helping professional who proceeds to use a **problem-solving** approach of some variety, augmented with **information** from formal sources and with some objective **evaluation** procedure. We presume the differences in outcome are due to the practitioner's use of her professional knowledge and skills. The underlying hypothesis of this book is that such differences (favoring the practitioner) may be maximized to the extent that she uses scientific practice. What is scientific practice?

Scientific practice, as described here, is a philosophy and a methodology for connecting two domains which some people perceive as involving or producing a fundamental antagonism. Practice connotes a humane art to some, a fraudulent ineffectiveness to others; science connotes knowledge and results to some, impersonality to others. The facts are that all of these may be true, depending on whose eye is viewing the matter, and whose hand is at the switch. The philosophy of scientific practice has as one of its foci the analysis of the apparent tension in the art/science relationship of the helping professions. My view of the matter is that both art and science, in combination, are necessary; when either is minimized, humane solutions to human problems suffer. But merely saying so—that art and science should be combined in the helping professions—does not make it happen in practice. For this to occur requires a methodology which enables the combination to emerge.

The major portion of this book has concerned the methodology for combining **professional action** with the best available **information** and objective **evaluation** components; these three components and their interrelationships represent my version of scientific practice (see Figure 21-1). It is the task of this chapter to suggest how aspects of these three components may be orchestrated.

The heart of scientific practice—both the literal and figurative sense—is professional action, with its seven steps of problem solving. But except for the initial orientation period and the point at which decisions have to be made, professional action is informed and monitored continually by the most retrievable relevant information and the most accurate evaluation procedures at hand. Problem definition utilizes the logical steps of identifying events and systems of events meaningful to the client as the basis of formulating concepts concerning the class of abstracted events problematic to the client. These concepts also serve as entry points in the professional literature, using the many information retrieval tools available. Evaluation begins immediately as the worker and client form some understanding about the priorities among problematic events. Translated into the sphere of action, these priorities become end goals and intermediate goals, and the worker moves to seek alternative plans for obtaining them.

Information on alternative causal explanations is located primarily through key concept systems of retrieval, as is research on related matters and pertinent practice wisdom. It is a major effort to sort through these alternatives, but having a clear conceptual picture of the problems and the goals helps to identify the plans with the greatest probability of being useful. Probability, or its opposite coin, level of risk, becomes a critical perspective in dealing with information-for-practice. In order to have maximal clarity concerning the problems, specific objective data are collected as the baseline for later comparisons of the effectiveness of intervention. Objective data include many naturally occurring indicators of the events meaningful to clients as well as some artificial indicators as are necessary, but unless some indicators are found as to what we are doing, we can never know how well it has been done.

Decision making is the stage at which the worker is on his own. He has been informed as fully as possible and has received objective assessment of the problem events. Now he has to make some decisions based on these types of information and the valued goals the client is seeking.

Implementation resumes the interchange between evaluation and information with professional action. A strategy is formed from the accumulated theoretical information, translated to fit the specific case situation. Strategy is a composite involving the decisions about what is usable (and at what risk) among the theoretical, research, and practice information. Such decisions are reached in the context of the goals, values, and problems of the particular client. Data continue to be collected and monitored during this period, providing information to the worker on the process as well as on the results of his intervention.

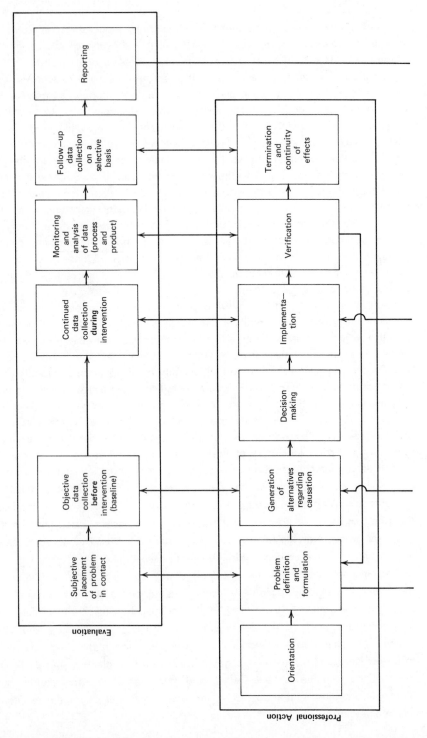

Figure 21-1—Summary schematic diagram of the components of scientific practice, showing details of suggested interrelationships.

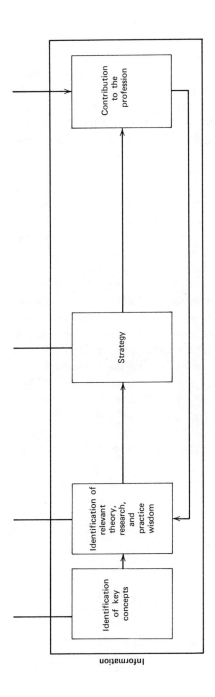

When the comparisons are made that indicate a congruence between the current state of affairs in relation to the desired goal state (and as contrasted to the preintervention state), then the termination process may begin. The termination may be with regard to a particular task or for the entire helping relationship; in either case, the final obligation on the part of the worker is to provide for continuity of the effects of intervention to the time when the helping professional is no longer present.

Thus professional action with the client comes to an end, while work on evaluation and information continues. The accountability of the entire case situation is reported to the agency in conventional recordings, but possibly also to the entire profession in the form of conceptualized and evaluated practice, at conferences, workshops, or in the professional literature, so that other helping professionals may draw on this knowledge as accumulated practice wisdom. And so the circle of action, information, and evaluation turns back onto itself.

Looking at Figure 21-1, we can observe another paradox, that although we can understand another person's abstractions, they remain foreign to us until we can reconstruct that person's abstractions into our own terms, into a practice model of our own. Thus, Figure 21-1 represents my schematization; I would fully expect that each reader would reassemble the pieces, add and subtract as fitted his or her experiences, but arrive at a systematic organization of the kinds of components discussed in this book. Then let Figure 21-1 be a challenge, a beginning rather than a final product. Scientific practice is a continually growing and changing process, but at each moment of practice we are the sum of our experiences, knowledge, and skills. Such is the paradox of helping.

References

Albert, E. M. & Kluckhohn, C. **A Selected Bibliography on Values, Ethics and Esthetics in the Behavioral Sciences and Philosophy, 1920–1958.** Glencoe, Ill.: Free Press, 1959.

Aldous, J. & Hill, R. **International Bibliography of Research in Marriage and the Family, 1900–1964.** Minneapolis: University of Minnesota Press, 1967.

Alinsky, S. D. **Rules for Radicals: A Pragmatic Primer for Realistic Radicals.** New York: Vintage, 1971.

Allen, B. T. & Horniman, A. B. **Child Welfare and the Computer: A Project of Potential.** New York: Edwin Gould Foundation for Children, 1969.

Allport, G. W. **Personality: A Psychological Interpretation.** New York: Holt, 1937.

Anastasi, A. **Psychological Testing** (3rd edition). New York: Macmillan, 1968.

Asch, S. E. **Social Psychology.** Englewood Cliffs, N.J.: Prentice-Hall, 1952.

Ban, T. A. **Conditioning and Psychiatry.** Chicago: Aldine, 1964.

Bandura, A. **Principles of Behavior Modification.** New York: Holt, Rinehart and Winston, 1969.

Barker, R. G. **Ecological Psychology: Concepts and Methods for Studying the Environment of Human Behavior.** Stanford, Cal.: Stanford University Press, 1968.

Bartlett, H. M. **The Common Base of Social Work Practice.** New York: National Association of Social Workers, 1970.

Bateson, G., Jackson, D. D., Haley, J., & Weakland, J. Toward a theory of schizophrenia. **Behavioral Science.** 1956, 1:251–264.

Berelson, B. & Steiner, G. A. **Human Behavior: An Inventory of Scientific Findings.** New York: Harcourt, Brace & World, 1964.

Bergin, A. E. & Strupp, H. H. **Changing Frontiers in the Science of Psychotherapy.** Chicago: Aldine & Atherton, 1972.

Bianchi, M. D. & Hampson, A. L. **The Poems of Emily Dickinson.** Boston: Little, Brown, 1935.

Blenkner, M., Bloom, M., & Nielsen, M. A research and demonstration project of protective services. **Social Casework,** 1971, 52:8, 483–499.

Bloom, B. S. & Broder, L. J. **Problem-Solving Processes of College Students.** Chicago: University of Chicago Press, 1950.

Bloom, M. Gerontological evaluation in the 21st century: A fable. **The Gerontologist,** 1973, 13:3 (Pt. 1), 318–321. (1973a)

Bloom, M. Information science in the education of social workers: The Indiana approach. Paper presented at the Annual Program Meeting of the Council on Social Work Education, San Francisco, 1973. (1973b)

Bloom, M. Evaluation instruments: Tests and measurements in long-term care. In S. Sherwood (Ed.), **Long-Term Care Research: A Review and Analysis of the Literature.** (DHEW/BHSR Contract HSM 110–71–141.) To be published.

Bonjean, C., McLemore, D., & Hill, R. **Sociological Measurements.** San Francisco: Chandler, 1967.

Bridgman, P. W. **The Way Things Are.** Cambridge, Massachusetts: Harvard University Press, 1927.

Brittain, J. M. **Information and its Users: A Review with Special Reference to the Social Sciences.** New York: Wiley, 1970.

Broadhurst, P. L. Coordinate indexing—A bibliographic aid. **American Psychologist,** 1962, 17, 137–142.

Browning, R. M. & Stover, D. O. **Behavior Modification in Child Treatment: An Experimental and Clinical Approach.** Chicago: Aldine & Atherton, 1971.

Buckley, W. (Ed.) **Modern Systems Research for the Behavioral Scientist: A Source Book.** Chicago: Aldine, 1968.

Buhler, C. **Values in Psychotherapy.** New York: Free Press of Glencoe, 1962.

Buros, I. K. (Ed.) **The Mental Measurement Yearbook** (7th edition). Highland Park, N.J.: Gryphon, 1970. (2 Vols.)

Burtt, E. A. **The Metaphysical Foundations of Modern Physical Science.** Garden City, N.J.: Doubleday Anchor, 1954.

Campbell, D. T. & Stanley, J. C. **Experimental and Quasi-Experimental Designs for Research.** Chicago: Rand McNally, 1963.

Cantril, H. **The Pattern of Human Concerns.** New Brunswick, N.J.: Rutgers University Press, 1965.

Carkhuff, R. R. **The Art of Helping.** Amherst, Mass.: Human Resources Development Press, 1972.

Carnap, R. Testability and Meaning. In H. Feigl & M. Brodbeck (Eds.) **Readings in the Philosophy of Science.** New York: Appleton-Century-Crofts, 1953.

Cartwright, D. Lewinian theory as a contemporary systematic framework. In S. Koch (Ed.) **Psychology: A Study of a Science.** Vol. 2. New York: McGraw-Hill, 1959.

Cassirer, E. **Substance and Function, and Einstein's Theory of Relativity.** New York: Dover, 1953. (As referred to by Cartwright, 1959)

Chaplin, J. P. **Dictionary of Psychology.** New York: Dell, 1968.

Cherry, C. **On Human Communication.** Cambridge, Mass.: MIT Press, 1957.

Churchman, C. W. **Prediction and Optimal Decision: Philosophical Issues of a Science of Values.** Englewood Cliffs, N.J.: Prentice-Hall, 1961.

Coan, R. W. Dimensions of psychological theory. **American Psychologist,** 1968, 23:10, 715–722.

Cockerill, C. C. The epidemiological approach to problem solving. In **Social Work Practice, 1962.** New York: Columbia University Press, 1962.

Combs, A. W., Avila, D. L., & Purkey, W. W. **Helping Relationships: Basic Concepts for the Helping Professions.** Boston: Allyn & Bacon, 1971.

Conant, J. B. **On Understanding Science: A Historical Approach.** New Haven, Conn.: Yale University Press, 1947.

Copi, I. M. **Introduction to Logic.** New York: Macmillan, 1953.

Cronbach, L. J. **Essentials of Psychological Testing** (2nd edition). New York: Harper & Row, 1960. (See also 3rd edition.)

Dalkey, N. C. (Ed.) **Studies in the Quality of Life: Delphi & Decision Making.** Lexington, Mass.: Lexington Books, 1972.

Davidson, P. O. & Costello, C. G. (Eds.) **N = 1: Experimental Studies of Single Cases.** New York: Van Nostrand Reinhold, 1969.

Day, P. R. **Communication in Social Work.** Oxford, England: Pergamon, 1972.

Dixon, J. C. Cognitive structure in senile conditions with some suggestions for developing a brief screening test of mental status. **Journal of Gerontology,** 1965, 20:1, 41–49.

Durkheim, E. **Suicide: A Study in Sociology.** Glencoe, Ill.: Free Press, 1951.

D'Zurilla, T. J. & Goldfried, M. R. Problem solving and behavior modification. **Journal of Abnormal Psychology,** 1971, 78:1, 107–126.

Eddington, A. S. **The Nature of the Physical World.** New York: Macmillan, 1929.

Edwards, W. & Tversky, A. (Eds.) **Decision Making.** Harmondsworth, Middlesex, England: Penguin, 1967.

Ellis, A. **Reason and Emotion in Psychotherapy.** New York: Lyle Stuart, 1962.

Franks, C. M. (Ed.) **Behavior Therapy: Appraisal and Status.** New York: McGraw-Hill, 1969.

Galbraith, J. K. **The Affluent Society.** New York: Mentor, 1963.

Gambrill, E. D., Thomas, E. J., & Carter, R. G. Procedure for sociobehavioral practice in open settings. **Social Work,** 1971, 16, 51–62.

Gerard, R. W. The biological basis of imagination, In B. Ghiselin (Ed.) **The Creative Process.** New York: Mentor, 1952.

Gibbs, J. R. The effects of human relations training. In A. E. Bergin & S. L. Garfield (Eds.) **Handbook of Psychotherapy and Behavior Change.** New York: Wiley, 1971.

Goffman, E. **Asylums.** Garden City, N.Y.: Anchor Books, 1961.

Golan, N. When is a client in crisis? **Social Casework,** 1969, 50:7, 389–394.

Goldberg, L. R. Simple models or simple processes? Some research on clinical judgments. **American Psychologist,** 1968, 23:7, 483–496.

Goldberg, L. R. & Rorer, L. G. Learning clinical inference: The results of intensive training on clinicians' ability to diagnose psychosis versus neurosis from the MMPI. Paper presented at the meeting of the Western Psychological Association, Honolulu, June 1965.

Goldstein, A. P., Heller, K., & Sechrest, L. B. **Psychotherapy and the Psychology of Behavior Change.** New York: Wiley, 1966.

Gouldner, A. W. Theoretical requirements of the applied social sciences. **American Sociological Review,** 1957, 22, 92–103.

Grannis, G. F. Demographic perturbations secondary to cigarette smoking. **Journal of Gerontology,** 1970, 25, 55–63.

Greenwood, E. **Lectures in Research Methodology for Social Welfare Students.** Berkeley: University of California Syllabus Series, No. 388, 1961.

Haley, J. **Strategies of Psychotherapy.** New York: Grune & Stratton, 1963.

Hall, E. T. **The Silent Language.** Greenwich, Conn.: Fawcett, 1959.

Hall, E. T. **The Hidden Dimension.** Garden City, N.Y.: Anchor, 1966.

Halpert, H. P., Horvath, W. J., & Young, J. P. **An Administrator's Handbook on the Application of Operations Research to the Management of Mental Health Systems.** Washington, D.C.: National Clearinghouse for Mental Health Information, 1970.

Hammond, K. R., Kelly, K. J., Castellan, N. J., Schneider, R. J., & Vancini, M. Clinical inference in nursing: Use of information seeking strategies by nurses. **Nursing Research,** 1966, 15:3, 330–336.

Hammond, K. R., Kelly, K. J., Schneider, R. J., & Vancini, M. Clinical inference in nursing: Revising judgments. **Nursing Research,** 1967, 16:1, 38–45.

Harvard Computational Laboratory. **Tables of the Cumulative Binomial Probability Distribution.** Cambridge: Harvard University Press, 1955.

Hayakawa, S. I. **Language in Thought and Action** (3rd edition). New York: Harcourt Brace Jovanovich, 1972.

Hoffer, J. Information science in the education of social work students: The National Conference on Social Welfare Approach. Paper presented to the Annual Program Meeting of the Council on Social Work Education, San Francisco, 1973.

Hollis, F. **Casework: A Psychosocial Therapy** (2nd edition). New York: Random House, 1972.

Holt, R. R. Yet another look at clinical and statistical prediction: Or, is clinical psychology worthwhile? **American Psychologist,** 1970, 25:4, 337–349.

Holtzman, W. H. & Sells, S. B. Prediction of flying success by clinical analysis of test protocols. **Journal of Abnormal and Social Psychology,** 1954, 49, 485–490.

Humphreys, L. **Tearoom Trade.** Chicago: Aldine, 1970.

Institute for Scientific Information. **Social Science Citation Index.** Philadelphia, 1973.

Jackson, D. D. (Ed.) **Communication, Family, and Marriage (Human Communication, Vol. 1).** Palo Alto, Cal.: Science & Behavior Books, 1968a.

Jackson, D. D. (Ed.) **Therapy, Communication, and Change (Human Communication, Vol. 2).** Palo Alto, Cal.: Science & Behavior Books, 1968b.

Jacobs, J. & Teicher, J. D. Broken homes and social isolation in attempted suicides of adolescents. **The International Journal of Social Psychiatry,** 1967, 8:2, 139–149.

Jones, M. **Social Psychiatry in Practice: The Idea of the Therapeutic Community.** Harmondsworth, Middlesex, England: Penguin, 1968.

Kadushin, A. **The Social Work Interview.** New York: Columbia University Press, 1972.

Kanfer, F. H. & Phillips, J. S. **Learning Foundations of Behavior Therapy.** New York: Wiley, 1970.

Kaplan, A. **The Conduct of Inquiry.** San Francisco: Chandler, 1964.

Kasl, S. V. Physical and mental health effects of involuntary relocation and institutionalization of the elderly—A review. **American Journal of Public Health,** 1972, 62:3, 377–384.

Katz, S., Downs, T. D., Cash, H. R., & Grotz, R. C. Progress in development of the Index of ADL. **The Gerontologist,** 1970, 10:1 (Pt. 1), 20–30.

Katz, S., Ford, A. B., Moskowitz, R. W., Jackson, B. A., & Jaffe, W. Studies of illness in the aged. The Index of ADL: A standardized measure of biological and psycho-social function. **Journal of the American Medical Association,** 1963, 185, 914–919.

Kelly, E. L. & Fiske, D. W. **The Prediction of Performance in Clinical Psychology.** Ann Arbor: University of Michigan Press, 1951.

Kiresuk, T. J. & Sherman, R. E. Goal attainment scaling: A general method for evaluating comprehensive community mental health programs. **Community Mental Health Journal,** 1968, 4:6, 443–453.

Kleinmuntz, B. (Ed.) **Problem Solving: Research, Method, and Theory.** New York: Wiley, 1966.

Kleinmuntz, B. (Ed.) **Clinical Information Processing by Computer.** New York: Holt, Rinehart and Winston, 1969.

Kluckhohn, C. Values and value-orientations in the theory of action: An exploration in definitions and classifications. In T. Parsons & E. A. Shils (Eds.) **Toward a General Theory of Action.** Cambridge: Harvard University Press, 1951.

Knickmeyer, R. A Marxist approach to social work. **Social Work,** 1972, 17:4, 58–65.

Kuhn, T. S. **The Structure of Scientific Revolutions** (2nd edition). Chicago: University of Chicago Press, 1971.

Lehman, R. S. & Bailey, D. E. **Digital Computing.** New York: Wiley, 1968.

Levin, G., Hirsch, G., & Roberts, E. Narcotics and the community: A system simulation. **American Journal of Public Health,** 1972, 62:6, 861–873.

Levine, A. S. Cost-benefit analysis and social welfare program evaluation. **Social Service Review,** 1968, 42:2, 173–183.

Levitt, E. E. **The Psychology of Anxiety.** Indianapolis: Bobbs-Merrill, 1967.

Lewin, K. **Field Theory in Social Science** (Ed. D. Cartwright). New York: Harper, 1951.

Licklider, J. **Libraries of the Future.** Cambridge, Mass.: MIT Press, 1965.

Lindzey, G. & Aronson, E. (Eds.) **Handbook of Social Psychology** (2nd edition, five volumes). Reading, Mass.: Addison-Wesley, 1968–1969.

Loehlin, J. C. **Computer Models of Personality.** New York: Random House, 1968.

Lyerly, S. B. & Abbott, P. S. **Handbook of Psychiatric Rating Scales (1950–1964).** Public Health Service Publication No. 1495. 1966.

MacCorquodale, K. & Meehl, P. E. On a distinction between hypothetical constructs and intervening variables. **Psychological Review.** 1948, 55, 95–107.

MacMahon, B., Pugh, T. F., & Ipsen, J. **Epidemiologic Methods.** Boston: Little, Brown & Company, 1960.

Marx, K. **Capital, The Communist Manifesto, and Other Writings.** New York Modern Library, 1932.

Mayer, J. **Overweight: Causes, Cost, Control.** Englewood Cliffs, N. J.: Prentice-Hall, 1968.

Mayer, J. E. & Timms, N. **The Client Speaks: Working Class Impressions of Casework.** New York: Atherton, 1970.

McGrath, J. E. & Altman, I. **Small Group Research: A Synthesis and Critique of the Field.** New York: Holt, 1966.

McLeod, D. L. & Meyer, H. J. A study of the values of social workers. In E. J. Thomas (Ed.) **Behavioral Science for Social Workers.** New York: Free Press, 1967.

McLuhan, M. **Understanding Media: The Extensions of Man.** New York: New American Library, 1964.

Mednick, S. A. The associative basis of the creative process. **Psychological Review.** 1962, 69, 220–232.

Meehl, P. E. **Clinical Versus Statistical Prediction: A Theoretical Analysis and a Review of the Evidence.** Minneapolis: University of Minnesota Press, 1954.

Meehl, P. E. When shall we use our heads instead of the formula? **Journal of Counseling Psychology,** 1957, 4, 268–273.

Meehl, P. E. The cognitive activity of the clinician. **American Psychologist.** 1960, 15, 19–27.

Meenaghan, T. M. What means 'community'? **Social Work,** 1972, 17:6, 94–98.

Meltzoff, J. & Kornreich, M. **Research in Psychotherapy.** New York: Atherton, 1970.

Merten, W. PERT and planning for health programs. **Public Health Reports,** 1966, 81:5, 449–454.

Miller, G. A., Galanter, E., & Pribram, K. H. **Plans and the Structure of Behavior.** New York: Holt, Rinehart and Winston, 1960.

Miller, J. G. Living systems: Basic concepts. **Behavioral Science.** 1965a, 10:3, 193–237.

Miller, J. G. Living systems: Structure and process. **Behavioral Science.** 1965b, 10:4, 337–379.

Miller, J. G. Living systems: Cross-level hypotheses. **Behavioral Science.** 1965c, 10:4, 380–411.

Mullen, E. J., Dumpson, J. R., & assocs. **Evaluation of Social Intervention.** San Francisco: Jossey-Bass, 1972.

Mullins, N. C. **The Art of Theory: Construction and Use.** New York: Harper & Row, 1971.

Newcomb, T. M., Turner, R. H., & Converse, P. E. **Social Psychology: The Study of Human Interaction.** New York: Holt, Rinehart and Winston, 1965.

Newell, A., Shaw, J. C., & Simon, H. A. Elements of a theory of human problem-solving. In R. J. C. Harper, C. C. Anderson, C. M. Christensen, & S. M. Hunks (Eds.). **The Cognitive Process: Readings.** Englewood Cliffs, N.J.: Prentice-Hall, 1964.

Ogden, C. K. & Richards, I. A. **The Meaning of Meaning.** London: Routledge & Kegan Paul, 1923.

Ohlin, L. E. & Cloward, R. A. **Delinquency and Opportunity.** New York: Free Press, 1960.

Osborn, A. F. **Applied Imagination: Principles and Procedures of Creative Problem-Solving** (3rd edition). New York: Scribner's, 1963.

OSS. **Assessment of Men: Selection of Personnel for the Office of Strategic Services.** New York: Rinehart, 1948.

Overall, J. E. & Williams, C. M. A computer procedure for the diagnosis of thyroid functioning. In K. Enslein (Ed.) **Data Acquisition and Processing in Biology and Medicine** (Vol. 2). New York: Macmillan, 1964.

Palmore, E. B. & Stone, V. Predictors of longevity: A follow-up of the aged in Chapel Hill. **The Gerontologist,** 1973, 13:1, 88–90.

Parsegian, V. L. **This Cybernetic World of Men, Machines, and Earth Systems.** Garden City, N.Y.: Doubleday, 1973.

Paul, G. L. **Insight Versus Desensitization in Psychotherapy: An Experiment in Anxiety Reduction.** Stanford, Cal.: Stanford University Press, 1966.

Paul, G. L. Strategy of outcome research in psychotherapy. **Journal of Consulting Psychology,** 1967, 31:2, 109–118.

Pelz, D. C. Environments for creative performance within universities. Paper presented at the Conference on Cognitive Styles and Creativity in High Education, Montreal, 1972.

Pelz, D. C. & Andrews, F. M. **Scientists in Organizations: Productive Climates for Research and Development.** New York: Wiley, 1966.

Perlman, H. H. The charge to the casework sequence. **Social Work,** 1964, 9:3, 47–55.

Perlman, H. H. The problem-solving model in social casework. In R. Roberts & R. Nee (Eds.) **Theories of Social Casework.** Chicago: University of Chicago Press, 1970.

Perlman, H. H. Social casework: A problem solving process. In R. Roberts & R. Nee. **Theories of Social Casework.** Chicago: University of Chicago Press, 1970.

Piven, F. F. & Cloward, R. A. **Regulating the Poor: The Function of Public Welfare.** New York: Pantheon, 1971.

Polya, G. **How to Solve It.** Garden City, N.Y.: Doubleday, 1957 (revised).

Reid, W. & Epstein, L. **Task-Centered Casework.** New York: Columbia University Press, 1972.

Reid, W. & Schyne, A. **Brief and Extended Casework.** New York: Columbia University Press, 1969.

Reik, T. **Listening with the Third Ear: The Inner Experience of a Psychoanalyst.** New York: Farrar, Straus, 1949.

Revusky, S. Some statistical treatments compatible with individual organism methodology. **Journal of the Experimental Analysis of Behavior,** 1967, 10:3, 319–330.

Reynolds, P. D. **A Primer in Theory Construction.** Indianapolis: Bobbs-Merrill, 1971.

Richmond, M. E. **Social Diagnosis.** New York: Russell Sage, 1917.

Richmond, S. B. **Operations Research for Management Decisions.** New York: Ronald Press, 1968.

Riesenfeld, M. J., Newcomer, R. J., Berlant, P. V., & Dempsey, W. A. Perceptions of public service needs: The urban elderly and the public agency. **The Gerontologist,** 1972, 12:2 (Pt. I), 185–190.

Ripple, L., Alexander, E., & Polemis, B. W. **Motivation, Capacity, and Opportunity: Studies in Casework Theory and Practice.** Chicago: University of Chicago Press, Social Service Monographs, 1964.

Robertson, R. J. & Banks, O. L. Indirect measurement of results in a project for improving socialization among the aged. **Journal of Gerontology,** 1970, 25, 265–267.

Robinson, J. P. & Shaver, P. R. **Measures of Social Psychological Attitudes.** Ann Arbor: Institute for Social Research, 1969.

Rogers, C. **Carl Rogers on Encounter Groups.** New York: Harper & Row, 1970.

Rommetveit, R. **Social Norms and Roles: Explorations in the Psychology of Enduring Pressures.** Minneapolis: University of Minnesota Press, 1955.

Rosow, I. & Breslau, N. A Guttmann health scale for the aged. **Journal of Gerontology,** 1966, 21, 556–559.

Ruesch, J. & Bateson, G. **Communication: The Social Matrix of Psychiatry.** New York: Norton, 1968.

Rychlak, J. F. **A Philosophy of Science for Personality Theory.** Boston: Houghton-Mifflin, 1968.

Sanazaro, P. & Williamson, J. End results of patient care: A provisional classification based on reports by internists. **Medical Care,** 1968, 6:2, 123–130.

Sarbin, T. R., Taft, R., & Bailey, D. E. **Clinical Inference and Cognitive Theory.** New York: Holt, Rinehart and Winston, 1960.

Satir, V. **Conjoint Family Therapy** (revised edition). Polo Alton, Cal.: Science and Behavior Books, 1967.

Sawyer, J. Measurement **and** prediction, clinical **and** statistical. **Psychological Bulletin,** 1966, 66:3, 178–200.

Schmitt, S. A. **Measuring Uncertainty: An Elementary Introduction to Bayesian Statistics.** Reading, Mass.: Addison-Wesley, 1969.

Schneider, J. H. Selective dissemination and indexing of scientific information. **Science,** 1971, 173:3994, 300–308.

Sellin, T. & Wolfgang, M. E. **The Measurement of Delinquency.** New York: Wiley, 1964.

Shock, N. W. **A Classified Bibliography of Gerontology and Geriatrics.** Stanford, Col.: Stanford University Press, 1951. (With supplements: **Supplement One,** 1949–1955, Stanford University Press, 1957: **Supplement Two,** 1956–1961, Stanford University Press, 1963.)

Shore, M. F. & Golann, E. S. (Eds.) **Current Ethical Issues in Mental Health.** Department of Health, Education, and Welfare Publication No. (HSM) /3–9029, 1973.

Skinner, B. F. **Science and Human Behavior.** New York: Macmillan, 1953.

Skinner, B. F. An operant analysis of problem solving. In B. Kleinmuntz (Ed.) **Problem Solving: Research, Method, and Theory.** New York: Wiley, 1966.

Skinner, B. F. **Beyond Freedom and Dignity.** New York: Knopf, 1971.

Spitzer, R. L., Endicott, J., Fleiss, J. L., & Cohen, J. The Psychiatric Status Schedule: A technique for evaluating psychopathology and impairment in role functioning. **The Archives of General Psychiatry,** 1970, 23, 41–55.

Stein, M. I. & Heinze, S. J. **Creativity and the Individual: Summaries of Selected Literature in Psychology and Psychiatry.** Glencoe, Ill.: Free Press, 1960.

Stevens, S. S. A metric for the social consensus. **Science,** 1966, 151:3710, 530-541.

Stuart, R. B. **Trick or Treatment: How and When Psychotherapy Fails.** Champaign, Ill.: Research Press, 1970.

Stuart, R. B. Research in social work: Social casework and social group work. In National Association of Social Workers, **Encyclopedia of Social Work,** Vol. II, New York: NASW, 1971.

Sutherland, E. H. **Principles of Criminology.** Chicago: Lippincott, 1934.

Szasz, T. S. **The Myth of Mental Illness.** New York: Hoeber-Harper, 1961.

Tharp, R. G. & Wetzel, R. J. **Behavior Modification in the Natural Environment.** New York: Academic, 1969.

Theodorson, G. A. & Theodorson, A. G. **Modern Dictionary of Sociology.** New York: Crowell, 1969.

Thomas, E. J. Selecting knowledge from behavioral science. In National Association of Social Workers, **Building Social Work Knowledge.** New York: NASW, 1964.

Thomas, E. J. (Ed.) **The Sociobehavioral Approach and Application to Social Work.** New York: Council on Social Work Education, 1967.

Thomas, E. J. & Walters, C. L. Guidelines for behavioral practice in the open community agency: Procedure and evaluation. **Behavior Research and Therapy,** 1973, 11, 193–205.

Tripodi, T., Fellin, P., & Epstein, I. **Social Program Evaluation: Guidelines for Health, Education, and Welfare Administrators.** Itasca, Ill.: Peacock, 1971.

Truax, C. B. & Carkhuff, R. R. **Toward Effective Counseling and Psychotherapy: Training and Practice.** Chicago: Aldine, 1967.

Turner, M. B. **Philosophy and the Science of Behavior.** New York: Appleton-Century-Crofts, 1967.

United States Senate. **Runaway Youth.** Hearings before the Subcommittee to Investigate Juvenile Delinquency, on S. Res. 32, Section 12, 92nd Congrss, 1st Session, January 13–14, 1972. U.S. Government Printing Office, 1972.

Vassey, I. T. Developing a data storage and retrieval system. **Social Casework,** 1968, 49:7, 414–417.

von Bertalanffy, L. General systems theory. **General Systems** (Yearbook of the Society for General Systems Research, 1962) 7, 1–20.

Wasser, E. Protective practice in serving the mentally impaired aged. **Social Casework,** 1971, 52:8, 510–522.

Watzlawick, P., Beavin, J. H., & Jackson, D. D. **Pragmatics of Human Communication: A Study of Interactional Patterns, Pathologies, and Paradoxes.** New York: Norton, 1967.

Weaver, W. **Science and Imagination: Selected Papers.** New York: Basic Books, 1967.

Webb, E. J., Campbell, D. T., Schwartz, R. D., & Sechrest, L. **Unobtrusive Measures: Nonreactive Research in the Social Sciences.** Chicago: Rand McNally, 1966.

Weber, M. **The Methodology of the Social Sciences.** Glencoe, Ill.: Free Press, 1949.

Weizenbaum, J. Contextual understanding by computers. **Communications of the ACM,** 1967, 10:8, 474–480.

Wiener, N. **The Human Use of Human Beings: Cybernetics and Society.** Garden City, N.Y.: Doubleday Anchor, 1950.

Wilson, I. C. Rapid approximate intelligence test. **American Journal of Psychiatry,** 1967, 123, 1289–1290.

Wolpe, J. & Lazarus, A. A. **Behavior Therapy Techniques: A Guide to the Treatment of Neuroses.** Oxford, England: Pergamon Press, 1966.

Young, E. F. **The New Social Worker's Dictionary.** Los Angeles, Cal.: Social Work Technique, 1939.

Zung, W. W. K. A self-rating depression scale. **Archives of General Psychiatry,** 1965, 12, 63–70.

Index of Names

Index of Subjects